MY
GREEK
TABLE

MY
GREEK
TABLE

Authentic Flavors and Modern Home Cooking
from My Kitchen to Yours

DIANE KOCHILAS

Food Photography by Vasilis Stenos
Atmospheric Photography by Christopher Bierlien
Food Styling by Carolina Doriti

ST. MARTIN'S GRIFFIN
NEW YORK

For Kyveli and Yiorgo

www.stmartins.com

FOOD PHOTOGRAPHY BY VASILIS STENOS

ATMOSPHERIC PHOTOGRAPHY BY CHRISTOPHER BIERLIEN

FOOD STYLING BY CAROLINA DORITI

ENDPAPER TILE DESIGN COURTESY OF KYVELI ZOI STENOS

DESIGN BY JAN DEREVJANIK

Library of Congress Cataloging-in-Publication Data

Names: Kochilas, Diane, author.
Title: My Greek table : authentic flavors and modern home cooking from my
kitchen to yours / Diane Kochilas ; food photography by Vasilis Stenos.
Description: First edition: December 2018. | New York : St. Martin's
Griffin, 2018. | Includes index.
Identifiers: LCCN 2018026435| ISBN 9781250166371 (paper over board) | ISBN
9781250166388 (ebook)
Subjects: LCSH: Cooking, Greek. | Cooking—Greece. | LCGFT: Cookbooks.
Classification: LCC TX723.5.G8 K5955 2018 | DDC 641.59495—dc23
LC record available at https://lccn.loc.gov/2018026435

ISBN 9781250166371 (paper over board)
ISBN 9781250166388 (ebook)

Our books may be purchased in bulk for promotional,
educational, or business use. Please contact your local bookseller or
the Macmillan Corporate and Premium Sales Department
at 1-800-221-7945, extension 5442, or by email at
MacmillanSpecialMarkets@macmillan.com.

First Edition: December 2018

10 9 8 7 6 5 4 3 2 1

ALSO BY DIANE KOCHILAS

The Food and Wine of Greece

*Ikaria: Lessons on Food, Life and Longevity from the
Greek Island Where People Forget to Die*

The Greek Vegetarian

CONTENTS

ACKNOWLEDGMENTS

I OWE A DEBT OF GRATITUDE, MUCH MORE THAN I'LL EVER BE ABLE TO REPAY BY AN INVI-
tation to my Greek table, to many people for many things over the years, although Lord knows
I've cooked for them time and again and have been grateful for every shared meal with friends
and colleagues.

My Greek Table, this book, evolved out of *My Greek Table*, the public television series that
debuted in 2017 across the United States. It was a labor of love to produce and host, and a life-
long dream come to fruition. The project began on a wintry day about three years ago, when Matt
Cohen, friend and coproducer, and I met at Molyvos, New York Greek restaurant, and agreed
to work together to create a show that would pay homage to my adopted country and ancestral
land, Greece. Without the trust, faith, and commitment by the whole team at Maryland Public
Television, our presenting station, none of this would have been possible. I specifically want
to thank Larry Unger, Steven Schupak, Jay Parik, and Stuart Kazanow for supporting the show
from its inception. Special thanks to production manager Gwenn Williams for always calling the
shots like they are. Thank you to Juliette Dannibale for directing a great show and making it all
fun, and to director of photography Chris Bierlien, aka Man of Iron, who was gracious enough
to let us use some of the many seductive images of Greece he shot while we were on location.
Thanks, too, of course, to Richard Dallett, for his expert eyes as DP during the second half of our
filming. To our entire crew, including Andreas Economakis, Gabriel Loukeris, Carolina Doriti,
Daphne Garcia, Vasili Parasamlis, Christina Panagopoulou, Vasilis Athanassas, and everyone else
who shared our long days with such good spirits and excitement, it was a pleasure for which I
will always be grateful. Special thanks to Ryan Kollmorgen, as well as to John Pappalardo, Dave
Elphick, and Cameron Shipmen, for the countless hours they spent in the editing room stitching
together all our amazing footage from Greece.

Many of the recipes in this book were collected on my travels for the show and over the years,
but some were created either in my home kitchen or at the stoves of Committee, the *meze* restaurant in Boston I've been a part of since it first opened in 2014. To managing partner Demetris
Tsolakis, chef de cuisine and fellow bull Theo Tsillipanos, and executive chef Jerry Pablo, thanks
for always welcoming my ideas and helping to bring them to a delicious end. I owe a debt of
gratitude to the myriad cooks and food artisans who shared their kitchens and recipes with me for
both the TV series and the book.

Many other people and institutions made the TV series, hence this book, possible: Elena
Kountoura, Greek minister of tourism; Lou, Joy, and Amber Moshakos; Pam Overton Skea;
Stelios Vasilakis; Nancy McKinstry; Ron Rexroth; Greta Kamaterou; Maria Kalitsi; the inimitable

Art Dimopoulos, executive director of the National Hellenic Society; and His Honorable Geoffrey R. Pyatt, United States Ambassador to Greece, and his wife, Mrs. Mary Pyatt, for graciously opening their residence to me when the series was first aired; and His Honorable Robert Peck, former ambassador of Canada to Greece and a quiet but steady support from the beginning. To George and Judy Marcus, Stelios Boutaris, Yianis Voyatzis, Maria Triantafyllou, Klairi Efkarpidou, Kostas Arkoumanis, Stathis Topouzoglou, Steve Raftopoulos, Ted Diamantis, Drake Behrakis, and Father Alex Karloutsos I owe many thanks for your embrace of the series and more. The series would not have been possible without the generous support of the Stavros Niarchos Foundation, Wines of Greece, Flying Olive Farms and Vrisi 36, the Greek National Tourism Organization, Arthur Schuman Cheeses and Dodoni Feta, The Fillo Factory, Grecian Delight Foods, the National Hellenic Society, the George and Judy Marcus Foundation, the Chabraja Foundation, Klio Teas, Grecian Delight and Peter Parthenis, Jr., Esti Fords and Konstantine Ifantis, Diamond Importers, Chefs Warehouse, Selonda Fisheries, the Santo Cooperative in Santorini, George Skouras, Yiannis Tselepos, Titan Foods, Aegean Airlines, and Hertz Hellas.

Without Carolina Doriti, friend, chef, and food stylist par excellence, and Daphne Garcia, the food cooked for each photo would have paled. Special thanks to Vasilis Stenos for bringing so much grace to his beautiful food photography.

Without the watchful eye of editor Michael Flamini *My Greek Table* would not have ever been possible. I am grateful for how hard my agent, Janis Donnaud, made me work and for going to bat with such resolve when needed, and thankful for copyeditor Ivy McFadden, with her hawk eyes combing through the manuscript with such care and knowledge. It was also by a propitious turn of fate that I met Karen Stiegler, who brought her meticulous eye and chef's training to bear when testing these recipes.

And, of course, last but never least, a deep thanks to my family, especially my kids, Kyveli and Yiorgo, and my sisters, Koko and Athena, and my entire family, who accept me warts and all and have been the best company anyone could ever ask for around the table and throughout life.

MY
GREEK
TABLE

INTRODUCTION

A MEAL AT MY GREEK TABLE—WHETHER IN ATHENS, ON MY ANCESTRAL ISLAND, IKARIA, or stateside—is noisy, chaotic, and usually filled with enough variety to satisfy a wide range of appetites, from vegans to carnivores. Meals *chez moi*, even on weekdays, are rambling, filled-plate, free-ranging affairs during which we linger over wine, mostly Greek with the hard-to-pronounce names of our indigenous grapes, and people talk for hours. Perhaps in less-expressive cultures, one would label these exchanges "shouting matches" or "arguments." For us Greeks, passionate table talk and unbridled grazing from a landscape that includes every food group and lots of plant-based dishes are part of our Mediterranean ways. The table in Greece is the perfect place to witness the spectrum of foods that make up one of the world's healthiest cuisines and the emotional well-being inherent in a way of eating that is inclusive, varied, and good for life.

My Greek Table is a celebration of these rituals. It is a feast of great Greek home cooking—my home cooking—served forth with generosity and abundance.

The book is a very personal paean to the healthful foods I make at home. Some dishes have crossed the Atlantic a few times, morphing anew in my restaurant work, but always starting and usually ending at home. My recipes are inspired by seasonal, regional, raw ingredients and the traditions from which they derive, and from the farmers, cheese makers, vintners, and other devoted artisans who produce them.

My goal with *My Greek Table* is to share great Greek recipes for home cooks, some regional classics, and my own interpretations and innovations, which happen to belong to a broad tradition of eating well and deliciously.

The beauty of Greek cuisine is that it combines innate nutrition with vibrant flavors. It is a cuisine of indulgence, not abstention. *My Greek Table* is the expression of the natural Greek way to eat that embraces health without anxiety.

I hope to open the window on a Greece that few people know by using traditional ingredients in time-honored but also innovative ways, attesting to the flexibility and timelessness of Greece's cuisine.

My Greek Table is different from the eight other Greek cookbooks I have written in that it is less a research project and more a subjective tale. I am not setting out to document the vast wealth of Greek regional dishes; I've already done that. *My Greek Table* is personal, and the recipes are inspired by my travels and deep-rooted knowledge of Greece and Greek products.

There is a famous novel in Greek called *Loxandra*, the story of a cook in Constantinople. She would wake up in the morning and think first thing about what she was going to make that day. That's me, and it's a role I relish even more than a svelte silhouette, more than dining out in

the starriest of restaurants, more than pretty much anything else. Cooks are givers, the sentimental orchestrators of that most civilized human activity: a meal shared with other people around a table.

In Greece, this activity is still sacred. We are fortunate to be blessed with an abundance of delicious, healthful recipes rooted in regional, religious, and social traditions that are also thoroughly modern and accessible. Everything, every individual and business decision, every milestone, every day in Greek culture is celebrated and calibrated around the table. There is something elemental and intrinsically good for us in eating and sharing food around a Greek table. I hope *My Greek Table* is a celebration of heartfelt Greek hospitality.

BASICS

*classic and contemporary greek
sauces & dressings*

De hortainei m'oraia logia y koilia

"The belly doesn't fill up on nice words."

In Greek cooking, the approach to sauces is simple. While there are a few technique-driven sauces, such as avgolemono, the egg-lemon liaison that laces so many stews and binds so many soups, most sauces are easy to make. Most dressings and many marinades are simple emulsions of acid whisked with olive oil, riffs on the theme of what the world knows as vinaigrette.

It is in the contemporary Greek kitchen, spun from the whisks of modern Greek chefs in Greece and in Greek restaurants around the globe, that a new range of sauces and dressings has emerged over the past decade or so. Many have been co-opted by home cooks. I love them all. For the most part, the new range is an evolution of the classics: avgolemono spiked with alcohol or reddened with a pinch of saffron; *ladolemono*, the basic lemon–olive oil emulsion, as an open invitation to tweak with herbs, cheeses, liqueurs, honey, ginger, and more; basic tomato sauces perked up with orange and ouzo. The variations are endless.

DRESSINGS AND MARINADES ON THE GREEK TABLE

It's safe to say that almost all dressings and marinades in the Greek kitchen call for olive oil, coupled with an assortment of other ingredients, from fresh citrus juices to alcohol (both deglazed and not) to yogurt, honey, mustard, herbs, garlic, ginger, and more. Marinades are used to "cure" raw fish dishes, a much-embraced newcomer to the Greek table, as well as to enhance grilled foods, from vegetables to fish, seafood, and meat. Dressings are mainly used over salads.

The Greek salad—that timeless assembly, in its purest, most authentic, seasonal form, of great tomatoes; unabashedly sharp onions; crunchy cucumbers; grassy, slightly bitter peppers; kalamata olives; and feta—need be dressed in nothing but olive oil and good sea salt. To my mind, any other addition in the dressing department (not to mention lettuce!) adulterates the clarity of flavor of this true Greek classic.

For boiled salads, such as those of wild greens, or *horta*, the rule of thumb is olive oil and lemon juice for sweet greens, olive oil and vinegar for bitter ones. Other cold boiled vegetable salads, such as of zucchini, cauliflower, broccoli, carrots, and potatoes, are typically dressed with a simple *ladolemono*. Boiled beets usually like vinegar rather than lemon juice.

The selection that follows is a reflection of my personal favorites and of the sauces and dressings I use most in my own home cooking.

Ladolemono

GREEK LEMON–OLIVE OIL DRESSING

yield varies

The most fundamental flavor profile in the Greek kitchen is the mixture of fresh lemon juice and olive oil called ladolemono. *When whisked and emulsified, the combination becomes a viscous, creamy elixir, the Greek answer to French vinaigrette but predating it by millennia; the ancient Greeks were fond of acidity and used vinegar in many different sauces and dressings. Lemons, while not the first citrus fruit to travel from the Arab world to Europe, were an early one, arriving on the shores of the Mediterranean some time around AD 1000 and faring well in the region's temperate climes.*

In Greece, circa 2018, lemon trees grow in country gardens, and the main variety is one that bears fruit twice a year. Commercially, there are a few places renowned for lemon cultivation, and these happen to be the same regions where the olive tree also flourishes best: the Peloponnese and Crete. Other varieties of citrus fruits abound in many parts of the country: kumquats in Corfu; mandarins in Chios; oranges of every sort in Argos and other parts of the Peloponnese; the odd citron and bergamot here and there. In Athens, city streets are lined and shaded by thousands of bitter orange trees, nerantzi *in Greek, the juice of which is a great substitute for the lemon juice called for in this recipe. Green, young, and whole, or ripe and carefully skinned for their the peel, bitter oranges become the stuff of spoon sweets, preserved in a sugar syrup and served forth as an offering to visitors at home.*

The perfumed travels of lemons and their like have been long and meandering in this sunny country. Like most Greek cooks, I use ladolemono *on a wide range of foods, from dressing a simple shredded cabbage slaw to drizzling over all manner of fish and seafood. Indeed, the creamy, almost yellowish-green, soothing but astringent mixture is the de facto dressing to be spooned over basic grilled fish and much, much more.*

Fresh lemon juice, strained	**Salt and freshly ground black pepper (optional)**
Extra-virgin Greek olive oil	

The basic ratio is 1:3—that is, one part fresh lemon juice to three parts olive oil. Put the lemon juice in a bowl and, while whisking vigorously, drizzle in the oil. Add a pinch each of salt and pepper, if you like, and *oriste*—that's "voilà" in Greece—you have *ladolemono*, the most basic Greek sauce and dressing.

NOTE: You may also add 1 teaspoon dried Greek oregano to this; whisk it into the lemon juice at the start before adding the oil.

Ladolemono me Meli kai Moustarda

Lemon-Honey-Mustard Dressing

This is my favorite dressing for simple, fresh greens salads. It's also great over grilled seafood, such as shrimp and squid. You can try adding a grated knob of fresh ginger to this, as well as some fresh herbs of your choice, such as chopped dill, parsley, mint, and/or basil.

I like to use Greek honey and Greek mustard in this dressing, but any good honey and pungent mustard will do. makes 1½ cups (360 ml)

⅓ cup (80 ml) strained fresh lemon juice

2 teaspoons Greek honey

1 tablespoon Greek, Dijon, or other pungent mustard

1 cup (240 ml) extra-virgin Greek olive oil

Salt

Whisk together the lemon, honey, and mustard in a medium bowl. While whisking, drizzle in the olive oil in a slow, steady stream and whisk until the mixture is smooth, creamy, and emulsified. Season to taste with salt.

Ladolemono me Portokali kai Skordo

Orange-Garlic Olive Oil Dressing

Orange adds a sweet note to this refreshing dressing. Try it over boiled or roasted beets or any leafy green salad. makes 1¾ cups (420 ml)

2 tablespoons strained fresh lemon juice

¼ cup (60 ml) strained fresh orange juice

1 garlic clove, minced

1¼ cups (300 ml) extra-virgin Greek olive oil

Pinch of salt

Freshly ground black pepper

Whisk together the lemon and orange juices and the garlic in a medium bowl. While whisking, drizzle in the olive oil in a slow, steady stream and whisk until the mixture is emulsified. Season with the salt and pepper to taste. Use immediately.

Vinaigrette me Elies

Greek Olive Vinaigrette

To either the Lemon-Ouzo-Garlic Dressing (opposite) or the Orange-Garlic Olive Oil Dressing (above), add 2 tablespoons finely chopped pitted kalamata or other Greek olives.

Ladolemono me Ouzo kai Skordo

Lemon-Ouzo-Garlic Dressing

This is a great combination to use as both a dressing and marinade-cure. See the note for changing the amount of lemon juice if you want to make crudo or seafood carpaccio at home.
makes 1½ cups (360 ml)

⅓ cup (80 ml) ouzo

3 tablespoons strained fresh lemon juice

1 garlic clove, minced

1¼ cups (300 ml) extra-virgin Greek olive oil

Salt and freshly ground black pepper

In a small saucepan or skillet, heat the ouzo over medium heat. (Keep the kitchen fan off and stand away from the saucepan because the ouzo may ignite, which is natural when heating alcohol; the flame will die down in a few seconds.) Cook until the ouzo has reduced by a little more than half, to about 3 tablespoons. Set aside to cool for a few minutes.

Whisk together the reduced ouzo, lemon juice, and garlic in a medium bowl. While whisking, drizzle in the olive oil in a slow, steady stream and whisk until the mixture is emulsified. Season to taste with salt and pepper. Use immediately.

NOTE: To use this combination of ingredients as a marinade cure for all manner of fresh filleted fish, increase the lemon juice to ½ cup (120 ml) and keep the ouzo as is, without heating it or reducing it. Try grating a little fresh ginger into the mixture and adding a few chopped fresh herbs, such as basil, oregano, and/or mint.

Ladolemono me Feta kai Myrodika

Feta-Herb Ladolemono

The addition of feta to the basic ladolemono *recipe considerably changes its consistency and character, transforming it from a refreshing, light dressing to a creamy, rich, substantial addition to any salad or cooked vegetable dish. I tend to use this recipe as the weather gets cooler, when the need to make even a simple salad more filling grows proportionately to the drop in mercury!*
makes 1⅔ cups (400 ml)

⅓ cup (80 ml) strained fresh lemon juice

⅓ cup (50 g) crumbled Greek feta

2 tablespoons chopped fresh oregano

1 garlic clove, minced (optional)

1 cup (240 ml) extra-virgin Greek olive oil

Salt and freshly ground black pepper

Whisk together the lemon juice, feta, oregano, and garlic, if using, in a medium bowl. While whisking, drizzle in the olive oil in a slow, steady stream and whisk until smooth and creamy. Season to taste with salt and pepper.

NOTE: You can reconstitute any of the above dressings and sauces by placing them in a jar with a tight-fitting lid and shaking or by rewhisking.

Ntressing me Yiaourti

✓ GREEK YOGURT RANCH SAUCE

makes 1⅔ cups (400 ml)

Greek Yogurt Ranch Sauce, sans mayonnaise and preservatives, of course, is a great way to enjoy a creamy salad dressing or cold sauce without the guilty burden of unhealthy calories.

⅓ cup (80 ml) strained fresh lemon juice

Scant 1 tablespoon Dijon or Greek mustard

1 cup (240 ml) extra-virgin Greek olive oil

⅓ cup (80 ml) Greek yogurt, preferably full-fat

1 garlic clove, minced

2 tablespoons chopped fresh herbs of your choice, such as dill, parsley, oregano, and/or mint

Salt and freshly ground black pepper

Put the lemon juice in a medium bowl and whisk in the mustard. While whisking, drizzle in the olive oil in a slow, steady stream and whisk until the mixture emulsifies. Whisk in the yogurt until smooth, followed by the garlic and herbs. Season to taste with salt and pepper. Use immediately or place in a jar with a tight-fitting lid and refrigerate for up to 3 days. To reconstitute, shake vigorously.

Saltsa Tartar me Yiaourti

GREEK YOGURT TARTAR SAUCE

makes about 1½ cups (360 ml)

One of the great qualities of Greek yogurt is the ease with which one can use it to replace or reduce the quantity of mayonnaise used. This is a classic example.

1 cup (240 ml) Greek yogurt, preferably full-fat

½ cup (120 ml) good-quality mayonnaise

3 tablespoons minced cornichon pickles

1 tablespoon chopped capers

2 teaspoons Dijon, Greek, or other pungent mustard

Grated zest of 1 lemon

Juice of ½ to 1 lemon, strained

Salt and freshly ground black pepper

Whisk together the Greek yogurt and mayonnaise in a small bowl. Using a spatula, mix in the cornichons, capers, mustard, and lemon zest. Taste and add lemon juice, salt, and pepper to taste.

Mayioneza me Eliopasta

KALAMATA OLIVE–GREEK YOGURT "MAYO"

makes about 2 cups (480 ml)

One of my all-time favorite new Greek recipes. I use this to "paint" over a pretty serving platter before placing keftedes (pages 78, 81, 84, and 97) or vegetable fritters (pages 76, 82, and 83) on top. It stands on its own as a dip with homemade pita chips, too!

1½ cups (360 ml) Greek yogurt, preferably full-fat

⅓ cup (80 ml) store-bought kalamata olive paste

Scant 1 tablespoon Dijon mustard

3 tablespoons extra-virgin Greek olive oil

1 garlic clove, minced

Grated zest of 1 small orange

Salt and freshly ground black pepper

Whisk together the yogurt, olive paste, mustard, and olive oil in a small bowl. Using a spatula or wire whisk, stir in the garlic and orange zest. Season to taste with salt and pepper. Chill before serving.

Kafteri Saltsa Meliou

GREEK HONEY HOT SAUCE

makes about 1½ cups (360 ml)

I've been working in restaurant kitchens for a long time, and one of the great things about the intense, heated, noisy environment of a busy kitchen is the intuitive blurring of lines when it comes to making a quick snack for oneself. Most Greek kitchens I've worked in have been blessed with great crews of Mexican cooks. La Morena brand cans of chipotles in adobo sauce hide behind the tarama *and feta; jalapeños have their place tucked behind the produce for Greek dishes; the Cholula hot sauce is drizzled with impunity over just about everything. So it stands to reason that a few Grec-Mex recipes have found their way into my own repertoire, Hellenized in a way, but also the products of an open palate and an open mind!*

This recipe is great with pita chips, grilled chicken or seafood, or used to baste chicken wings on the grill.

1 cup (240 ml) extra-virgin Greek olive oil

10 fresh jalapeños, seeded and chopped

4 garlic cloves, crushed

3 tablespoons strained fresh lemon juice, plus more for seasoning

2 cups (100 g) coarsely chopped fresh cilantro

2 to 3 tablespoons good-quality honey, preferably raw Greek pine honey

Several drops of hot sauce, to taste

Salt

Place all the ingredients in the bowl of a food processor and puree until smooth. Taste and season with more lemon juice, hot sauce, and/or salt as needed. Serve.

NOTE: You can store the sauce in a jar with a tight-fitting lid in the refrigerator for up to a week.

Saltsa Mparmpekiou me Vyssino

MY SOUR CHERRY BARBECUE SAUCE

makes about 2½ cups (600 ml)

The inspiration for this sauce goes back many years to the first experience I had dining at Kefi, chef Michael Psilakis's first Greek restaurant in New York. He served us a range of crudo, one of which was tuna paired ingeniously with Greek vyssino, the sour cherry preserves usually reserved for a sweet pick-me-up over afternoon coffee in a typical Greek home. The pairing catapulted me out of my comfort zone, pushing me beyond the purist's probity into a boundless horizon of fearless new uses for traditional old recipes. And a barbecue sauce was thus born. I make it every summer in batches, to be brushed over lamb and goat chops, burgers, and eggplant on the grill. You can find the Greek sour cherry spoon sweet and sour cherry syrup in Greek food shops or online. You can also substitute other sour cherry syrup.

3 tablespoons extra-virgin Greek olive oil

1 large onion, finely chopped

2 shallots, chopped

2 garlic cloves, minced

1 tablespoon ground cumin

2 teaspoons ground cinnamon

½ to 1 teaspoon red pepper flakes

⅔ cup (160 ml) tomato paste

4 cups (1 L) dry red wine

1 cup (240 ml) *vyssino* syrup or other sour cherry syrup

1 heaping tablespoon Dijon mustard

3 tablespoons sherry vinegar or apple cider vinegar

Salt and freshly ground black pepper

Heat the olive oil in a medium saucepan over medium heat. Add the onion and shallots and cook until soft and lightly colored, 10 to 12 minutes. Stir in the garlic. Add the cumin, cinnamon, and red pepper flakes and cook, stirring, for a minute or two to release the flavors of the spices.

Add the tomato paste and stir. Add the wine, *vyssino* syrup, mustard, and vinegar and season to taste with salt and black pepper. Simmer the barbecue sauce over low heat until it thickens and has reduced by one-third; it should be the consistency of ketchup.

Remove from the heat and either transfer to the bowl of a food processor and process until smooth or puree directly in the pot with an immersion blender until smooth. Pass the barbecue sauce through a fine-mesh strainer and let cool. If it is too thin, return it to the saucepan after it's been strained and cook to thicken it further, then let cool before storing. Store in an airtight container in the refrigerator for up to 2 weeks.

Avgolemono kai y Parea Tou

AVGOLEMONO AND COMPANY

No doubt the most sophisticated sauce in the Greek kitchen is avgolemono, the egg-lemon liaison that calls for tempering a mixture of eggs and lemon juice with hot broth, which results in a creamy, foamy, thick, soul-satisfying addition to soups and stews. It has a long history in the eastern Mediterranean, perhaps tracing its roots to the *agristada* or *salsa blanca* of the Sephardic Jews who settled en masse in Greece in the fifteenth century, during the Spanish Inquisition.

There are several traditional ways to make it, either with yolks, whole eggs, or separated yolks and whipped whites, each resulting in liaisons of varying density and thickness. There are also a few delicious contemporary variations, which call for additions such as saffron, wine, and other seasonings. You may also use the juice of bitter oranges, or even verjuice, in place of the lemon juice; both are old renditions of this dish, rehatched in the hands of contemporary chefs.

One thing to keep in mind when making any of the following versions is that the eggs should always be at room temperature. With room-temperature eggs, the whites and yolks combine easier when whisking. This means that the eggs will disperse more evenly into the mixture. You can soak cold eggs in warm water for 10 to 15 minutes to bring them down to room temperature. Instead of whisking by hand, you can mix the avgolemono in the bowl of a stand mixer fitted with the whisk attachment or in a large bowl using the whisk attachment of an immersion blender.

Aplo Avgolemono

THE SIMPLEST AVGOLEMONO

makes 3 to 4 cups (720 to 960 ml)

This rendition with whole eggs is the easiest. As a rule of thumb, for every quart (liter) of liquid, use 2 large whole eggs and the juice of 1 large lemon, which amounts to about ¼ cup (60 ml).

2 large eggs, at room temperature

Pinch of salt

¼ cup (60 ml) strained fresh lemon juice

2 to 3 cups (480 to 720 ml) hot broth, from the cooking liquid of any soup or stew to which you wish to add the avgolemono

Vigorously whisk together the eggs and salt in a metal bowl until frothy. While whisking, slowly add the lemon juice and whisk until the mixture changes color and texture, becoming pale yellow and creamy.

Take a ladleful of the hot broth and, while whisking, very slowly, almost drop by drop, drizzle it into the egg-lemon mixture. Continue drizzling and whisking until all the hot broth has been added and incorporated into the mixture.

Pour the avgolemono back into the soup (or the pot you used to heat the broth), tilt the pot back and forth to distribute the avgolemono evenly, and heat very gently, stirring, for a few minutes to warm through. One caveat: Do not cover the pot unless you want an omelet!

NOTE: You can make avgolemono using just egg yolks following the same directions as those for whole eggs. You can also borrow a trick from many a restaurant and stabilize the mixture by whisking 1 teaspoon cornstarch into the egg-lemon mixture before adding the hot broth.

AVGOLEMONO
with meringue and yolks

makes 5 to 6 cups (1.2 to 1.4 L)

This version of avgolemono, with the egg yolks and whites separated and the latter whipped into a meringue, results in a thicker, denser sauce or liaison. It is used the same way The Simplest Avgolemono (page 17), added to soups and stews to bind and thicken them, and to add that characteristic creamy texture and lemony flavor that defines so many Greek dishes.

2 large eggs, at room temperature, separated

Pinch of salt

Juice of 1 large lemon (about ¼ cup / 60 ml), strained

3 cups (720 ml) hot broth, from the cooking liquid of any soup or stew to which you wish to add the avgolemono

Place the egg whites and salt in a medium, preferably metal, bowl and whisk vigorously until the whites hold soft peaks. Set aside until ready to use.

Vigorously whisk the egg yolks in a separate, clean, preferably metal bowl until frothy. While whisking, slowly add the lemon juice and whisk until the mixture is creamy and dense. Using a large spoon or spatula, add the whipped egg whites to the yolk mixture in big plops, whisking well after each addition.

Take a ladleful of the hot broth and, while whisking, very slowly, almost drop by drop, drizzle it into the egg-lemon mixture. Continue drizzling and whisking until all the hot broth has been added and incorporated into the mixture.

Pour the avgolemono back into the soup (or the pot in which you heated the broth), tilt the pot back and forth to distribute the avgolemono evenly, and heat very gently, stirring, for a few minutes to warm through. One caveat: Do not cover the pot unless you want an omelet!

NOTE: You can borrow a trick from many a restaurant and stabilize the mixture by whisking 1 teaspoon cornstarch into the egg lemon mixture before adding the hot broth.

VARIATIONS

FOR A SAFFRON AVGOLEMONO, add a pinch of saffron threads to the egg-lemon mixture after drizzling in the first ladleful of hot broth. Continue whisking and adding the broth as indicated. *Other spices that work nicely are a pinch of ground turmeric, cayenne pepper, or ground cumin.*

TO ADD WINE OR SPIRITS TO THE AVGOLEMONO, in a small saucepan, heat ½ cup (120 ml) of the alcoholic beverage of your choice (such as ouzo, mastiha liqueur, white wine, or brandy) to burn off the alcohol, then let it cool to room temperature. Whisk it into the egg-lemon mixture after the first ladleful of hot broth. Continue whisking and adding the broth as indicated.

OTHER CITRUS FRUITS: Try adding a combination of lemon and orange, lemon and blood orange, or lemon and bitter (Seville) orange juice to the eggs.

Saltsa Fetas

FETA CHEESE SAUCE

makes about 3 cups (720 ml)

This is a standby in my home kitchen, an easy, rich, and elegant sauce to pour over pasta for a quick meal or to serve with meatballs and vegetable fritters. You can make the sauce ahead of time and keep it refrigerated in a tight-lidded jar for 2 to 3 days.

2 tablespoons extra-virgin Greek olive oil

1 heaping tablespoon all-purpose flour

2 cups (480 ml) milk

1½ cups (225 g) crumbled Greek feta

½ cup (55 g) grated kasseri or other soft, mild sheep's-milk cheese

Grated zest of 1 lemon

Freshly ground black pepper

½ cup (25 g) chopped fresh mint or basil

Heat the olive oil in a medium saucepan over medium heat. Add the flour and stir vigorously with a wire whisk until the mixture is a very light yellow-beige color, about 5 minutes. Add the milk and cook, whisking continuously, for about 7 minutes, until slightly thickened and smooth.

Add the cheeses and lemon zest and season with pepper to taste. Reduce the heat to low and cook, whisking gently, until the cheeses have melted and the sauce is thick and creamy. Add the mint, then immediately remove from the heat.

Vasiki Saltsa Kima

BASIC GROUND MEAT SAUCE

makes 8 cups (2 L)

3 tablespoons extra-virgin
Greek olive oil

1 large onion, chopped

2 garlic cloves, minced

1½ pounds (680 g) ground beef,
lamb, turkey, chicken, or pork, or any
combination

1 recipe My Secret Classic Cinnamon-
Tomato Sauce (page 22)

1 small cinnamon stick

Cooked spaghetti, tubular spaghetti,
or tubini, for serving

Grated myzithra or Kefalotyri cheese,
for serving

Heat the olive oil in a large saucepan over medium heat. Add the onion and cook, stirring, until wilted, 8 to 10 minutes. Add the garlic and stir. Add the ground meat and cook, stirring, until browned, 10 to 12 minutes. Pour in the tomato sauce and add the cinnamon stick. Reduce the heat to low, cover, and simmer for 45 minutes, until the meat is cooked through. Remove the cinnamon stick before serving. Toss the sauce with cooked pasta and grated cheese.

Y Mystiki mou Saltsa Tomatas me Kanella

MY SECRET CLASSIC CINNAMON-TOMATO SAUCE

makes 5 cups (1.2 L)

It's been my experience that all cooks have their little cooking secrets, ingredients they embrace often to add that something special (and unidentifiable) to a dish. I have a few! Lemon zest is something I add to all sorts of dishes, especially those with rice or in which herbs are a major component; a dash of cocoa, a spoonful of dried mushroom powder, a tablespoon of pureed prunes, (which thicken and season), and a drizzle of either honey or petimezi (grape molasses) are a few of my other little secrets, amassed over the years in an effort to achieve that elusive balance between sweetness and acidity that is the fundamental test of most good recipes.

A few of those little secrets come into play in this classic Greek tomato sauce, seasoned with the trio of cinnamon, allspice, and nutmeg. It's wonderful with pasta and is also the basic support sauce for ground meat dishes from moussaka to pastitsio to good old galley cook's spaghetti with kima (ground meat).

¼ cup (60 ml) extra-virgin Greek olive oil

2 large red onions, finely chopped

4 garlic cloves, minced

1 tablespoon dried mushroom powder (see Note)

Pinch of unsweetened cocoa powder

6 cups (1.4 L) chopped or pureed fresh or good-quality canned tomatoes

⅔ cup (180 ml) white wine

1 large cinnamon stick

8 allspice berries

½ teaspoon freshly grated nutmeg

2 bay leaves

Salt and freshly ground black pepper

1 to 2 tablespoons *petimezi* (grape molasses) or honey

1 to 2 tablespoons balsamic vinegar

Cooked pasta or rice, for serving

Grated Greek myzithra or Kefalotyri cheese or Greek yogurt, for serving

Heat the olive oil in a medium saucepan over low heat. Add the onions and cook until wilted and lightly browned, 12 to 15 minutes. Add in the garlic and stir a few times to soften it. Stir in the mushroom powder and cocoa and cook for a minute or so to release their flavors.

Add the tomatoes, wine, cinnamon stick, allspice, nutmeg, and bay leaves. Bring to a simmer and add 2 cups (480 ml) water. Bring back to a simmer. Season to taste with salt and pepper. Cover and cook over low heat for 45 minutes to 1 hour, until the sauce is thick and has reduced to about 5 cups (1.2 L). Add additional water during the cooking if the sauce thickens too much.

Taste the sauce and add the *petimezi* and vinegar as needed to adjust the balance of flavors. Season with salt and pepper as needed. Remove the cinnamon stick, allspice berries, and bay leaves before serving.

Serve the sauce over pasta or rice, accompanied by grated cheese or Greek yogurt. Or use it as the base in a ground meat sauce that stands on its own or to make pastitsio or moussaka.

NOTE: You can buy dried mushroom powder online or in gourmet shops, or make your own by grinding any dried mushrooms of choice (I like porcini best) in the bowl of a food processor or coffee grinder until broken down into a fine powder.

*Y Agapimeni mou Vasiki Tomatosaltsa
me Ouzo kai Portokali*

MY FAVORITE BASIC GREEK TOMATO SAUCE
with ouzo and orange zest

makes about 5 cups (1.2 L)

This is my go-to Greek-inspired tomato sauce that can be served with almost anything.

It's great over pasta, of course. Make it in a large batch, say, three or four times the recipe, and keep it on hand in the fridge or freezer. It goes beautifully with chicken and pork: for example, sauté chunks of either meat, then add them to the sauce for an easy stew. This recipe makes enough sauce for 1½ pounds (680 g) of meat.

You can also add a handful of chopped kalamata olives to this, which pair well with both the orange and ouzo flavors, or a (drained) can of tuna packed in water, to make a more substantial pasta sauce. Fresh or dried oregano, thyme, marjoram, and mint also go well and may be added toward the end, right before you remove the sauce from the heat.

3 tablespoons extra-virgin Greek olive oil

2 large red onions, finely chopped

4 garlic cloves, minced

½ cup (120 ml) ouzo

2 tablespoons *petimezi* (grape molasses)

6 cups (1.4 L) chopped or pureed fresh or good-quality canned tomatoes

⅔ cup (180 ml) white wine

2 (3 x 1-inch / 7.5 x 2.5 cm) strips orange zest, preferably from organic oranges (peeled with a vegetable peeler)

1 star anise pod

4 allspice berries

2 bay leaves

1 (3- to 4-inch / 7.5 to 10 cm) fresh rosemary sprig

1 whole dried chile, plus more as desired

2 tablespoons balsamic vinegar

Salt and freshly ground black pepper

1 tablespoon dried Greek oregano, or ½ cup (25 g) chopped fresh herbs, such as oregano, marjoram, thyme, basil, or mint (optional)

Heat the olive oil in a medium saucepan over low heat. Add the onions and cook until wilted and lightly browned, 12 to 15 minutes. Add the garlic and stir a few times to soften it.

Carefully pour in the ouzo. As soon as it steams up (deglazes), add the *petimezi* and stir. Add the tomatoes and bring the mixture to a simmer. Add the wine, increase the heat to bring the mixture to a boil, then add 2 cups (480 ml) water. Bring back to a boil, reduce the heat to maintain a simmer, and stir in the orange zest, star anise, allspice, bay leaves, rosemary, chile, and vinegar.

Season to taste with salt and pepper. Cover and simmer the sauce for 1 hour, adding a little more water over the course of cooking so that by the end you have about 5 cups (1.2 L) of thick sauce.

Taste and adjust the seasoning with additional salt, pepper, *petimezi*, and/or vinegar. Remove the star anise, allspice berries, bay leaves, rosemary, and chile. Stir in the fresh oregano or herbs, if using, then immediately remove from the heat.

Serve the sauce as desired, or let it cool and store in an airtight container in the refrigerator for up to 3 days or in the freezer for up to 1 month.

BREAKFAST
FUN
FOR GREEK HEROES

Greek Farmers' Breakfast Porridge 31

Whole Wheat Baklava Muffins
with Greek Yogurt 33

Baklava Oatmeal 34

Eggs in a Hole {Cooked in Beet Greens} 37

Zucchini Omelet with Greek Yogurt, Lemon Zest, and Feta 38

Tsoureki French Toast 39

Greek Yogurt Pancakes 40

H kaly mera apo to proi fainetai

"A good day starts from the morning."

In the Greek kitchen, there are two tiers of breakfast. There is the *proino* (pronounced *pro-ee-NO*), breakfast proper; and the *kolatsio* (*ko-lat-si-O*), sometimes also called *dekatiano*, which means "tenth," for the approximate time of the morning most people, whether at work in an office or a field, or at school, start to feel peckish and in need of a snack. More recently, a third breakfast tier—brunch—has taken hold in Athens and beyond.

Greeks of another generation wisely used to say it's best to eat like a king at breakfast, a prince at lunch, and a pauper at dinner. In these days of fraying traditions, most urban Greeks do pretty much the opposite, forgoing the filling porridges of yore for something to grab on the go in the morning: one of the sweet or savory dunking biscuits called *voutimata*; or a small *frigania*, something akin to melba toast; or *paximadia*, rusks, that are enjoyed with coffee or with an herbal infusion—the latter woven into the tapestry of traditional customs that are still going strong.

But there are dozens of great foods, culled from Greek traditions or inspired by older recipes, that make excellent breakfast choices. Any of the savory pies (page 257), for example, provide substantial morning fare. The range of Greek cheeses and olives, accompanied by a slice or two of good tomatoes or fruit and rusks or good bread, are easy choices for a quick but healthy morning meal.

The traditional farm breakfast used to be a dense, steaming bowl of porridge made either from cracked wheat, bulgur, or *trahana* (see page 214). There is a tepid revival of this heady fare, and the recipe in this chapter, inspired by the offering at Avli restaurant in Rethymnon, Crete, is a delicious concoction of creamy bulgur studded with pomegranate seeds and raisins and perfumed with cinnamon.

Egg dishes are endless and delineated either by region or by ingenuity. Everyone loves a good omelet, for example, which makes for an easy first meal and just as easy an evening one. There are plenty of local, regional omelet dishes all around Greece, and some of them are included here.

My favorite Greek egg recipe is a kind of local egg-in-a-hole, the hole being not carved from bread slices but a hollow made in a skillet full of sautéed greens.

Breakfast, at least to my mind, is also an opportunity to have some fun in the kitchen. On my table, there's usually something sweet and relatively healthy: an olive oil–lemon cake, nut-studded muffins inspired by the flavors of baklava, some of those dunking biscuits mentioned earlier.

The idea is to leave the house sated each morning, better able to face the world! In this chapter, I offer up a few of my personal favorite Greek or Greek-inspired breakfast goodies.

GREEK YOGURT FOR BREAKFAST

The popularity of Greek yogurt has opened up a whole new world of breakfast possibilities. Most "Greek yogurt" in the United States bears little resemblance to the range of yogurts one finds in Greece. These include the thick, protein-rich cow's-milk yogurt now ubiquitously called Greek yogurt around the globe but distinguished in Greece as *strangisto* or "drained," because once the yogurt is set, it is placed in large muslin bags and hung overnight so the whey drains out, resulting in the thick texture that has won over the world. Few of the American facsimiles of this product are actually drained, which is something to note when reading labels. (Most are thick because protein and thickening agents have been added to the product.)

Greek yogurt in Greece can be made from cow's, sheep's, or goat's milk. Any of these yogurts can also be strained. Then there is a range of plain (and flavored) unstrained yogurts that are creamy and light, but not particularly thick. There is also my personal favorite, the selection of traditional yogurts usually set in small clay pots, and characterized by the delicious sour, thin, but almost leathery skin that forms on the surface.

One thing is for sure everywhere: Greek yogurt of every ilk is delicious with honey—preferably also Greek—and the two combined are an ancient and timeless breakfast pair.

Other things to mix into a bowl of Greek yogurt run the gamut from *peti-mezi* (grape molasses) or *vyssino* (sour cherry) syrup to fresh herbs combined with fruit or any combination of refreshing vegetables. Throw in some ice and press start on a blender to open up a whole world of smoothies or, as this scribe might pen them—Greek Yogurt Grab-and-Gos!

GREEK FARMERS' BREAKFAST PORRIDGE

serves 4

I stumbled upon this remake of a true Greek farm breakfast at Avli, a lovely sprawling restaurant situated in a five-hundred-year-old house in Rethymnon, Crete. Katerina, the owner, has resuscitated many old Cretan recipes, and this hearty porridge is a hit even in the heat of a Greek summer.

Whole wheat, bulgur wheat, and trahana *(see page 214), a milk-based, pebbly grain product that is one of the oldest foods in the world, are the main grains for Greece's traditional breakfast porridges. The latter imparts a delicious sour flavor and can be interchanged with the bulgur or whole wheat kernels called for in the recipe. I sometimes also make this with buckwheat; the proportion of water to grain is the same, about 3 parts water to 1 part grain. Note that if you're using whole wheat kernels, you'll need to soak them overnight, so plan ahead.*

2 cups (280 g) bulgur wheat or whole wheat kernels (see headnote)

1 cinnamon stick

2 cups (480 ml) milk

Pinch of salt

4 to 6 tablespoons (60 to 90 ml) Greek honey

½ cup (25 g) finely chopped fresh parsley

½ cup (25 g) finely chopped fresh mint

⅔ cup (95 g) seedless raisins

1½ cups (350 ml) pomegranate seeds

Ground cinnamon

If using whole wheat kernels, rinse them, put them in a bowl with water to cover, and soak them overnight. Drain.

Place the bulgur or whole wheat kernels in a medium saucepan with 6 cups (1.4 L) water. Bring to a simmer over medium heat and add the cinnamon stick and milk. Reduce the heat to low and simmer, stirring, until creamy, about 10 minutes for bulgur and 45 minutes to 1 hour for whole wheat kernels.

Season with the salt and honey, using more or less according to your taste. Just before removing from the heat, stir in the parsley, mint, raisins, and pomegranate seeds. Remove the cinnamon stick.

Serve in shallow bowls, sprinkled with cinnamon.

BREAKFAST INSPIRED BY BAKLAVA

Baklava, the classic Greek dessert of phyllo dough filled with nuts, flavored with cinnamon, cloves, and allspice, and dampened with simple honey or sugar syrup, is a dish that has inspired my cooking in more than the dessert department.

The combination of all those warm spices, evocative of the East, translates well to so many other recipes. If you've got baklava on hand, try cutting it up into small chunks and mixing it into a container of softened good vanilla ice cream, then refreezing it. I've made baklava ice cream sandwiches and baklava-flavored flans. But it's in the day's first meal that those warm spices inspire me the most. Here are two recipes for classic American fare flavored with the aromas of Greek baklava.

Mafins me Mavro Glevri, Yiaourti kai Yefsi Mpaklava

WHOLE WHEAT BAKLAVA MUFFINS
with greek yogurt

makes 12 muffins

Olive oil, for greasing (optional)

FOR THE FILLING

⅔ cup (80 g) chopped walnuts

⅔ cup (90 g) chopped pistachios

6 tablespoons (85 g) packed brown sugar

2 teaspoons ground cinnamon

½ teaspoon ground cloves

Pinch of freshly ground black pepper

¼ teaspoon freshly grated nutmeg

Grated zest of 1 small orange

3 tablespoons unsalted butter, melted

FOR THE MUFFINS

2½ cups (315 g) whole wheat flour, preferably pastry flour

¾ cup (150 g) granulated sugar

2 teaspoons baking powder

¼ teaspoon baking soda

¼ teaspoon salt

½ cup (120 ml) extra-virgin Greek olive oil

1 cup (240 ml) mashed or pureed banana

1 large egg, beaten

½ cup (120 ml) Greek yogurt, preferably full-fat

½ cup (120 ml) whole milk

½ cup (120 ml) Greek honey, for brushing

Preheat the oven to 375°F (190°C). Lightly oil two 6-cup muffin tins or line them with paper liners.

Make the filling: Mix all the filling ingredients together in a small bowl and set aside.

Make the muffins: Mix together the flour, granulated sugar, baking powder, baking soda, and salt in a large bowl.

In a separate medium bowl, whisk together the olive oil, banana, egg, yogurt, and milk. Fold the wet mixture into the dry mixture and stir until just combined.

Fill the prepared muffin cups one-third of the way with the batter. Add a heaping tablespoon of the nut filling to each (reserve any remaining filling), then fill the cups with the remaining batter to just below the level of the tin, covering the filling. Bake for 25 to 30 minutes, until the muffins are puffed and golden brown on top. Remove from the oven and transfer to a wire rack. Brush or drizzle with the honey and sprinkle with any remaining filling.

Kwaker me Yefsi Mpaklava

BAKLAVA OATMEAL

serves 4

It's hard to dress up oatmeal, but such was the task when my colleague Demetris Tsolakis, of Committee restaurant in Boston, asked me to spruce up the brunch menu and to think up something with oatmeal for those cold New England winter weekends. Baklava oatmeal, with all the warm spices that pair beautifully with oatmeal and are part of the flavor palette of baklava, was the result. My favorite part is the crunch!

1 tablespoon unsalted butter or olive oil

1½ cups (150 g) walnuts, coarsely chopped

½ teaspoon ground cinnamon, plus more for garnish

Pinch of ground cloves

Pinch of salt

½ cup (75 g) Corinthian currants or other raisins

6 tablespoons (90 ml) Greek honey

2 cups (180 g) rolled oats

2 cups (480 ml) whole milk, goat's milk, or unsweetened almond or coconut milk (optional)

2 pieces store-bought baklava, cut into slivers or chopped

In a medium skillet, melt the butter or warm the olive oil over medium heat. Add the walnuts and toast, stirring, until they begin to emit their earthy aroma, about 3 minutes. Stir in the cinnamon, cloves, and salt and stir for a minute to release the aromas of the spices. Stir in the currants. Drizzle in 2 tablespoons of the honey and cook until the nuts are gooey and slightly caramelized, 2 to 3 minutes more.

While working the walnuts, cook the oatmeal: In a medium saucepan, combine the oatmeal and 7 cups (1.7 L) water (or 4 cups / 1 L] water plus the milk). Cook over medium heat, stirring occasionally, until the oatmeal thickens to a creamy consistency, 5 to 7 minutes.

Divide the oatmeal among four bowls and sprinkle with the chopped baklava and the walnut-raisin mixture. Sprinkle with cinnamon and drizzle with the remaining 4 tablespoons (60 ml) honey. Serve hot.

Avga Matia Mageiremena se Lakouva apo Horta

EGGS IN A HOLE
{cooked in beet greens}

serves 2

Vegetables and eggs are a beloved combination in the Greek kitchen, and there are endless combinations served for breakfast, lunch, or a light supper. This is one of my favorites because it's easy but it looks stunning.

1 pound (450 g) beet greens

3 tablespoons extra-virgin Greek olive oil

1 medium onion, chopped, or 1 small leek, trimmed, thoroughly washed, and chopped

1 small fennel bulb, chopped

1 garlic clove, chopped

½ teaspoon sweet paprika

½ teaspoon cayenne pepper or hot paprika

½ cup (25 g) chopped fresh mint

½ cup (85 g) chopped peeled plum tomatoes (canned is fine)

Salt and freshly ground black pepper

4 large eggs

Crusty bread, for serving

Wash the greens thoroughly in several changes of water and spin dry or drain in a colander. Remove the stems and discard or save for another use (see Note). Coarsely chop the leaves.

In a large deep nonstick skillet, heat the olive oil over medium-low heat. Add the onion and fennel and cook until wilted and lightly browned, about 10 minutes. Add the garlic, paprika, and cayenne and cook, stirring, for 3 to 4 minutes. Add the greens, cover the pot, and cook until wilted, about 8 minutes. Stir in the mint, add the tomatoes, and simmer for 10 to 15 minutes, until most of the liquid has evaporated. Season to taste with salt and black pepper.

Using a wooden spoon, make four wells in the cooked greens. Carefully break an egg into each of the wells. Cook until the yolks and whites are set, 10 to 12 minutes. Remove and serve immediately, with a good piece of crusty bread.

NOTE: You can use the beet stems to make a version of tzatziki, the classic Greek yogurt–garlic dip that usually contains grated cucumbers: Chop the beet stems and blanch them briefly in boiling water, then drain. Combine the stems, 1½ cups (360 ml) Greek yogurt, 1 to 3 finely chopped garlic cloves, 2 tablespoons extra-virgin Greek olive oil, and 2 teaspoons red wine vinegar and season to taste with salt. This ad hoc beet stem tzatziki goes nicely with the Eggs in a Hole and is a good way to make use of something ordinarily discarded.

Omeleta me Kolokythaki, Yiaourti kai Feta

ZUCCHINI OMELET
with greek yogurt, lemon zest, and feta

serves 2

2 tablespoons extra-virgin Greek olive oil

2 scallions or spring onions, chopped

1 medium zucchini (about 6 inches / 15 cm long), cut into ¼-inch-thick (6 mm) rounds or diced

½ cup (25 g) chopped fresh wild fennel fronds, dill, or mint

½ teaspoon grated lemon zest

4 large eggs

2 tablespoons Greek yogurt

½ cup (75 g) crumbled Greek feta

Salt and freshly ground black pepper

In a 10- or 12-inch (25 or 30 cm) nonstick skillet, heat the olive oil over medium-high heat. Add the scallions and cook, stirring, until soft and translucent. Add the zucchini and cook, stirring gently, until al dente. Stir in the fennel fronds and lemon zest.

Reduce the heat to medium. Whisk together the eggs, yogurt, and 2 tablespoons water and pour the mixture into the skillet, tilting the skillet back and forth for a few minutes so that the egg cooks evenly. As the egg begins to set, sprinkle in the feta. Season to taste with salt and pepper. Cover the pan and cook over low heat for about 10 minutes, or until the omelet is set and lightly golden. Flip onto a large plate, cut into wedges, and serve.

Tiganites me Tsoureki

TSOUREKI FRENCH TOAST

serves 4

This is a great way to make use of leftover Greek Easter or New Year's breads, called tsoureki *and* vasilopita, *respectively. You can also buy the bread throughout the year online from Greek shops or at any Greek or Middle Eastern shop near you. It resembles challah and brioche, both of which make an easy substitute.*

2 large eggs

½ cup (120 ml) whole milk

Scant 1 teaspoon ground cinnamon, plus more for garnish

3 to 4 tablespoons (45 to 55 g) unsalted butter

12 slices stale leftover *tsoureki* or *vasilopita* (Greek Easter or New Year's bread) or challah

Greek honey, for garnish

Whisk together the eggs, milk, and cinnamon in a wide, shallow bowl.

In a large skillet, melt 1 tablespoon of the butter over medium heat.

One at a time, dip 3 of the bread slices into the egg-milk mixture. As soon as the butter stops bubbling and before it turns brown, place the bread in the skillet and cook until golden brown on both sides. Transfer to a platter and cover or tent with aluminum foil to keep warm. Repeat with the remaining bread, adding another tablespoon or so of the butter to the skillet between batches as needed.

Serve the *tsoureki* French toast hot, drizzled with Greek honey and dusted with a little cinnamon.

Tiganites me Yiaourti

GREEK YOGURT PANCAKES

serves 4

1½ cups (190 g) all-purpose flour

½ cup (65 g) whole wheat flour

1½ teaspoons baking powder

¼ teaspoon baking soda

½ teaspoon salt

¾ cup (180 ml) Greek yogurt, preferably full-fat

1 large egg, lightly beaten

¾ cup (180 ml) whole milk

Butter or olive oil, for the skillet

Toppings (see Note)

Mix together the flours, baking powder, baking soda, and salt in a large bowl.

In a separate medium bowl, whisk together the yogurt, egg, and milk. Add the dry ingredients to the wet ingredients in three or four increments, whisking until smooth. Cover with plastic wrap and let the batter rest in the refrigerator for at least 15 minutes or up to overnight.

When ready to make the pancakes, in a nonstick skillet, melt 2 teaspoons butter over medium-high heat, tilting the pan so the butter is evenly distributed over the surface.

Pour the batter into the skillet, a ladleful at a time, to form pancakes that are about 4 inches (10 cm) in diameter. Don't overcrowd the skillet. Flip the pancakes when the underside is golden brown and continue to cook until both sides are golden. Transfer to a plate, dabbing each pancake with a little butter as you stack them. Continue until the all the batter has been used, adding butter to the skillet between batches as needed. Serve hot.

NOTE: Try topping these fluffy pancakes with a dollop of Greek yogurt, a drizzle of honey, and some fresh fruit or Greek spoon sweet preserves, such as bergamot or lemon rind, which go beautifully with yogurt.

FUN DIPS

TO DIVE INTO

Ψωμοτύρι και γλυκιά ζωή

Psomotyri kai glykia zoi

"Bread, cheese, and a sweet life."

The Greek love affair with bread is one of the reasons there are so many delicious, traditional dips in the cuisine. Nothing is quite as comforting (at least to me) as that moment, say, in a favorite Greek restaurant, when the *taramosalata* arrives accompanied by a basket of warm pita wedges swaddled in a dinner napkin, then the first taste of the two together. It is one of my favorite combinations in the world. The Greeks' love of bread was tempered by a reverence for it as well; it is sacred in this culture; hence, wasting it is anathema. It isn't by chance that many of the classic dips are made with a base of dried or stale bread, a custom found throughout the Mediterranean.

Dips are part of the larger landscape of *mezedes*, small plates meant to be shared in a convivial atmosphere, on the Greek table. Traditionally, some are meant to be served with specific accompaniments: *skordalia*, the garlicky dip, with fried fish or boiled beets; tzatziki, the Greek yogurt classic with cucumbers and garlic, is often served with crispy fried vegetable rounds or fritters.

Mostly, though, the range of traditional Greek dips is both a celebration of regional distinctions in the cuisine and an opportunity to experiment. In the recipes that follow, the old and the new are whipped up together. Serve them forth with your own pita chips, bread sticks, vegetable chips, or fresh vegetable sticks.

HOMEMADE PITA CHIPS

makes 32 pieces, to serve 4 to 6

¼ cup (60 ml) extra-virgin Greek olive oil, plus more for greasing, if needed

6 garlic cloves, thinly sliced

4 pocketless pita bread rounds, cut into 8 triangular wedges each

2 or 3 pinches of coarse sea salt or kosher salt

1 teaspoon dried Greek oregano

Preheat the oven to 400°F (200°C). Lightly oil two large baking sheets or line them with parchment paper.

Strew the garlic slices over the baking sheets, dividing them evenly.

Using your hands, toss together the pita wedges, olive oil, salt, and oregano in a large bowl. Divide the pita chips between the baking sheets. Bake for 7 minutes or so, turning once, until golden and crisp. Remove from the baking sheet, transfer to a serving bowl, and serve hot or at room temperature.

NOTE: You can discard the garlic pieces, but I find them rather tasty and like to toss them into the serving bowl with the pita chips.

SKORDALIA

Skordalia, from *skordo*, the Greek word for garlic, is one of the classic dips in the Greek kitchen. It is almost always served with fried fish, such as anchovies or cod, but also pairs classically with boiled beets and cooked greens.

There are numerous traditional recipes for *skordalia* which vary from region to region; some, like the *aliada* of the Ionian islands, call for a base of potatoes; others are made with stale bread, and/or almonds. One, from the Dodecanese, is made into a thin sauce. The combination of bread and walnuts as a base distinguishes the *skordalia* of Thessaloniki. One interesting recipe deriving from Ithaca calls specifically for octopus broth.

So basic is the marriage of starch, garlic, and olive oil that *skordalia* has moved beyond tradition. I've played around with a few of my own versions, some developed for restaurant menus but all easy and suitable for making in a home kitchen.

Skordalia apo Kastana

CHESTNUT SKORDALIA

makes about 2½ cups (600 ml)

This unusual rendition of skordalia *is actually an old recipe from the region of Arcadia in the Peloponnese. All over Greece's mountainous regions, chestnut trees flourish; indeed, the chestnut has long been revered as an addition to pilafs and stuffings, candied, transformed into spoon sweets (preserved in sugar syrup), and pureed, as in this recipe, which attests to the ingenuity of traditional cooks who know how to make use of everything that nature provides.*

I like to serve this with a pile of floured and lightly fried strips of winter squash or grilled vegetables.

20 peeled vacuum-packed, frozen, or fresh chestnuts

½ cup (50 g) coarse stale bread crumbs or plain croutons

4 garlic cloves, finely chopped

¾ to 1 cup (180 to 240 ml) extra-virgin Greek olive oil

2 tablespoons red wine vinegar

2 tablespoons strained fresh lemon juice

Salt and freshly ground black pepper

If using vacuum-packed chestnuts, simmer according to the package instructions; for frozen, bring to room temperature before using. For fresh chestnuts: Score the shells with a sharp paring knife and place in a pot with enough water to cover by 2 inches (5 cm). Bring to a boil over high heat, reduce the heat to medium, and simmer until the chestnuts are soft, 35 to 40 minutes. Drain, let cool briefly until cool enought to handle, and peel.

Put the stale bread cubes in a bowl, dampen them with water, and squeeze out the excess moisture using either the palms of your hands or by wrapping the crumbs in cheesecloth and twisting to extract the liquid. Place the dampened crumbs in the bowl of a food processor. Crumble the chestnuts into the food processor and add the garlic. Pulse a few times to combine well.

With the motor running, slowly drizzle in the olive oil, vinegar, and lemon juice, alternating between each and using as much of the olive oil as needed until the chestnut *skordalia* is very creamy. Add a little warm water if necessary to achieve the desired smooth texture. Season to taste with salt and pepper and serve.

Skordalia me Ouzo kai Elies Kalamon

POTATO SKORDALIA
with ouzo and kalamata olives

makes about 3 cups (720 ml)

Here's a riff on the classic potato-based skordalia, spiked with ouzo and a handful of chopped kalamata olives. In most skordalia recipes, a little acid, usually vinegar, is added to help balance the headiness of the garlic. Here the briny flavor of kalamata olives does the job. This recipe makes a nice accompaniment to, or a bed on which to serve crispy grilled or fried fish.

1 pound (450 g) boiling potatoes (about 4), such as russets or waxy varieties, peeled and quartered

⅓ cup (80 ml) ouzo

½ cup (120 ml) hot cod broth or other fish broth, plus more as needed (you can substitute clam juice for the fish broth)

4 to 6 garlic cloves, smashed

½ teaspoon salt, plus more as needed

Extra-virgin Greek olive oil (approximately ⅔ cup / 160 ml)

Juice of 1 lemon, strained

½ cup (75 g) chopped pitted kalamata olives

Freshly ground black pepper

Put the potatoes in a large pot of salted water and bring to a boil. Reduce the heat to medium and simmer until the potatoes are fork-tender, 15 to 20 minutes. Turn off the heat and cover the pot to keep the potatoes warm.

While the potatoes are cooking, place the ouzo in a small pot and bring it to a boil over medium heat. (Keep the kitchen fan off and stand away from the saucepan because the ouzo may ignite, which is natural when heating alcohol; the flame will die down in a few seconds.) Cook for about 45 seconds, then remove from the heat. If using clam juice, warm it in a separate small pot or skillet.

In a large mortar, pound the garlic and salt to a thick paste using the pestle. Add several tablespoons of the hot broth (or clam juice) and pound until smooth. (Alternatively, combine the garlic and salt in the cool bowl of a small food processor, add some of the broth, and process until smooth.)

Using a slotted spoon, remove a few chunks of potato from the hot water, place them in a large bowl, and mash with the pestle or a fork until chunky, then transfer the mashed potato to the mortar and pound it together with the garlic paste. In alternating turns, drizzle in some of the olive oil, lemon juice, ouzo, and additional broth as needed, pounding and adding more potatoes and liquids as you go until the mixture is smooth. Using a spatula, fold in the olives at the end. Taste and adjust the seasoning with salt and pepper as needed.

NOTE: You can also make this in the bowl of a stand mixer fitted with the paddle attachment: Pound the garlic-salt mixture by hand or puree it in the bowl of a small food processor, then transfer it to the mixer and add the potatoes. As the paddle attachment is pounding the hot potato-garlic mixture, add the liquids in alternating turns until the mixture is creamy. Fold in the olives at the end.

TIP: It's important to use hot potatoes when making *skordalia* so that they more readily absorb the olive oil and other liquids. You can bring a pot of water to a boil and reheat the potatoes for a few minutes if they are cold.

Fava me Fresko Araka, Myrodika kai Ladi

SPRING FRESH PEA PUREE
with herbs and olive oil

makes about 3 cups (720 ml)

Fava is one of the all-time classic Greek meze recipes, most often made with yellow split peas cooked until they disintegrate into a puree (see page 245). There are a few regional fava recipes: for example, a green split pea puree from the island of Lesvos, and koukofava, broad bean puree, from Crete. Here's a contemporary idea that calls for using fresh or frozen peas. It works well as a sandwich spread or spooned over bruschetta, and it pairs beautifully with ouzo-seared shrimp (see page 334) or grilled or fried seafood.

2 cups (290 g) fresh or frozen shelled peas

½ cup (120 ml) ouzo, or 1 star anise pod

¼ cup (13 g) chopped fresh parsley

2 tablespoons chopped fresh tarragon

½ to ⅔ cup (120 to 160 ml) extra-virgin Greek olive oil

Juice of 1 lemon, plus more as needed, strained

Greek sea salt or kosher salt

Freshly ground black pepper

2 tablespoons chopped fresh chives or red onion

Scant 1 teaspoon whole pink peppercorns

2 tablespoons crumbled Greek feta

Place the peas in a medium saucepan and add water to cover and the ouzo or star anise. Cover and bring to a boil over medium-high heat. Reduce the heat to low and simmer until tender, about 3 minutes for fresh peas, 3 to 5 minutes for frozen. Drain (discard the star anise, if you used it).

Transfer the hot peas to the bowl of a food processor. Add the parsley and tarragon. While pulsing on and off, add enough of the olive oil and lemon juice in alternating increments to achieve a smooth, silky puree. Season with salt and black pepper to taste.

Transfer the fava to a serving dish and garnish with the chives, pink peppercorns, and feta.

TIP: Do not salt the water when boiling peas because doing so toughens them up.

Tahinosalata me Avokanto

AVOCADO-TAHINI SPREAD

makes about 2½ cups (600 ml)

One of the best dishes during periods of fasting in Greece is tahinosalata, *a deeply satisfying, velvety spread made with tahini (sesame paste), lemon juice, garlic, and cayenne pepper. Avocado enhances the texture and pairs beautifully with the nutty flavor of the tahini. Try this as a sandwich spread. It works well with grilled vegetable sandwiches and vegetable patties (see page 81). It's also great with falafel!*

2 cups (480 ml) mashed ripe avocados

3 tablespoons tahini

3 garlic cloves, finely chopped

3 tablespoons extra-virgin Greek olive oil

2 to 3 tablespoons strained fresh lemon juice

Dash of hot sauce or Aleppo pepper

Pinch of ground cumin

Salt

Place the mashed avocado and tahini in the bowl of a food processor and pulse until smooth and thick. Add the garlic and olive oil and pulse to puree and combine. Add water and lemon juice in 1 tablespoon increments, pulsing after each addition, until the mixture is creamy, smooth, and spreadable (you may use 3 to 6 tablespoons water). Season with the hot sauce, cumin, and salt to taste. Serve.

AVOCADOS ON THE GREEK TABLE

Avocados are not native to Greece, but over the last decade or so, there has been a concerted effort to farm them there, as the country's temperate climate is conducive to their cultivation. Most Greek avocados grow in Crete and the Peloponnese.

Greek cooks have embraced the avocado, too. For one, its rich texture has the same satisfying appeal as many of the country's traditional olive oil–based vegetable dishes, a smooth, buttery quality to which the Greeks are naturally accustomed. Avocados are also surprisingly compatible with many of the most basic ingredients in the Greek kitchen, from the fish roe called *tarama* to feta, Greece's national cheese, to the range of herbs, spices, and citrus fruits used most in the cuisine, to tahini and even olive oil.

Taramosalata me Avokanto

AVOCADO TARAMOSALATA

makes about 2 cups (480 ml)

Nutrient-dense tarama, *the savory, salty fish roe (usually of cod or carp) that forms the basis of* taramosalata, *one of Greece's best-known dips, inspires recipes that in this day and age move far beyond tradition. The roe itself is a superfood in its own right, packed with omega-3 fatty acids and vitamins D, A, K, E, and B$_{12}$. It's a powerhouse of minerals including potassium, selenium, phosphorous, and copper. No wonder it's one of the foods almost always on the table during Lent, a period of abstention from all animal products, but one rich in some of the healthiest foods of the Greek diet nonetheless.*

Most traditional recipes call for emulsifying tarama *with olive oil and lemon juice, typically bound with a bread or potato base. This unusual version was born in the kitchen of Committee restaurant in Boston, where I am consulting chef. We serve it as a dip. It's also one of the Greek dips that works well as a sandwich spread.*

1 medium potato, peeled and cubed

Salt

1 ripe large avocado

¼ cup *tarama* (fish roe)

½ to ⅔ cup (120 to 160 ml) extra-virgin Greek olive oil

Juice of 1 large lemon, strained

Hot sauce (optional)

Homemade Pita Chips (page 46) or crudités, for serving

Place the potato in a small pot and add enough water to cover by about 1 inch (2.5 cm). Bring to a boil, season the water with salt, reduce the heat to medium, and simmer until the potato cubes are fork-tender, 12 to 15 minutes. Turn off the heat but leave the potatoes in the hot water and cover to keep them warm.

Halve the avocado and remove the pit. Score the flesh with a paring knife.

Use a slotted spoon to transfer the hot potato cubes to the bowl of a food processor or the bowl of a stand mixer fitted with the paddle attachment (reserve the potato cooking water). Add the *tarama* and use a spoon to scoop the avocado flesh out of the skins and add it as well. Pulse or beat to combine, then add the olive oil and lemon juice in alternating increments, a few tablespoons at a time, until the mixture is smooth and has the consistency of mayonnaise. Loosen the mixture to the desired consistency by adding some of the reserved potato cooking water. Season to taste with salt and a few drops of hot sauce, if desired. Serve with pita chips or crudités.

Y Taramosalata tou Mezen ston Volo

MEZEN'S TARAMOSALATA

makes about 2 cups (480 ml)

Mezen, one of the most cutting-edge meze *restaurants in Greece as of this writing, is located in Volos, a small port city in central Greece renowned for its* tsipouradika *(casual restaurants that served* tsipouro, *aka Greek firewater or grappa) and the variety of* mezedes *served at them.*

Salty tarama—*fish roe—is the perfect* meze *with which to wash down shot glass after shot glass of strong, grapy Greek* tsipouro. *The roe is typically culled from cod or carp and sometimes from grey mullet, and is cured (in other words, salted and preserved). There are two main varieties: white roe (usually cod), and cheaper pink or red roe consisting of a blend of cured roes that have been dyed pink.*

Traditionally the dish was pounded in a mortar with a pestle. Many contemporary chefs and home cooks use a combination of olive and sunflower or corn oil to help emulsify the mixture and keep its flavor balanced, without too much of the headiness that would be imparted by using extra-virgin Greek olive oil alone. The final taste is pleasantly fishy and sharp, with a sweet after-taste. Taramosalata *is one of the staple dishes of Greek fasting periods.*

2½ ounces (71 g) white or pink *tarama* (fish roe; about 3 tablespoons)

3 tablespoons finely chopped red onion

Scant ⅓ cup (70 ml) strained fresh lemon juice

1⅓ cups (4½ ounces / 125 g) fresh white bread crumbs (preferably from sourdough bread)

¾ cup plus 1 tablespoon (200 ml) sunflower oil

3 tablespoons plus 1 teaspoon (50 ml) extra-virgin Greek olive oil

Homemade Pita Chips (page 46) or crudités, for serving

Place the *tarama*, onion, and lemon juice in a blender and blend on high speed to form a loose paste. Add the bread crumbs in four ⅓-cup (40 g) increments, alternating with the sunflower and olive oils and pulsing after each addition. Continue until the *taramosalata* is a dense but smooth paste. Add enough water, a tablespoon at a time, to loosen the mixture to a creamy, spreadable consistency, as light and fluffy as mayonnaise. Serve as a dip, with pita chips or crudités.

Tzatziki me Tsakpinia

TZATZIKI
with a twist

makes about 2 cups (480 ml)

Tzatziki is one of the most iconic Greek dishes, and changing it is akin to painting a mustache on the Mona Lisa. So . . . I'll say this is an homage to Marcel Duchamp: tzatziki with a few cornichons tossed in.

1 large seedless cucumber, peeled and grated on the large holes of a box grater

Salt

2 cups (480 ml) Greek yogurt, preferably full-fat

4 to 6 garlic cloves, minced

3 tablespoons extra-virgin Greek olive oil

3 small cornichons, minced

1 tablespoon red wine vinegar

¼ cup (13 g) chopped fresh dill

Place the grated cucumber in a fine-mesh sieve lined with cheesecloth, sprinkle lightly with salt, and toss. Cover and let stand in the sink for 1 hour to drain. Gather up the ends of the cheesecloth and twist as far down as possible, squeezing out as much water as possible from the cucumber. Do this several times, until the grated cucumber has exuded most of its liquid.

Empty the yogurt into a medium bowl. Add the cucumber, garlic (use more or less to taste), olive oil, cornichons, vinegar, and dill and stir to combine. Taste and adjust the seasoning with salt if necessary. Cover and refrigerate for 15 minutes before serving.

The tzatziki will keep, covered and chilled, for a day or two before the garlic starts to impart an unpleasant bitterness to the dip.

Ktipiti Kafteri

FETA FIRE

makes about 3 cups (720 ml)

Feta whipped into a dip is a popular meze *all over Greece, and there are countless variations on the theme. This one is both spicy and creamy, thanks to the addition of Greek yogurt to smooth out the mixture. This is also great as a sandwich spread and goes wonderfully as an accompaniment to grilled vegetables, meat, or shrimp.*

2 chopped roasted red peppers, either freshly roasted or brined Greek Florina peppers, rinsed and drained

1 or 2 fresh chiles, seeded

1 pound (450 g) Greek feta, crumbled or otherwise broken up

Juice of ½ to 1 lemon, strained

A few drops of hot sauce

1 teaspoon dried Greek oregano

½ to ⅔ cup (120 to 160 ml) extra-virgin Greek olive oil

Freshly ground black pepper

2 to 3 tablespoons Greek yogurt, preferably full-fat, as needed

Homemade Pita Chips (page 46) or crudités, for serving

Put all the peppers in the bowl of a food processor and process until pulverized.

Add the feta and pulse until the mixture is a thick cream. Add half the lemon juice, hot sauce to taste, the oregano, ½ cup (120 ml) of olive oil, and black pepper to taste. Pulse to combine well. The mixture should be creamy. Add the remaining olive oil and lemon juice and the yogurt as needed to adjust the flavor and consistency to your preference. Serve as a dip with homemade pita chips or crudités.

Ktipiti me Mexikaniki Pinelia

GREC-MEX WHIPPED FETA

makes about 3 cups (720 ml)

Having grown up in New York, with the world of international ingredients at my fingertips, I often cast a blind eye to tradition in order to embrace a little fun and experimentation. Here is a rendition of a pretty classic Greek dip, spicy whipped feta, not unlike the one on page 57. It is also sometimes called tyrokafteri. *The heat comes from Mexican peppers.*

1 garlic clove

1 slim fresh chile, such as árbol, seeded and chopped

1 to 3 pickled jalapeños, drained, seeded, and chopped

3 tablespoons chopped canned chipotles in adobo sauce

½ cup (25 g) chopped fresh cilantro

3 cups (450 g) crumbled Greek feta

½ to ⅔ cup (120 to 160 ml) extra-virgin Greek olive oil

Grated zest of 1 small lemon

2 to 3 tablespoons strained fresh lemon juice

Freshly ground black pepper

Pita chips, store-bought or homemade (page 46)

Place the garlic clove, chile, pickled jalapeños, and chipotles in the bowl of a food processor and pulse to a paste. Add the cilantro and pulse to combine.

Add the feta. With the motor running, steadily stream in enough of the olive oil to make a smooth, spreadable paste. Add the lemon zest, 2 tablespoons of the lemon juice, and black pepper to taste. Pulse to combine, taste, and adjust the texture and flavor with the remaining olive oil and/or lemon juice. Serve as a dip with pita chips.

OTHER USES FOR
KTIPITI IN THE KITCHEN

You can use *ktipiti* (whipped feta) as a dip, but you can also use it to stuff long green peppers for baking, or even as a topping for broiled fish or chicken. It's great between slices of cooked beet, or as a dip for crispy fried potatoes. You can thin and warm the *ktipiti* with a little cream as well and serve it with a piece of grilled steak.

To stuff peppers: Add ½ cup (50 g) plain dried bread crumbs to the *ktipiti* mixture. Remove the crowns from 6 to 8 long green peppers; set the crowns aside. Carefully remove as many of their seeds as possible without tearing the peppers (a long, dull butter knife does the trick). Using your thumb, press as much of the cheese mixture as possible into each hollowed-out pepper, leaving about ½ inch (1.5 cm) from the top unfilled. Place the crown inside each pepper opening, stem-side in. Place the stuffed peppers in an oiled pan, drizzle with olive oil, and bake in a preheated 375°F (190°C) oven until tender but al dente and lightly charred. Serve hot.

As a topping for fish such as salmon or sea bass, or for chicken: Add 1 large egg, ½ cup (50 g) plain dried bread crumbs, and ⅔ cup (35 g) chopped fresh herbs such as mint, parsley, and oregano to the mixture. Season the fish or chicken with salt and black pepper and brush it with olive oil and a little mustard, if desired. Press a few tablespoons of the cheese mixture onto the surface of each piece of fish or chicken and bake until done. If desired, switch the oven to broil for a few minutes just before removing the fish or chicken from the oven to get some color on the cheese crust.

Kopanisti me Psites Tomates

ROASTED TOMATO "KOPANISTI"

makes about 3 cups (720 ml)

Kopanisti, *which means "beaten," is the name for several cheese specialties in the Greek kitchen. It sometimes refers to a fermented cheese that is a traditional product throughout the Aegean islands, and it also refers to a whipped feta spread seasoned with herbs, olive oil, and sometimes some heat in the form of black pepper or chiles. This is a mild, tangy version of* kopanisti *and is excellent spread on bruschetta or as a base for meatballs.*

1 garlic clove, chopped

1 cup (150 g) crumbled Greek feta

1 cup (150 g) crumbled manouri or ricotta salata cheese

2 tablespoons Greek yogurt, preferably full-fat

1½ cups (250 g) roasted cherry or teardrop tomatoes (see Note)

3 tablespoons extra-virgin Greek olive oil

1 teaspoon grated lemon zest

2 teaspoons chopped fresh oregano leaves

Pita chips, store bought or homemade (page 46)

Combine the garlic, feta, manouri, and yogurt in the bowl of a food processor and pulse to combine.

Add the roasted tomatoes, olive oil, lemon zest, and oregano and pulse until the mixture is a slightly chunky paste.

Transfer to a bowl or plastic container, cover, and refrigerate for at least 30 minutes or up to 1 week before serving. Serve as a dip with pita chips.

NOTE: To make the roasted cherry or teardrop tomatoes, preheat the oven to 350°F (175°C) and line a baking sheet with parchment paper. Halve 3 cups (300 g) of cherry or teardrop tomatoes and place them in a large bowl. Add 3 sliced garlic cloves, 1 teaspoon sugar, 2 tablespoons balsamic vinegar, 3 tablespoons extra-virgin Greek olive oil, 2 tablespoons chopped fresh oregano, 2 tablespoons chopped fresh thyme, and salt to taste and toss to coat the tomatoes. Spread the mixture over the prepared baking sheet and roast for 30 to 45 minutes, turning the tomatoes once, until they are caramelized and just starting to form a charred crust on top. Remove and set aside. Let cool before using. You can store these in a jar with a tight-fitting lid, covered with olive oil, in the refrigerator for up to a week.

MEZE

TO SHARE

Φάγαμε ψωμί και αλάτι μαζί

Fagame psomi kai alati mazi

"We ate bread and salt together."
(Representing friendship)

The story of *mezedes* is the story of one of the most convivial aspects of the Greek table. The *meze* tradition is one of grazing and socializing; the savory, varied, small dishes that make up a *meze* table are meant to be shared and sipped with alcohol. The quaffs of choice are typically wine, ouzo, *tsipouro*, or raki. The latter two, grape distillates akin to grappa, are a long-standing tradition in this grape-growing, wine-making culture.

Mezedes are enjoyed all over Greece. The lively atmosphere that generally permeates the *meze* table makes for one of the most essential dining experiences in the country. Indeed, the tradition traces its roots to the symposia of the distant, ancient past. *Symposium*, in Greek, actually means "to drink together."

For the most part, it's the drink of choice that determines the selection of small plates served up on a *meze* table. That means making a distinction between distillates, such as ouzo and *tsipouro* or raki, and wine. The basic (flexible) rule of thumb is that whatever swims goes well with ouzo, *tsipouro*, and raki, and whatever grazes on land is better with wine.

Regardless of the quaff, however, variety is a key element. Almost anything can be served as a *meze*, from a simple plate of olives to savory dips (pages 44–51) to a whole array of seafood, aromatic meat dishes, vegetable fritters, and more.

I've separated dips from the *meze* chapter because there are many of them, and I like to think of them as dual purpose: they're great as *mezedes*, but most of them are also great as sandwich spreads or even accompaniments for more substantial proteins. "Painting" a swath of, for example, tzatziki or whipped feta onto a serving platter as a bed or base for, say, Greek meatballs or even a lamb chop or two is a little trick from my work in restaurant kitchens that I often carry over to my table at home.

In this section, the *meze* selection is composed of an array of small plates, from spiced aromatic feta wrapped in phyllo to fritters, savory seafood dishes, and a few meat-based *mezedes*. Enjoy them with a glass of Greek wine or a sip of a Greek distillate, clinking glasses with good company and savoring lively conversation.

Elies Psites sto Tigani me Portokali kai Myrodika

PAN-SEARED OLIVES ON TOAST
with oranges and herbs

makes 4 to 6 meze servings

During the height of the first financial crisis in Greece, Greeks used to say, not altogether in jest, that "at least we have olives." Olives, one of nature's greatest superfoods, have always been an integral part of the Greek table. Ironically, with the exception of breads and sauces to which olives might be added, there are very few traditional Greek recipes calling for olives. Mostly, olives are just there, ever present on the table during every meal of the day. They are also the country's number one agricultural export.

This recipe is one of the few in which olives are featured prominently. Pan-fried or pan-grilled olives are a popular quick meze *in many parts of Greece where table olives are cultivated.*

Of all the table olive varieties in Greece, the ones called "raisin olives," which mature on the tree until they are wrinkled but still retain their meaty texture, are best for this dish. Wrinkled black olives are generally less salty than brined olives, and the oiliness inherent in their flesh makes them most suitable for sautéing.

½ small orange, preferably organic

2 tablespoons extra-virgin Greek olive oil

2 cups (310 g) wrinkled black Greek olives, preferably either Thassos or Halkidiki

1 large garlic clove, cut into very thin slivers

Scant 1 teaspoon dried Greek oregano, or 2 teaspoons chopped fresh oregano leaves

Keep the peel on the orange and cut the orange into 3 wedges. Cut each wedge into small triangular slices, about ⅛ inch (3 mm) thick.

In a heavy skillet or stovetop grill pan, heat the olive oil over medium heat. Add the olives and orange wedges to the pan and shake the pan back and forth to combine them. Stir in the garlic. Continue to shake the pan back and forth or gently stir for about 5 minutes, until the olives are warmed through, the garlic is soft and shiny, and the orange slices are slightly wilted. Stir in the oregano and transfer to a bowl. Serve.

KALAMATA OLIVES, FROM TREE TO TABLE

The world's most famous olive is a bit of a misnomer. The kalamata olive, that purplish-brownish-black olive with the smooth, taut skin and the almond shape, the one that punctuates Greek salads the world over, is named not for the region it comes from but the port from which most were once shipped. The vast majority of Greece's annual production is actually produced in another part of the Peloponnese, Laconia, especially in the region around Sparta. Kalamata olives are produced in other parts of Greece as well, with a large harvest in the area around Agrinio, in Western Mainland Greece.

The best kalamata olives, indeed the best olives of any variety, are what the Greeks call *kserikes* or "dry," as in watered only by natural rainfall. When there is a drought, conditions can be severe enough to cause the loss of up to 70 percent of olive production. Such are the olives produced by Manousos and Manolis Manousakis on their gently sprawling estate in Selasia, a few kilometers outside Sparta, a town that once acted as gatekeeper for the ancient warrior city-state.

Harvesting olives is one of the most arduous yet therapeutic acts. There is a rhythm to it, honed over generations. Constant movement as you move up and down the trees, bending, stretching to reach the highest branches, protects against the chill of November and December days in the Laconian mountains. The winter sun is sweet. No one harvests in the rain.

To start, the women in the family prep and trail, laying green tarpaulin nets on the ground beneath the trees to cover the area under the leaf sprawl so that as many olives as possible can be collected. The men do the more demanding physical labor, first rattling the branches with a kind of giant vibrating pole, shaking down the olives, which fall onto those nets. Any errant fruit left on the branches is raked down by hand with a special wide, comb-like tool. There are about 250 olives to a kilogram. At this writing, a kilogram wholesales for 2 euro, so losing even a few, whether squashed underfoot or rolled downhill, means losing precious income.

The harvest always happens in the fall, sometime between October and December, when the fruit has turned from green to bluish black. Each tree at least ten years old produces about 10 kilograms (22 pounds) of olives. The variety of olive sizes on a given tree is mind-boggling, but these are sorted through later on, either by hand or mechanically.

Once a tree has been harvested, the women get back into action, picking up the edges of the nets, rolling the olives into the middle to collect them into crates. Then they roll up the nets and spread them under the next few trees in line for harvesting.

From the tree, the crates of olives go directly to a nearby processing plant where a series of machines simulate the home curing, or fermentation, process, slitting and then soaking them in a salt brine, where they sit for about three weeks before being transferred to a vinegar-salt solution for a few days. Once sufficiently fermented and brined—the extent of which is a matter of personal taste when done at home and commercial profile when done at a processing plant—the olives are packed and shipped to the four corners of the globe. Of course some stay local, in which case the region's home cooks are more likely to put them up in olive oil, which is ample in this part of Greece, and which softens their sharp flavor over time.

Everywhere one looks in Laconia, there is almost nothing else but olive trees and mountains. But despite the ubiquity of the olive tree and the importance of its famed fruit in the local economy, it is oddly absent from the kitchen. "We just serve them as they are for breakfast, lunch, and dinner. They are always on the table," Maria Stefanopoulou told me. She is the caretaker on Manoli's land, and I had the pleasure of watching and learning as her nimble hands slit basin after basin of olives: three slits for the large ones, two for the medium, and one for the smallest. She moved fast and rhythmically with an easy agility she jokingly said was from the three generations of olive growers in her DNA. She may not have been far from the truth. Olives, an ancient superfood, are a great source of anti-inflammatories, which help keep us nimble like Maria.

Feta Psiti se Fyllo Me Baharika kai Meli

PHYLLO-WRAPPED FETA
with cumin, poppy, or caraway seeds and honey

makes 4 meze servings

The salty, briny flavor of feta goes surprisingly well with honey, a combination that contemporary Greek chefs have been experimenting with for about the last decade. This recipe is a variation on several cheese-based specialties that are traditional Greek mezedes. One of those specialties is saganaki, *its most common iteration the pan-fried cheese that is a traditional and popular Greek dish; the other is baked cheese, either crumbled and baked in a small pan, or wrapped in parchment paper or phyllo, sometimes seasoned with herbs, spices, or vegetables. Melting cheese, wrapped in phyllo or not and regardless of the additions, is always a welcome dish on my Greek table!*

3 tablespoons extra-virgin Greek olive oil, plus more for greasing

2 sheets (14 x 18-inch / 35 x 45 cm) #7 commercial phyllo, defrosted overnight in the refrigerator, then brought to room temperature

2 (4-inch / 10 cm) square pieces Greek feta, each about ½ inch (1.5 cm) thick

½ to ¾ cup (145 to 215 g) caraway, cumin, or poppy seeds

1 egg white, lightly beaten

½ cup (120 ml) Greek honey

1 small fresh or dried chile, seeded and finely chopped

1 tablespoon strained fresh lemon juice

Preheat the oven to 350°F (175°C). Lightly oil a small baking dish large enough to hold the two squares of feta.

Take the first phyllo sheet and place it horizontally in front of you on a clean work surface. Brush the phyllo lightly with some of the olive oil. Place a feta square in the middle. Fold in the sides, brushing each unoiled surface of the phyllo with a little of the olive oil and pressing lightly to seal. Repeat with the second phyllo sheet and feta square.

Spread the caraway seeds over a large flat plate. Lightly brush the top of each phyllo-wrapped feta square with a little of the egg white and dip the egg-washed side into the caraway seeds. Place the feta square seed-side up on the prepared baking dish. Repeat to coat the top of the second feta square.

Bake the feta for about 20 minutes, or until the phyllo is puffed and golden.

While the feta is baking, whisk together the honey, chile, and lemon juice in a small bowl.

Remove the feta squares from the oven and let cool for a few minutes. Cut each square into two triangles and serve, drizzled with the spiced honey.

DOLMA HEAVEN

For all the ubiquity of dolmades (stuffed, rolled leaves, usually grape leaves) in the Greek kitchen—they are, after all, one of the most iconic Greek *mezedes*—it is heartening to know that a few places in Greece are home to some of the most unusual renditions of this classic. The most common filling for Greece's famous stuffed grape leaves is the aromatic combination of onions, rice, fresh herbs, and sometimes pine nuts and/or raisins. Ground beef and rice are also a classic filling, especially in the winter, and the dolmades filled with them tend to be served with béchamel or avgolemono sauce.

But there are a few genuinely unusual regional recipes for stuffed leaves, most of which are found in the island kitchens of the Dodecanese. In Kalymnos, for example, where grape leaves are preserved by drying them like garlands, which to this day still dangle from hooks in country groceries, vegetable mixtures like pumpkin and rice or bulgur wheat and spices are the local filling specialties. I discovered my favorite dolmades recipes in an unlikely place: Rhodes, one of the most heavily touristed islands in Greece, where much of the food one encounters at first glance is, unfortunately, tailored to the tourism industry, with little or no regional character. But leaving the overcrowded capital and venturing into the interior of the island is a journey that reveals some of the most fascinating and original local fare in Greece.

Traditional cooks on the island have long had a penchant for making highly original stuffed leaves. I've included two of my favorite recipes: grape leaves filled with fresh broad beans and with mushrooms, respectively. Ground pork and onions are another popular filling for grape or cabbage leaves there.

But the biggest surprise was discovering old recipes from Rhodes for dolmades rolled in leaves other than those plucked off the grapevine. Cyclamen and apricot leaves are also used to make dolmades. I've even come across a very old recipe for rolled geranium leaves, cooked in the same pot with translucent, delicious, stuffed rolled onions.

Today, dolmades are open to all sorts of modern interpretations. Even Greek producers of classic dolmades, sold in either cans or vacuum packs, have broadened the range of their product line to include quinoa, bulgur, sriracha, and other ingredients in commercial reinterpretations of this time-honored Greek dish.

RHODES-STYLE GRAPE LEAVES
stuffed with broad beans and bulgur

makes 8 to 12 meze servings

The most common recipes for vegetarian stuffed grape leaves in Greece call for rice and herbs. This is an old recipe from Rhodes and attests to the place of wheat in the traditional Greek diet, before rice became prevalent enough to be affordable on the everyday table.

1 (16-ounce / 475 ml) jar grape leaves in brine, drained

2 large, firm tomatoes

10 ounces (285 g) shelled fresh or defrosted frozen baby broad beans

½ cup (70 g) coarse bulgur wheat

4 red onions, finely chopped

4 scallions, finely chopped

2 garlic cloves, minced

1 cup (50 g) chopped fresh dill

1 cup (50 g) chopped fresh parsley

1 cup (50 g) chopped fresh mint

1 tablespoon ground cumin

Salt and freshly ground black pepper

1 cup (240 ml) extra-virgin Greek olive oil

Bring a large pot of water to a rolling boil. Fill a large bowl with ice and water. Add the grape leaves to the boiling water and blanch for 3 minutes to soften. Remove with a slotted spoon and transfer to the ice water.

Grate the tomatoes on the large holes of a box grater. Place the tomatoes, broad beans, bulgur, onions, scallions, garlic, dill, parsley, and mint in a large bowl and toss to combine. Add the cumin and season generously with salt and pepper. Mix in ½ cup (120 ml) of the olive oil and 1 cup (240 ml) room-temperature water. Let the mixture stand for 15 minutes.

Drain the grape leaves and place them vein-side up on a work surface. Using kitchen scissors or a small knife, snip off the stems. Place as many grape leaves as will fit in neat rows in front of you, arranging them vein-side up, with the pointy part at the top and the stem end at the bottom, nearest you. Place any torn or very small leaves in a wide pot, arranging them to cover the bottom.

Take a heaping teaspoon of the filling and place it in the center of the bottom of the first leaf. Fold in the sides, then roll the leaf around the filling to form a small cylinder. Place the roll seam-side down in the pot, along the outer rim. Repeat to fill and roll the remaining grape leaves. You can layer the dolmades on top of one another in the pot, so long as they are placed snugly next to one another in each layer. Pour in the remaining ½ cup (120 ml) olive oil and enough water to cover the leaves by ¼ inch (6 mm).

(CONTINUED)

Cut a piece of parchment paper to the circumference of the pot and place it over the pot. Cover the pot with a lid and bring the liquid to a simmer over medium heat. Reduce the heat to low and simmer for 50 minutes to 1 hour, until the grape leaves are tender.

VARIATION

GRAPE LEAVES STUFFED WITH MUSHROOMS: This iteration is from a small village in the interior of Rhodes called Laerma, about 64 kilometers (40 miles) from the island's capital: Simply replace the broad beans with 1 pound (450 g) chopped button, oyster, or portobello mushrooms.

NOTE: Try peeling and slicing potatoes to place on the bottom of the pot, under the grape leaves. You can remove them and serve them separately as a salad or side dish. They take on the delicious briny flavor of the leaves and make a very unique dish.

Tomatokeftedes Santorinis me Mpakaliaro

MARGARITA'S TOMATO FRITTERS
with cod

makes 6 to 8 meze servings

Santorini is one of the most astoundingly beautiful—and deeply troubled—places in the world. When I first visited the island almost thirty years ago, it was on the cusp of becoming one of the world's most popular tourist destinations. As of this writing, the island is inundated with more than two million tourists a year, about a tenth of the total number of people who visit Greece yearly. Land prices on this tiny island, only 76 square miles, are exorbitant, making it more and more difficult for farmers and vintners to survive.

I visited one of the last working family farms, run by Margarita Alefrangki and her family, who also operate one of the island's best fish tavernas, Y Spilia tou Nikola. They grow Santorini's famed anydra, *or waterless, tomatoes, a small variety that flourishes in chalky volcanic soil and needs almost no water to survive. They are among the most intensely flavored tomatoes in Greece and the main ingredient in one of the island's signature dishes. This is Margarita's recipe. The cod will need to be desalted for 48 hours before it can be used, so be sure to plan ahead.*

1 salt cod fillet, about 1½ pounds (680 g)

2 red onions, finely chopped

10 scallions, chopped

Salt

3 pounds (1.4 kg) firm but not juicy small tomatoes, such as grape tomatoes

3 small round or oblong zucchini, quartered, seeded, and finely chopped

1 cup (50 g) chopped fresh basil leaves

3 tablespoons dried mint

Freshly ground black pepper

3 to 6 cups (375 to 750 g) all-purpose flour, as needed

Corn oil, for frying

Two days before preparing the recipe, desalt the cod: Break up the cod into pieces about 2 inches (5 cm) square. Place the cod in a bowl and fill with cold water to cover. Refrigerate for 48 hours, changing the water every few hours. Drain the cod and break the pieces apart into shreds and chop them. Set aside.

Put the onions and scallions in a large bowl. Add a scant 1 teaspoon salt and knead the onion-scallion mixture until soft. Add the tomatoes, zucchini, basil, and mint. Add the cod to the bowl. Season to taste with salt and pepper.

Knead the mixture, adding the flour as you go until you've added enough that the mixture forms a dense mass that holds its shape on a spoon when scooped up and held upside down.

In a large, deep skillet or wide pot, heat 2 inches (5 cm) of corn oil over medium-high heat until it registers 350°F (175°C) on an instant-read or deep-fry thermometer. Scoop up a teaspoon of the cod mixture and, using a second teaspoon, slide it into the hot oil. Repeat to fill but not overcrowd the pan. Fry the fritters for about 2 minutes, then turn them and fry on the other side until nice and golden, 2 to 3 minutes. Use a slotted spoon to transfer the fritters to a paper towel–lined plate to drain. Repeat with the remaining cod mixture. Serve hot or at room temperature.

Melitzanokeftedes apo to Molyvo

MOLYVOS EGGPLANT KEFTEDES

makes 4 to 6 meze servings

Lesvos, Greece's third largest island, is one of my favorite places. The island's natural environment overflows with wildlife. Over a million olive trees blanket the island; Lesvos's rich natural flora and plankton-rich bays and coves have been renowned since antiquity.

The philosopher Aristotle was so moved by the island's rich flora and teeming waters that he wrote one of the world's first masterpieces of natural history there, inspiring Darwin thousands of years later.

Lesvos found itself in the eye of the European migration crisis, inundated with thousands of refugees who washed up on its shores from the war-torn Middle East as they made their way across the Aegean from the coast of Turkey.

Indeed, the island's proximity to Turkey has shaped its long history, and food is part of that. During the final throes of the Ottoman Empire in 1922, the Greek army, with the blessing of the British, invaded Asia Minor (present-day Turkey) to help liberate the four million Greeks who had been living there since ancient times. Two million were killed, and two million fled. Thousands settled in Lesvos, revitalizing the local economy and cuisine. With them came a rich, urbane, aromatic cooking style and a love for the eggplant, for which Lesvos claims at least twenty-two unique local recipes.

I first tried these eggplant keftedes in Molyvo at the family home of my good friend Nick Livanos, where they were prepared by Nick's cousin Maria, a fabulous cook.

5 Japanese or other long eggplant variety, each about 6 inches (15 cm) long

1 large egg, lightly beaten

1½ cups (150 g) grated aged myzithra or Kefalotyri cheese (see Note)

1 heaping tablespoon dried Greek oregano

1 cup (50 g) chopped fresh mint

3 to 4 tablespoons sour *trahana* (see page 214) or fine bulgur wheat

Salt and freshly ground black pepper

2 to 8 tablespoons (15 to 50 g) plain dried bread crumbs, as needed

1 cup (125 g) all-purpose flour, or more as needed, for dredging

Olive or vegetable oil, for frying (see Note)

Bring a pot of water to a boil and season it with salt. Trim and peel the eggplants. Add them to the boiling water, reduce the heat to maintain a simmer, and cook the eggplants until soft, 15 to 20 minutes. Remove with a slotted spoon and drain well. Transfer to a large bowl.

Mash the eggplant with a fork and add the egg, grated cheese, oregano, mint, and 3 tablespoons of the *trahana*. Season to taste with salt and pepper. Add the bread crumbs judiciously, starting with a couple of tablespoons and adding more only if the mixture is loose and needs help holding its shape. You can also add the remaining 1 tablespoon *trahana*.

Shape 1 tablespoon of the eggplant mixture into a patty about 1½ inches (4 cm) in diameter. Place it on a platter or baking sheet(s) and repeat with the remaining eggplant mixture. Refrigerate the patties for 30 minutes to help firm them up even more.

Place 1 cup (125 g) of the flour on a flat dish. In a large deep skillet, heat 2 inches (5 cm) of olive oil over medium-high heat. Test the heat with a small cube of bread: when tossed into the oil, it should sizzle and brown lightly; remove and discard the test cube. Working in batches, lightly dredge the eggplant patties in the flour and, using a spatula or slotted spoon, slide them into the hot oil, being careful not to crowd the pan. Fry until lightly browned on one side, then flip them carefully and cook until lightly browned on the other side. Use a slotted spoon to transfer the patties to a paper towel–lined plate. Repeat with the remaining patties, replenishing the frying oil if necessary. Serve immediately.

NOTE: You can use any other hard grating cheese, such as regato or pecorino, or a combination of crumbled feta and Kefalograviera cheeses.

NOTE: You can also bake the patties: Preheat the oven to 350°F (175°C). Line two baking sheets with parchment paper. Shape and refrigerate the patties as above. Place them on the prepared baking sheets and bake, turning once to brown on both sides, for about 15 minutes, or until cooked through and golden. Remove from the oven, let cool slightly, and serve.

VARIATION

ARTICHOKE HEART KEFTEDES: This is a recipe from the opposite side of Greece, Lefkada, in the Ionian Sea. Follow the recipe as above, but replace the eggplant with 10 large artichoke hearts (you can use defrosted frozen ones or good-quality canned artichoke hearts in olive oil, drained) and omit the *trahana*, using extra bread crumbs as needed.

Karotokeftedes

CARROT KEFTEDES

makes 4 to 6 meze servings

Greek vegetable fritters, or pseftokeftedes, *as they are sometimes called, are one of the great gifts from the Greek table to vegetable lovers the world over. All over the country, seasonal vegetable patties and fritters are part of the culinary tradition, a way to take simple, accessible, inexpensive, healthy ingredients and transform them into something delectable. All sorts of greens, tomatoes, onions, leeks, squashes, and beans are turned into crispy fritters. Most can be either baked or fried. These carrot* keftedes *are something I whipped up for Committee, the meze restaurant in Boston I've been working with for several years.*

4 cups (440 g) coarsely shredded carrots (6 to 8 medium carrots)

1 garlic clove, very finely chopped

½ cup (25 g) finely chopped fresh fennel fronds or dill

½ cup (25 g) finely chopped fresh parsley

2 heaping tablespoons dried mint

⅔ cup (100 g) crumbled soft Greek feta

¼ cup (25 g) grated graviera cheese

Salt and freshly ground black pepper

1 teaspoon ground cumin

1 large egg, lightly beaten

⅓ cup (35 g) plain dried bread crumbs

½ cup (65 g) all-purpose flour

Tzatziki or plain Greek yogurt, for serving

Preheat the oven to 350°F (175°C). Line a baking sheet with parchment paper.

Combine all the ingredients except the tzatziki in a large bowl and knead by hand until firm and a bit sticky. Shape into 1½-inch (4 cm) patties. Place on the prepared baking sheet and bake for 20 to 25 minutes, flipping once.

Serve hot, warm, or at room temperature, with a bowl of tzatziki or plain yogurt on the side.

Pseftokeftedes me Karydia

NORTHERN GREEK WALNUT FRITTERS

makes 6 meze servings

One of my favorite aspects of the Greek table is the wealth of dishes that simulate meat but are oftentimes totally vegan. These dishes generally evolved as a way to fill the belly during times of fasting, when all animal products are prohibited. This is an old recipe from the traditions of the Vlachs, a once itinerant shepherd tribe that calls northern Greece home. Serve it over a bed of frisée with a little Greek yogurt on the side.

1 medium potato, peeled

1½ to 2 cups (190 to 250 g) all-purpose flour, as needed, plus extra for coating the fritters

Scant 1 tablespoon baking soda

2 cups (160 g) coarsely ground walnuts

2 garlic cloves, minced

1 large red onion, finely chopped

½ cup (25 g) finely chopped fresh mint

Salt and freshly ground black pepper

Olive oil or other oil, for frying

Greek yogurt, for serving (optional)

Grate or shred the potato on the large holes of a box grater or using a food processor fitted with the grating disc. Squeeze the excess liquid out of the potato by hand or wrap it in cheesecloth and wring out as much liquid as possible. Place the potato in a bowl. Mix in 1½ cups (190 g) of the flour, baking soda, walnuts, garlic, onion, and mint. Season to taste with salt and pepper. Knead the mixture until firm enough to hold its shape, adding the remaining flour as needed. Shape 1 tablespoon of the mixture into a ball and flatten it lightly to form a patty. Set aside on a large platter or tray and repeat with the remaining mixture.

In a large deep skillet, heat about 2 inches (5 cm) of olive oil over medium-high heat until it registers about 365°F (185°C) on an instant-read or deep-fry thermometer.

Spread the flour over a large plate or platter and lightly dredge the patties, shaking off the excess. Working in batches, fry the patties in the hot oil until deep golden brown on both sides, flipping once. Drain on paper towels and serve, accompanied, if desired, by Greek yogurt.

CRISPY LEEK FRITTERS

makes 6 to 8 meze servings

Even something as simple as leeks, and their relatives, onions and scallions, inspire the simple mezedes found all over Greece. Onion, leek, or scallion fritters are very popular in the regional traditions of Rhodes, Evia, and Macedonia, among other places, and the variations on this theme are endless, from simple onion-batter crisps to an unusual scallion fritter from Rhodes, seasoned with cinnamon and drizzled with honey. This recipe is a bit of a hybrid, but it makes a great meze for many of Greece's dry white or rosé wines, as well as for tsipouro.

5 large leeks, white and light green parts only, washed well and coarsely chopped

2 teaspoons salt

4 large eggs

Scant 1 teaspoon baking powder

1 teaspoon paprika

½ teaspoon freshly ground black pepper

2 teaspoons dried Greek oregano

2 teaspoons dried mint

3 tablespoons chopped fresh parsley

1½ cups (190 g) all-purpose flour

Olive oil or other oil, for frying

Put the leeks in a colander and sprinkle with the salt. Knead for 5 to 6 minutes, pressing out as much of the leeks' natural moisture as possible. Do not rinse. Transfer the leeks to a large bowl and add the eggs, baking powder, paprika, pepper, oregano, mint, and parsley.

In a separate bowl, whisk together the flour and 1 cup (240 ml) water until smooth. Add the chopped leek mixture to the batter and stir to combine well.

In a large wide pot or a deep heavy skillet, heat 3 inches (7.5 cm) of olive oil over medium-high heat until it registers about 350°F (175°C) on an instant-read or deep-fry thermometer. Take a spoonful of the mixture and slide it into the hot oil, using another spoon to push it off the first, if necessary. Do this several times to make about 4 fritters. Fry, turning once, until browned on both sides. Remove with a slotted spoon and drain on paper towels. Repeat with the remaining leek mixture, replenishing the oil if needed. Serve hot.

Kotopoulo Keftedes

BAKED CHICKEN KEFTEDES

makes 6 meze servings

Classic Greek meatballs are made with either ground pork, lamb, beef, or a combination thereof. Here's a lighter version, flavored the classic way with plenty of onions, a little garlic, and a lot of mint, the telltale herb in all Greek meatballs. Serve these with tzatziki (page 56), fresh pea fava (page 50), or any of the feta cheese dips in chapter 3 or yogurt dressings in chapter 1.

2 pounds (900 g) ground chicken or turkey

3 garlic cloves, minced

2 red onions, finely chopped

1 large egg, lightly beaten

2 tablespoons extra-virgin Greek olive oil, plus more for frying

½ teaspoon paprika

⅔ cup (35 g) chopped fresh mint

½ cup (25 g) chopped fresh parsley

½ to 1 cup (40 to 80 g) panko bread crumbs

Salt and freshly ground black pepper

In a large bowl, combine the ground chicken, garlic, onions, egg, olive oil, paprika, mint, parsley, and ½ cup (40 g) of the panko. Season with salt and pepper and mix to combine. Test for firmness by shaping one meatball. If it holds its shape, don't add any more of the panko; if it comes apart, add more of the panko, a tablespoon at a time, until the mixture is firm enough to hold its shape when formed into a meatball.

Heat a little olive oil in a small skillet. Take a teaspoon of the mixture and fry it to test for seasoning; adjust accordingly.

Line a baking sheet with parchment paper. Form the mixture into 1-tablespoon meatballs. Place them on the prepared baking sheet in neat rows. Cover loosely with plastic wrap and refrigerate for at least 30 minutes or up to 6 hours.

Preheat the oven to 350°F (175°C).

Uncover and bake the meatballs for 20 to 25 minutes, until golden brown, turning gently with a spatula or kitchen tongs, until browned on all sides. Remove from the oven and serve.

Tragana Sardelokokala

CRISPY SARDINE BONES

makes 4 meze servings

Sardines are one of the most important, and economical, fish in the Aegean, and are a popular, nutritious source of protein on the weekly table all over Greece. Greek cooks like their sardines in many different ways: fried whole, baked with herbs and olive oil, stuffed and roasted, and filleted and salt-cured. No matter which way they're prepared, the bones are always left! I fell in love with this recipe for salted, crispy sardine bones when I tried it at Mezen, a cutting-edge meze *restaurant on a nondescript side street in the small city of Volos, in central Greece. Odd as the idea might sound, I really think this is a genius recipe. They go down like chips!*

2 tablespoons sea salt, plus more to taste

Whole sardine bones from 20 to 30 small fresh sardines (see Note)

Sunflower oil, for frying

1 to 1½ cups (125 to 190 g) all-purpose flour, for dredging

Scant 2 tablespoons smoked paprika

Lemon wedges, for serving

Salt the bones with 2 tablespoons of the sea salt and leave them out at room temperature, covered with paper towels, for 2 hours.

In a deep wide pot or skillet, heat ½ inch (1.5 cm) sunflower oil over medium-high heat until just below the smoke point. In a wide shallow bowl, combine the flour with salt to taste and the smoked paprika. Dredge the sardine bones lightly in the seasoned flour and shake off the excess. Fry the bones in the hot oil for a few minutes, until they turn lightly golden. Remove and drain on paper towels. Serve as is, with lemon wedges for squeezing over the top.

NOTE: It's important to use small fresh sardines, which are what is prevalent in Greece. You can also make this with anchovies.

Ktapodi stin Skara

ALL-TIME CLASSIC GRILLED OCTOPUS

makes 8 to 12 meze servings

It would be hard to imagine the Greek meze *table without a few slightly charred, smoky grilled octopus tentacles. If you're using a frozen octopus, it will need to thaw in the refrigerator overnight, so plan ahead.*

1 medium fresh or frozen octopus, about 4 pounds (1.8 kg)

3 garlic cloves, crushed

1 bay leaf

2 fresh rosemary sprigs

2 or 3 fresh thyme sprigs

½ cup (120 ml) dry red wine

½ cup (120 ml) red wine vinegar

¼ cup (60 ml) balsamic vinegar

½ cup (120 ml) plus 2 to 3 tablespoons extra-virgin Greek olive oil, plus more for brushing grill

1 teaspoon cracked black pepper

2 heaping teaspoons dried Greek oregano

2 tablespoons Greek capers, drained and rinsed

2 tablespoons chopped fresh parsley or oregano

If using frozen octopus, defrost it in the refrigerator overnight.

Using a large, sharp knife, cut off the octopus's sack-like hood just below the eyes and either discard or use to make a few servings of octopus *keftedes* (see page 90). Divide the octopus into 8 pieces, keeping the tentacles intact. Place it in a large heavy saucepan with the garlic, bay leaf, rosemary, thyme, wine, red wine vinegar, balsamic vinegar, ½ cup (120 ml) of the olive oil, and the pepper. Cover and bring to a boil. Reduce the heat to low and simmer for 45 to 50 minutes, or until the tentacles are tender but al dente and not at all stringy.

Remove the octopus from the pot and place it in a bowl with enough of the liquid from the pot to cover. Strain the remaining liquid from the pot and discard the solids. Set aside until ready to grill. (At this point, you can let the octopus cool to room temperature, then refrigerate it in its cooking liquid for up to 24 hours; refrigerate the strained cooking liquid as well. Bring the octopus to room temperature before grilling.)

When ready to grill, heat a grill to medium-high.

Return the strained octopus cooking liquid to the pot and simmer over medium-low heat until reduced to a loose, syrupy consistency.

Brush the grill grates with a little olive oil. Grill the octopus tentacles for 8 to 12 minutes, turning to char lightly on all sides.

Transfer the tentacles to a serving platter. Drizzle with the reduced cooking liquid and the remaining 2 to 3 tablespoons olive oil, sprinkle with the capers and a little fresh parsley or oregano, and serve.

TO MAKE OCTOPUS KEFTEDES: Turn the hood inside out and rinse it under cold running water. Using a paring knife or your fingers, remove and discard the viscera. Place the hood in a small pot, add water to cover, and bring to a boil. Reduce the heat to maintain a simmer, cover, and cook until cooked through, about 40 minutes. Remove from the pot and let cool. Chop the hood and place it in the bowl of a food processor. Add ¼ cup (25 g) chopped fresh parsley, 2 tablespoons chopped fresh dill, 1 tablespoon tomato paste, ¼ cup (35 g) chopped red onion, 1 tablespoon ouzo, ¼ to ½ cup (25 to 50 g) plain dried bread crumbs, and salt and freshly ground black pepper to taste. Pulse on and off a few times until the mixture forms a dense mass. Remove with a spatula and transfer to a bowl. Take a scant tablespoon and shape it into a small ball, 1 to 1½ inches (2.5 to 4 cm) in diameter. Place on a baking sheet. Repeat with the remaining mixture, cover loosely with plastic wrap, and refrigerate for 1 hour to firm up.

Heat 1 inch (2.5 cm) of olive or other oil over medium-high heat. Lightly dredge the octopus *keftedes* in all-purpose flour, shaking off the excess, and fry in the hot oil, turning, until browned on all sides. makes 12 to 14 keftedes

Skoumbri Pasto

GREEK MACKEREL "GRAVLAX"

makes 6 meze servings

Andreas Diakodimitris, co-owner of Mezen, is a passionate food lover and one of Greece's fore-most authorities on meze *and* tsipouro, *the grape distillate similar to grappa that is part of the culinary heritage of Andreas's hometown, Volos. When I tasted this dish at his restaurant, he told me that "Salt has incredible properties when it comes to raw meat or fish. It penetrates the flesh, drawing out moisture, resulting in a more intense taste. If other aromas are present, such as lemon and pepper, they are drawn together in the flesh, spreading the flavors even more."*

6 skin-on mackerel fillets, about 3 ounces (100 g) each

2 tablespoons coarse salt

2 teaspoons coarsely ground black pepper

2 teaspoons sugar

Finely grated zest of 1 lemon

Olive oil, for brushing

Place 3 fillets skin-side down in one layer in a glass or plastic container. Spread half the salt, pepper, and sugar evenly over them. Sprinkle half the lemon zest on top. Place the remaining 3 fillets skin-side down on top and repeat with the remaining salt, pepper, sugar, and zest. Cover and refrigerate for 3 to 4 hours. Gently rinse the fillets and dry them with a paper towel.

Preheat the broiler, heat a grill to medium, or brush a grill pan lightly with a little olive oil and heat it over medium heat.

Lightly oil the mackerel fillets. If broiling, place the fillets in a lightly oiled shallow pan and slide the pan under the broiler. If grilling, set the fillets on the grill grates. If pan-grilling, when the pan is hot, place the fillets in the pan, flesh-side down. Whether broiling, grilling, or pan-grilling, cook the fillets for a few minutes, turning them gently with a spatula to cook evenly on both sides, 6 to 7 minutes total.

Serve the mackerel, accompanied by a few tomato slices, arugula, or lettuce and drizzled with olive oil and lemon juice.

Garides Saganaki

SHRIMP IN A SKILLET
with feta and tomatoes

makes 4 to 6 meze servings

1½ pounds (680 g) large fresh shrimp, peeled, heads and tails kept on, and deveined

6 tablespoons (90 ml) ouzo

Juice of ½ lemon, strained

4 tablespoons (60 ml) extra-virgin Greek olive oil

1 large red onion, finely chopped

1 green chile, finely chopped

2 garlic cloves, chopped

2 cups (480 ml) grated fresh tomatoes (see Note) or chopped canned tomatoes

Salt and freshly ground black pepper

1 teaspoon grated lemon zest

⅔ cup (100 g) crumbled Greek feta

2 teaspoons dried Greek oregano

2 tablespoons finely chopped fresh parsley

Place the shrimp, 3 tablespoons of the ouzo, and the lemon juice in a bowl, cover, and refrigerate for at least 15 minutes or up to 2 hours.

In a large, deep skillet, heat 2 tablespoons of the olive oil over medium heat. Add the onion and chile and cook, stirring, until wilted, about 8 minutes. Stir in half the garlic. Add the toma-toes and bring to a simmer. Season lightly with salt and pepper. Raise the heat to medium-high and cook for 15 minutes, until most of the watery liquid from the tomatoes has evaporated.

In a separate large skillet, heat the remaining 2 tablespoons of olive oil over medium-high heat. Add the shrimp and remaining garlic, toss to combine, and cook until the shrimp turn pink. Carefully spritz with the remaining 3 tablespoons ouzo; it may flame up a bit. Add shrimp and pan juices to the tomato sauce. Stir in the lemon zest and feta. When the feta starts to melt, gently stir in the oregano and parsley. Remove from the heat and serve.

NOTE: To grate the tomato: Keep the tomato whole and unpeeled. Cut off a quarter-size piece from the root end and grate the tomato along the teeth of a box grater into a bowl.

Sardeles Sto Alati apo tin Lesvo

LESVOS-STYLE MARINATED RAW SARDINES OR ANCHOVIES

makes 6 to 8 meze servings

In the small seaside village of Skala Sikaminias, on the northern coast of Molyvos, there is a great little seafood taverna called I Mouria tou Myrivilli, "The Mulberry Tree of Myrivilis," after a famous Greek writer who used to sit under the shade of that tree penning his novels. It was there that I met Stratis Vamianos, a local fisherman and the taverna's cook, who was cast into the unlikely role of superhero when his efforts to save refugees from the war-torn Middle East, who washed up on the shores of the little beachfront where he works, got him nominated, together with a couple of local grandmothers who cared for the countless children on those dinghies, for the Nobel Peace Prize.

The refugee crisis, as of this writing, has more or less subsided, and Stratis is back to his favorite things: fishing and cooking. I met him for lunch at the taverna, where he prepared a sea lover's feast, among which were his rendition of what is arguably Lesvos's most famous seafood dish: salt-cured raw sardines. Indeed, those waters that saw so much turmoil happen to be teeming with local fish, mainly but not exclusively sardines; the Bay of Kalloni, among other coves and bays that sculpt the coastline of Lesvos, have been renowned since antiquity.

2 pounds (900 g) very fresh sardines, about 4 inches (10 cm) long, rinsed but not gutted

2 pounds (900 g) coarse sea salt

Extra-virgin Greek olive oil

Wash the sardines very well, but do not gut them.

Sprinkle a layer of coarse sea salt in container large enough to hold the sardines in one or two layers. Place the sardines in a large basin or bowl and toss gently with about 2 cups (546 g) of the sea salt. The salt should cling to the sardines' skin like an uneven crust. Place the sardines over the salt-covered surface of the container and refrigerate for 24 hours.

The next day, remove them from the refrigerator. Taking one sardine at a time, rake over the skin with the tines of a fork to remove the skin. Discard the skin. Using the fork or a small paring knife, remove the heads. As you pull away each of the heads, the viscera will come with it. Using your index finger, wipe the small belly cavity of the sardines to remove any remaining viscera. Rinse them very well under cold running water to remove any remaining salt.

Place the skinned, salt-cured sardines in a clean container and add olive oil to cover. Marinate in the refrigerator for at least 2 hours or up to 1 week. Serve as is, with a little ouzo and a bevy of other great Greek *mezedes*!

Kalamari Psito me Feta

RETRO FETA-STUFFED GRILLED CALAMARI

makes 4 to 6 meze servings

One of the great seafood mezedes of the Greek table is calamari (squid) served in almost any way, shape, or form. But a particularly easy—and dramatic—preparation is stuffing a whole squid with feta and herbs, then scoring it like ribs and serving it on a platter, the cheese oozing, tummies growling, appetites stirring, exactly what is supposed to happen when you sit down for a meal of mezedes. It's a bit retro, in that it's a classic one rarely finds nowadays in the seafood tavernas of, say, Athens, but readily encounters in less urbane eateries all over Greece. It's easy to make at home, too.

1 pound (450 g) squid, preferably fresh, cleaned (6 to 8 pieces, 6 to 8 inches / 15 to 20 cm long)

2 tablespoons extra-virgin Greek olive oil, plus more as needed

1 red or yellow onion, chopped

2 garlic cloves, finely chopped

1½ cups (225 g) crumbled Greek feta

½ cup (50 g) coarsely grated graviera or Kefalograviera cheese, or any mild, nutty sheep's-milk cheese

½ cup (120 ml) fresh anthotyro or ricotta cheese, drained

Finely grated zest of 1 lemon

½ cup (25 g) chopped fresh dill

½ cup (25 g) chopped fresh mint

1 medium egg

1 teaspoon crushed pink peppercorns

Salt and freshly ground black pepper

2 to 6 tablespoons plain dried bread crumbs, as needed

2 lemons, quartered

Keep the cleaned squid in the refrigerator until ready to use.

In a medium skillet, heat the olive oil over medium heat. Add the onion and cook until wilted and lightly golden. Stir in the garlic. Transfer the mixture to a bowl and let cool.

Add all the cheeses, the lemon zest, dill, mint, and egg to the bowl with the onion and toss to combine. Season with the pink peppercorns and salt and black pepper to taste. (The mixture will likely be salty enough with the feta, so you may not need to add any.)

Stir in 2 tablespoons of the bread crumbs to help bind the mixture. Test it by shaping a small ball with your hands; if it is still too loose to hold its shape, add more of the bread crumbs, 1 tablespoon at a time, until firm enough. Cover and refrigerate the mixture for 30 minutes to help firm it up.

Remove the squid and filling from the refrigerator. Stuff each of the squid tubes with enough of the filling to come up to about ¼ inch (6 mm) from the top so that when the stuffed squid shrinks during cooking, it doesn't burst. Using a toothpick, close the open end of the tube securely.

(CONTINUED)

Heat a grill until quite hot or heat a grill pan over high heat. Brush the grill grates or pan with a little olive oil. Place the stuffed squid and tentacles (separately) on the grill or in the hot grill pan and cook for 5 to 7 minutes, turning with kitchen tongs a few times, until lightly browned all over. Transfer to a platter.

Serve as is or, for a more dramatic effect, using a sharp knife score the top of each squid tube so that the surfaces fan open a bit, revealing the cheesy filling. Remove the toothpick and serve with lemon quarters.

VARIATIONS

Try stuffing the squid with any of the whipped feta recipes from the dips chapter, starting on page 57. Add 1 large egg and a few tablespoons of bread crumbs to firm up the feta mixture, then refrigerate as directed before using to stuff the squid.

You can also try stuffing the squid with about 2 cups of the spanakopita filling from page 264.

For an added twist, try mixing 3 tablespoons ouzo or mastiha liqueur into the cheese filling.

MY FAMILY KEFTEDES RECIPE

makes 30 to 35 keftedes

The secret is to make the mixture as loose as possible, while still enabling it to hold its shape. I add both grated tomatoes and milk to my meatball recipe, which lend moisture to the final mix. The bread crumbs give the keftedes *a fluffy texture.*

1 pound (450 g) ground beef	Salt and freshly ground black pepper
1 pound (450 g) ground pork	¾ to 1 cup (180 to 240 ml) milk
2 large red onions, grated or minced (about 2 cups / 250 g)	¼ to ½ cup (25 to 50 g) plain dried bread crumbs, as needed
1 large tomato, grated (see Note, page 92)	1½ cups (190 g) all-purpose flour, for dredging
2 tablespoons ground dried Greek mint	Olive oil, for frying

Combine the ground meat and onions in a bowl. Add the tomato and mint, season with salt and pepper, and knead well for about 3 minutes to combine. Pour in the milk and knead until the milk has been completely absorbed. If the mixture is so loose that the *keftedes* do not retain their shape, add the bread crumbs, a few tablespoons at a time, until it does. Cover and refrigerate for at least 1 hour or up to 6 hours to allow the flavors to meld.

Spread the flour over a large plate and season with salt and pepper. Have a clean plate ready nearby. Take 1 tablespoon of the meat mixture and form it into a ball about the size of a golf ball. Roll it in the flour to coat and shake off any excess. Place the dredged meatball on the clean plate. Repeat with the remaining meat mixture.

In a large, heavy skillet, heat about 1 inch (2.5 cm) of olive oil over medium heat. Using a tablespoon or small spatula, gently place as many meatballs in the pan as will fit without crowding. Fry, turning once or twice, until all sides are browned. Remove with a slotted spoon, drain slightly on paper towels, and repeat with the remaining meatballs. Serve hot or at room temperature. The meatballs may be cooked several hours ahead of serving and stored, covered, at room temperature.

VARIATION

Make the meatball mixture a tad firmer by adding some additional bread crumbs, and stuff each meatball with a pitted olive or a small cube of feta or Kefalotyri cheese to make meatballs that are literally bite-size surprises.

Yemista Loukanika

TOTALLY OVER-THE-TOP STUFFED SAUSAGES

makes 6 meze servings

There is a whole world of sausages and other charcuterie all over Greece. Most sausages are prepared simply, either grilled or stewed. This recipe is inspired by a dish I had at one of the many tsipouradika—meze *restaurants that specialize in dishes to pair with the Greek firewater* tsipouro—*in Volos, the port city on central Greece.*

2 tablespoons extra-virgin Greek olive oil

1 large red onion, halved and thinly sliced

3 garlic cloves, finely chopped

3 roasted red bell or Italian peppers, peeled and seeded

2 tablespoons chopped fresh oregano, or 2 teaspoons dried Greek oregano

Salt and freshly ground black pepper

1 package haloumi cheese (about 8 ounces / 225 g), drained and cut into ¼-inch (6 mm) cubes

6 fresh pork sausages, about 1¼ pounds (565 g) total

Olive oil or other oil, for the baking pan

In a large nonstick skillet, heat the olive oil over medium heat. Add the onion and cook until lightly browned, about 12 minutes. Stir in the garlic.

While the onion is cooking, slice the roasted peppers crosswise into ¼-inch-wide (6 mm) strips. Gently stir the peppers into the onion. Add the oregano, season with salt and black pepper, and stir to combine. Remove from the heat. Set aside to cool slightly, then mix in the haloumi cubes.

Heat a nonstick grill pan over medium-high heat or heat a grill to medium-high. Slit the sausages lengthwise down the middle, without halving them completely. Place them open and facedown like a book in the hot grill pan or on the grill grates and grill until cooked through, turning once. Remove carefully.

Preheat the broiler with a rack positioned about 6 inches (15 cm) from the heat source. Lightly oil a baking pan that will fit the sausages in a single layer.

Place the sausages open and face up on the prepared baking pan. Spoon equal mounds of the onion-pepper mixture over the surface of the sausages and broil for a few minutes, just until the haloumi starts to melt and the onion and peppers start to char. Remove from the oven and serve hot.

Bekri Meze me Meli kai Baharika

SKILLET PORK
with honey and spices

makes 6 meze servings

This Cretan specialty is wonderful with a glass of red wine on a winter day. You can serve it as a meze or make it into a more substantial meal by cooking up some rice and serving it with a salad.

6 tablespoons (90 ml) extra-virgin Greek olive oil

2 leeks, trimmed, washed well, and finely chopped

1 small onion, finely chopped

1½ pounds (680 g) boneless pork shoulder, cut into 1½-inch (4 cm) cubes

Salt and freshly ground black pepper

2 bay leaves

2 fresh rosemary sprigs

5 or 6 fresh thyme sprigs

Finely grated zest of 1 orange

1 star anise pod

1 whole dried chile

1½ cups (360 ml) dry white wine

Water or chicken broth, as needed

3 tablespoons Greek pine honey or thyme honey

In a large wide pot or deep skillet, heat 3 tablespoons of the olive oil over medium heat. Add the leeks and onion and cook until soft and lightly golden, about 12 minutes. Remove with a slotted spoon and set aside.

Rinse the pork and pat dry.

In the same pan, heat the remaining 3 tablespoons olive oil over medium heat. Add the pork pieces, raise the heat to medium-high, and cook, stirring occasionally, until browned on all sides. Reduce the heat to medium-low, return the leek-onion mixture to the pan, and season lightly with salt and pepper. Add the bay leaves, rosemary, thyme, orange zest, star anise, and chile and stir gently to release the aromas of the herbs and spices.

Raise the heat to medium-high and pour in the wine. Deglaze the meat; let the alcohol in the wine steam off, then add enough water or broth to barely cover the contents of the pot. Cover, reduce the heat to low, and simmer until the meat is completely cooked and very tender, 2 to 2½ hours, stirring in the honey about an hour before the meat is done. (The honey will slowly caramelize in the pot; by the end of cooking, the contents should be deeply colored and the pan juices should be thick, almost syrupy.)

Remove the herb sprigs, star anise, and chile before serving. Serve hot or warm.

MORE THAN

GREEK
SALAD

Ta ekanes salata

"You made a salad of it."
(Meaning: You made a mess of something.)

There is no better way to understand the importance of seasonality on the Greek table than to take a look at the range of Greek salads, both traditional and contemporary.

Each season has its salads. In winter, leafy greens such as spinach, cruciferous vegetables such as cabbage, and a whole range of roots, from carrots to celeriac, are mainstays of the salad bowl. Spring means a tender lettuce salad on the Greek table, made with romaine or any variety of Bibb lettuces, most often seasoned with fresh dill and a lemony dressing. In summer and through the early fall, without a doubt, the tomato rules the salad bowl, together with crunchy peppers and cucumbers and a whole bevy of fresh herbs.

Salad is a part of every Greek table and sometimes is a whole meal in itself. Greek salads fall into several broad categories: There is an enormous range of seasonal raw vegetable salads, from the famed *horiatiki*, or Greek village salad, to leafy green salads enhanced with nuts, dried and fresh fruits, cheeses, herbs, and more. Cooked dried beans are a classic protagonist in hearty salads, and there are plenty of great salads made with chickpeas, lentils, Greek giant beans, or any number of other beans. Grains, too, such as bulgur and nowadays buckwheat and quinoa, have found their way into the contemporary Greek salad bowl.

A whole category of dips are qualified as salads in Greek, including dishes like *taramosalata* (fish roe spread), and I have given recipes for those in the dips chapter. And finally, there is the entire universe of cooked salads on the Greek table, from boiled beets to *horta* (wild greens) to boiled broccoli, cauliflower, potatoes, carrots, and zucchini. These are typically dressed very simply with a little olive oil, salt, and lemon juice.

The contemporary Greek table has made room for additions to the salad bar, with fish and seafood, charcuterie, marriages of sweet and savory ingredients, or unusual uses for traditional foods now par for the salad course.

In this chapter, old and new come together in a collection of some of my personal favorite Greek salads. Enjoy!

Roka Salata me Ksera Syka, Throumbes kai Pasteli

ARUGULA SALAD
with dried figs, wrinkled olives, and pasteli

serves 4 to 6

This is not a salad my grandmother would have ever dreamed of making! Arugula, called roka *in Greek, is a favorite leafy green and is especially pungent and peppery when cultivated in the sunny dry climate of Greece. It is traditionally chopped or julienned and tossed into tomato or cabbage salad. Here it is the main vegetable, married, untraditionally, with sweet dried figs and* pasteli, *a sesame-honey brittle that is one of the oldest confections in Greece. I love the contradicting flavors and textures in this salad, a balance of peppery and mild (the manouri cheese), sweet and salty, chewy and crunchy, refreshing and creamy.*

8 cups (160 g) fresh wild (if possible) arugula, trimmed

1 small red onion, halved and thinly sliced

6 dried Greek figs, cut into slivers

3 tablespoons (45 g) chopped *pasteli* (sesame-honey brittle)

⅔ cup (105 g) Greek wrinkled black olives, such as throumbes

1½ cups (220 g) teardrop tomatoes, halved lengthwise

1 recipe Lemon-Honey-Mustard Dressing (page 8)

Salt and freshly ground black pepper (optional)

2 teaspoons extra-virgin Greek olive oil

1 (¾-inch-thick / 2 cm) round manouri, ricotta salata, or haloumi cheese

Wash the arugula and spin dry in a salad spinner. Place in a bowl with the onion, figs, *pasteli*, olives, and tomatoes. Toss with the dressing and place in a large salad bowl or on individual plates. Taste and season with salt and pepper, if desired.

In a nonstick grill pan, heat the olive oil over medium heat, tilting the pan so the oil is evenly distributed over the surface. Place the cheese round carefully on the hot pan. Sear for a minute or two, then carefully flip the cheese using a spatula and cook until nicely seared on the other side.

Place the cheese over the salad in the bowl, or transfer it to a cutting board, cut it into 4 or 6 wedges, and place one wedge on each serving. Serve immediately.

Spanaki Salata me Portokali, Avokanto, Revithia kai Feta

SPINACH SALAD
with oranges, avocado, chickpeas, and feta

serves 4

Spinach salad is a relative newcomer to the Greek table. Indeed, enjoying spinach raw is a fairly recent phenomenon, since it is among the greens most commonly consumed cooked into pies and casseroles. This hearty salad can easily double as a main course.

8 cups (160 g) fresh spinach, trimmed

1 ripe but firm avocado

1 red onion, halved and thinly sliced

1 cup (160 g) cooked chickpeas (canned are fine)

½ cup (75 g) crumbled Greek feta

½ cup (75 g) Greek wrinkled black olives, such as throumbes

1 navel or blood orange, peeled and cut into sections

1 recipe Greek Lemon–Olive Oil Dressing (page 7)

Coarsely chop the spinach, if preferred. Wash and spin dry in a salad spinner. Transfer to a serving bowl.

Cut the avocado into slices, peel, and cut each slice in half. Add to the bowl with the spinach.

Add the onion, chickpeas, feta, olives, and orange slices to the bowl. Toss with the salad dressing and serve.

Salata me Spanaki, Kankiofoles kai Feta

SPINACH SALAD
with jerusalem artichokes and feta

serves 4 to 6

This is an old recipe from Corfu. The Jerusalem artichoke was introduced to Corfu in the eighteenth century by the French, who occupied the island at the time and had first encountered this nutritious tuber in North America. It has become something of a local legend on the island, and a cottage industry of artisan producers has sprung up, creating a bevy of lovely dishes using the Jerusalem artichoke.

1 pound (450 g) fresh spinach, trimmed

1 red onion, halved and thinly sliced

1 garlic clove, minced

1 pound (450 g) Jerusalem artichokes, trimmed, peeled, and thinly sliced (see Note)

1 recipe Greek Lemon–Olive Oil Dressing (page 7)

Salt

Crushed pink peppercorns

Wash the spinach and spin dry in a salad spinner. Coarsely chop it and place in a large bowl. Add the onion, garlic, and Jerusalem artichokes.

Pour in the dressing, season to taste with salt and pink peppercorns, toss, and serve.

NOTE: Peel and slice the Jerusalem artichokes just before serving the salad to keep them from discoloring.

Salata me Keil, Milo kai Feta

KALE, APPLE, AND FETA SALAD

serves 4 to 6

While there are many vegetables in the Brassica family that are native to Greece, kale is a relative newcomer, not quite having taken this country of salad lovers by storm. I find it at the small, local organic farmers' markets that have been cropping up more and more frequently around Athens. I like to chop it and toss it with a combination of salty-sour and sweet additions, like feta and figs. You can dress this salad with almost anything, from a simple lemon–olive oil dressing to a creamy Greek yogurt–based sauce. My favorite is the lemon-honey-mustard vinaigrette on page 8.

8 cups chopped kale leaves

1 small red onion, halved and thinly sliced

1 tart, preferably organic apple, such as Granny Smith or McIntosh

⅔ cup (100 g) crumbled Greek feta

4 dried Greek figs, stemmed, minced

1 tablespoon toasted sesame seeds

Dressing of your choice

Salt and freshly ground black pepper (optional)

Mix the kale and onion in a serving bowl. Quarter the apple lengthwise, core it, and cut it into small triangular wedges. Add it to the bowl with the kale and onion, then add the feta, figs, and sesame seeds on top. Drizzle with the dressing of your choice. Taste and adjust the seasoning with salt and pepper, if needed. Serve.

Salata apo Omo Kolokythaki, Tomata kai Koukounari

SHAVED RAW ZUCCHINI-TOMATO SALAD
with toasted pine nuts

serves 4

This is one of my favorite summer salads. We usually have a glut of zucchini in our garden on Ikaria, where we spend the summer. The pine nuts add a bit of substance to this fairly light salad. When the temperature rises, it's a very refreshing dish.

½ cup (65 g) pine nuts

3 medium, preferably organic zucchini

1½ cups (220 g) teardrop or cherry tomatoes, halved

½ cup (25 g) chopped fresh mint leaves

Grated zest of 1 small lemon

1 recipe Greek Lemon–Olive Oil Dressing (page 7) or, for something richer, Feta-Herb Ladolemono (page 9)

Salt and freshly ground black pepper (optional)

Toast the pine nuts in a small, preferably cast-iron or nonstick skillet over medium heat, shaking the pan back and forth for a few minutes, until lightly browned.

Using a vegetable peeler or a mandoline, shave the zucchini lengthwise into strips. Place in a bowl. Add the tomatoes, mint, and lemon zest. Drizzle in the dressing and toss. Taste and adjust the seasoning with salt and pepper, if desired. Serve.

Trimmeni Salata me Ntresingk Yiaourtiou

THREE-VEGETABLE SLAW
with greek yogurt ranch dressing

serves 4

Shredded and grated salads in the Greek kitchen are typically limited to the classic cabbage-carrot winter salad, perked up with a simple ladolemono *(lemon vinaigrette). This three-root slaw was born of the Greek financial crisis, in that during these last few years here in Greece many of us have become keenly aware of food waste. There have been campaigns to teach people how to use ingredients they might otherwise discard, such as the broccoli stems used in this recipe.*

Juice of 1 lemon, strained

1 small celery root (celeriac; about ½ pound / 225 g)

1 pomegranate

3 large carrots

Stem from 1 large broccoli head

¼ cup (25 g) chopped fresh parsley or cilantro

2 tablespoons snipped fresh dill

1 recipe Greek Yogurt Ranch Sauce (page 10)

Salt and freshly ground black pepper

Fill a bowl with cold water and stir in the lemon juice. Peel the celery root with a large sharp knife or vegetable peeler and cut it into quarters. Place the celery root in the lemon water to prevent discoloration and set aside until ready to use.

Cut the pomegranate in half. Hold one half cut-side down in the palm of one hand, over a bowl. Tap the exterior of the pomegranate with a teaspoon all over, until the seeds have dislodged and fallen into the bowl. Repeat with the remaining half. Set aside.

Using a vegetable peeler, trim any tough knobs off the broccoli stem.

Grate the carrots and broccoli stem using a food processor fitted with the grating disc. Set aside in a bowl. Remove the celery root from the water and grate it as well; add it to the bowl with the carrots and broccoli.

Add the pomegranate seeds, parsley, and dill. Add the yogurt dressing and toss to coat. Season to taste with salt and pepper and serve.

Y Horiatiki Salata kai Oi Parallages tis

GREEK SALAD AND FRIENDS

serves 6

Most classics become so for a reason, and Greek salad—that savory mix of good tomatoes, crunchy cucumbers, kalamata olives, green peppers, onions, feta, olive oil, and oregano—is no exception. The combination is universally appealing, timeless, and never tiresome.

There are a few rules of thumb, at least in my book, when it comes to making a real Greek salad, aka horiatiki *(which literally translates as "village" salad): Make it in season with really good tomatoes. Make sure the feta is Greek. Never cut iceberg or any other lettuce into it—that's an American aberration. Serve it with a little salt, preferably Greek sea salt, and great extra-virgin Greek olive oil. Don't even think about drizzling vinaigrette over it!*

That said, it is tempting to experiment a little with a classic, and in the past decade or so, Greek chefs have turned Greek salad inside out and upside down in an attempt to add a personal touch to this time-honored, iconic dish. Is that like scrawling graffiti on the Parthenon? Maybe! But the combination of ingredients in a Greek salad is so appealing that it lends itself, at the very least, to alternative uses and a few variations. Here's my classic recipe, as well as a few ideas for how to tweak and serve this classic while staying true to its core flavors.

1 pound (450 g) ripe but firm juicy tomatoes	1 (3 x ½-inch / 7.5 x 1.5 cm) wedge Greek feta
1 red onion	Optional additions (see page 16), as desired
2 medium green bell peppers	
1 large firm cucumber	1 teaspoon dried Greek oregano
Salt	6 to 8 tablespoons (90 to 120 ml) extra-virgin Greek olive oil
12 kalamata olives	

Working over the bowl in which you plan to serve the salad in order to retain all the juices, use a sharp paring knife to cut the tomatoes in half through their stem end and core them. Cut into uneven chunks by first slicing them into wedges, then halving the wedges and dropping them into the bowl.

Halve the onion. Following the onion's natural contours, cut the onion into ⅛-inch-thick (3 mm) slices and place them in the salad bowl over the tomatoes.

Remove the crowns from the peppers. Using a paring knife or small spoon, remove the seeds and ribs. Cut the peppers into ⅛-inch-thick (3 mm) rings and place in the salad bowl over the tomatoes and onions.

Peel the cucumber, if you prefer it peeled (personally, I like it with the peel on). Cut the cucumber in half lengthwise and scrape out the seed bed if it is too large and wet. Cut the halves into roughly ⅛-inch-thick (3 mm) crescents or half-moons. Place them in the bowl with the tomatoes, onion, and peppers.

Season to taste with salt. Add the olives and place the feta wedge on top of the salad. Add optional additions as desired. Sprinkle with the oregano and drizzle with the olive oil, using more or less to your liking. Toss and serve.

NOTE: The best part is on the bottom, after the salad has been consumed and all that's left is the satisfying mixture of vegetable juices and olive oil. There's a word for this in Greek: *papara*, which refers to the act of dunking good bread into all those juices.

OPTIONAL ADDITIONS

Peperoncini peppers, capers, pickled sea fennel, fresh oregano, and broken-up chunks of the rusks called *paximadia* (see page 120) are all great additions to a Greek salad.

One of my favorite additions is something I borrowed from an Indian friend, which has become a signature salad at Committee, the Greek restaurant in Boston where, as of this writing, I am consulting chef: crispy fried fresh okra. To use okra, you'll need ½ pound (225 g) fresh okra pods. With a sharp paring knife, trim around and discard the top, right under the stem. Soak the pods in vinegar for 15 minutes. Meanwhile, heat 1 inch (2.5 cm) of vegetable oil in a large skillet over medium-high heat until it registers 350°F (170°C) on an instant-read or deep-fry thermometer. Drain the okra pods, pat dry, and cut them in half lengthwise. In a medium bowl, season ½ cup (65 g) all-purpose flour with a little salt and freshly ground black pepper. Toss the okra in the seasoned flour to coat. Working in batches, fry the okra in the hot oil until crisp and golden. Using a slotted spoon, transfer the okra to paper towels to drain. Sprinkle over the salad as a garnish.

WHAT ELSE CAN YOU DO
WITH A GREEK SALAD?

Make a sandwich. Mash olives with some feta cheese and spread it over some good bread and layer it with sliced tomatoes, cucumbers, peppers, and red onions.

Make a cold soup. The ingredients of a Greek salad make a great iced soup. Make sure you use pitted olives, and blend everything but the feta and olive oil together in the bowl of a food processor. Chill. Right before serving, garnish with the feta and drizzle with the olive oil.

Make a heartier Greek salad with bread or rusks. Toss all the ingredients for a Greek salad with 1 broken-up barley rusk or a handful of homemade pita chips (page 46).

HOW TO CHOOSE THE RIGHT TOMATO
FOR A GREEK SALAD

The hardest part of perfecting a Greek salad is finding the right tomato. Sweet or acidic? Firm-fleshed or juicy? Thin- or thick-skinned? These choices are all really a matter of personal taste.

If you lean toward tomatoes that have a sweet, almost fruity flavor, look for Campari tomatoes. They're a hybrid variety and easy to find and recognize: Camparis are usually sold attached to their stems and vine in neat rows.

If you're like me, wanting a slightly more complex tomato flavor, then look for any of the heirloom beefsteak varieties or the dark-purplish Black Cherry tomato, which has a mouth-watering acidic quality. My favorite heirloom tomato is the Lucky Cross, which closely resembles a variety in Greece called Vravrona or Batales. It is uneven and ribbed, with a beautiful balance of both sweetness and acidity.

Ntakos me Milo, Seleri, Ntomates kai Feta

BARLEY RUSK SALAD (DAKO)
with apples, celery, tomatoes, and feta

serve 2

Dako is a term of some confusion. It refers to a traditional Cretan salad made with a round barley rusk, grated tomatoes, feta or a local Cretan cheese called myzithra, oregano, and olive oil, as well as — at least according to some sources — the rusk itself, which in turn takes its name from the Cretan word for "shim," alluding, I would assume, to its hardness. Barley rusks, as well as those made from other grains, were once the ultimate traditional bread product, but they have become something of a trend in modern Greek restaurants, as chefs top these earthy, nutty hardtacks with everything from bananas to seafood. This recipe is derivative of the original Cretan dish and makes a light but filling salad, seasoned with a bit of culinary license.

2 Cretan barley rusks, preferably round

2 teaspoons plus ⅓ cup (80 ml) extra-virgin Greek olive oil

1 small, preferably organic Granny Smith or other tart apple

½ celery stalk, cut into thin crescents

1 cup (145 g) red and/or yellow teardrop or cherry tomatoes, halved

2 tablespoons chopped fresh mint, plus 2 whole leaves for garnish if desired

1 tablespoon drained and rinsed capers

Salt

½ cup (100 g) crumbled Greek feta, Cretan xinomyzithra cheese, or a combination of crumbled feta and fresh ricotta or anthotyro cheeses

Run the rusks under cold water. Hold them vertically to let the last drops of water drain off. Place each rusk on an individual serving plate or on a small platter large enough to hold them both. Drizzle each with 1 teaspoon of the olive oil.

Core the apple, then grate it on the large holes of a box grater. Place it in a large bowl and add the celery, tomatoes, mint, capers, remaining ⅓ cup (80 ml) olive oil, and salt to taste and toss gently.

Mound the mixture in equal parts over each of the rusks. Spoon the crumbled cheese(s) on top. Garnish each with a mint leaf, if desired, and serve.

Paximadia me Ahino kai Tomata

RUSK SALAD
with sea urchin, tomatoes, and onions

serves 2

Kalymnos, the sponge-fishermen's island, has a long and passionate association with all the treasures of the sea. Some of the most unusual seafood in Greece can be found here, as well as some of the country's most delicious octopus recipes. Local cooks have a way with sea urchin, too, plucking this spiny, iodine-rich creature from the cleanest waters, cracking it open, and enjoying it on the spot, or tossing it with summer tomatoes, onions, and rusks for a bit of Aegean umami.

2 large barley rusks

6 tablespoons (90 ml) extra-virgin Greek olive oil

2 ripe but firm large tomatoes, cored and diced

1 red onion, halved and very thinly sliced

Roe from 10 sea urchins, cleaned, or about 1 cup (250 ml) prepacked sea urchin roe (uni)

2 teaspoons strained fresh lemon juice

Pinch of sea salt

Freshly ground black pepper

Run the rusks under cold water. Hold them vertically to let the last drops of water drain off. Place the rusks on a serving plate and drizzle with 2 tablespoons of the olive oil.

In a small bowl, mix together the tomatoes, onion, sea urchin, lemon juice, and remaining 4 tablespoons (60 ml) olive oil. Season with the salt and pepper to taste. Spoon this mixture evenly over the rusks and serve.

RUSKS AND RUSK SALADS

Rusks, aka hardtack, are called *paximadia* in Greek, after a first-century-AD monk named Paximus who improved on the ancient recipe for *dipyros*, or twice-baked bread, which is essentially what *paximadia* are.

The *paximadia* dough is scored into wedges before being baked, removed from the oven while still soft enough to break apart, then rebaked, typically in a wood-burning oven that is warm but not fired up. *Paximadia* were a way for home bakers in the Greek countryside to bake long-keeping breads. They were and still are something fishermen carry with them and farmers snack on in the field.

The range of Greek rusks is enormous: barley, wheat, rye, and chickpea flour are all used to make rusks. Crete is famous in Greece for its range of *paximadia*, but there are regional variations everywhere, sometimes seasoned with cumin or fennel seed, nigella, and herbs or spices. They come in all sorts of shapes and sizes, from the round Cretan *dako* to large, thick wedges to small nuggets, and they can be used interchangeably to enhance a fresh salad or make a soup more substantial.

Large rusks make a great bed or base over which you can build a salad. You have to soften them, either by topping them with juicy vegetables such as tomatoes and letting them stand for 10 to 15 minutes before serving, or by rehydrating them under running tap water and letting all the water drip off before using them.

Nugget-size rusks can be tossed into salad and will soften with the vegetables' natural juices and some olive oil.

In the last few years, Greek bakers have developed a rusk basket, similar to the idea of a Parmesan basket, in which you can serve a salad.

A good rule of thumb when using rusks as a base or bed is to top them with 1 to 1½ cups (250 to 325 ml) of salad fixings. Here are some ideas for salad combos:

- Good juicy tomatoes, capers, crumbled feta, herbs, and olive oil

- Diced watermelon, mixed with any combination of feta, capers, red onions, tomatoes (especially cherry or teardrop tomatoes), and olive oil. Try using yellow teardrop tomatoes to contrast with the color of the watermelon.

- Tomatoes, green or red apple, red onion, lots of fresh mint, olive oil, and, if desired, crumbled feta

- Raw shaved artichokes; shaved or diced graviera cheese; fresh mint, dill, or oregano; fresh lemon juice; and olive oil

- For a filling, healthy Greek breakfast: fresh orange or tangerine juice (to dampen the rusks), chopped apples, raisins, and ground cinnamon

Mavromatika Salata me Spanaki, Praso kai Rodi

BLACK-EYED PEA SALAD
with spinach, leeks, and pomegranate

serves 6

Black-eyed peas are a traditional good-luck dish at New Year's throughout much of the American South and elsewhere. In Greece, it doesn't have to be New Year's to enjoy them. This is a modern take on a traditional Greek stew of black-eyed peas and greens, gussied up with some delicious pomegranate.

2 cups (320 g) dried black-eyed peas, picked over for debris and rinsed

2 leeks, trimmed

⅔ cup (160 ml) extra-virgin Greek olive oil

Salt

2 tablespoons Greek balsamic vinegar

1 pound (450 g) spinach, trimmed

2 garlic cloves, finely chopped

¼ cup (25 g) chopped fresh mint

Freshly ground black pepper

1 cup (250 ml) pomegranate seeds

Bring a kettle or saucepan of water to a boil.

Place the black-eyed peas in a separate medium saucepan and add water to cover by 2 inches (5 cm). Bring to a boil over high heat, then drain.

Return the black-eyed peas to the pot. Pour in enough boiling water to cover them by 2 inches (5 cm). Simmer the black-eyed peas over low heat for about 35 minutes, or until tender but al dente. Drain immediately in a colander and rinse.

While the black-eyed peas are cooking, cut the leeks into ½-inch-thick (1.5 cm) rounds. Rinse them very well to remove any grit. Spin dry in a salad spinner.

In a large skillet, heat 2 tablespoons of the olive oil over medium-high heat. Add the leeks, season lightly with salt, and cook, stirring occasionally, until the leeks begin to brown lightly. Add 1 tablespoon of the vinegar and cook until the leeks are soft and caramelized.

In a separate skillet, heat 2 tablespoons of the olive oil over medium heat. Add the spinach and cook, stirring occasionaly, until the leaves are wilted and the liquid they have released has cooked off. Add the garlic and cook until fragrant. Remove from the heat.

Combine the black-eyed peas, spinach-garlic mixture, leeks, and mint in a serving bowl. Add the remaining olive oil and remaining 1 tablespoon vinegar. Season to taste with salt and pepper, garnish with the pomegranate seeds, and serve.

Salata apo Psito Kremmydi

ROASTED ONION SALAD

serves 4

I've come across recipes in Greece that have startled me for the sheer simplicity of their preparation and natural elegance once served. This old country dish from Rhodes is one such recipe. I can imagine the flavor of onions just dug out of the ground and cooked under embers in the fireplace, skins crinkled and charred, revealing an almost blushingly delicate flesh, translucent and tender. With a sprinkling of parsley and a drizzle of olive oil and vinegar, this salad will win you over. It's also incredibly easy to make.

6 medium onions, unpeeled

4 to 6 tablespoons (60 to 90 ml) extra-virgin Greek olive oil

3 tablespoons red wine vinegar

1 garlic clove, minced

1 teaspoon dried Greek oregano, or 2 tablespoons chopped fresh oregano leaves

3 tablespoons chopped fresh parsley

Salt and freshly ground black pepper

Preheat the oven to 350°F (170°C).

Place the onions in a shallow baking pan and roast for 1 to 1½ hours, until soft and lightly charred. Remove from the oven and let cool. Peel the onions and break them apart or cut into wedges. Place in a serving bowl.

Whisk together the olive oil (use more or less to your liking), vinegar, garlic, oregano, and parsley in a small bowl. Season to taste with salt and pepper and drizzle over the onions. Toss to combine and serve.

Patatosalata me Sardeles apo tin Naxo

POTATO SALAD
with tomatoes and sardines from naxos

serves 4 to 6

Naxos, one of the major islands in the Cyclades, is home to some of the best food in Greece, thanks mainly to its fertile soil, cheese-making traditions, and wide-open plains where cattle can graze.

One of the island's major crops is the New World potato, which has flourished on the island's potassium-rich, sandy soil since the mid-nineteenth century. Four villages in the western-central part of the island are particularly renowned for potato cultivation. A center for potato seed production was founded on the island in the 1950s and provides seedlings to farmers all over Greece. Today, Naxos's potatoes are recognized by the European Union as an agricultural product with Protected Geographical Indication (PGI) status. The main varieties are the Spunta, Liseta, Marfona, Vivaldi, and Alaska potatoes.

For this salad, look for waxy potato varieties, such Yellow Finn or Yukon Gold.

1½ pounds (680 g) waxy, preferably organic potatoes, scrubbed

Sea salt

3 ripe but firm large tomatoes, cored and cut into 6 wedges each

2 large red onions, halved and thinly sliced

1 medium cucumber, peeled, halved lengthwise, seeded, and thinly sliced

4 to 6 salted sardine fillets, rinsed

FOR THE DRESSING

½ cup (120 ml) extra-virgin Greek olive oil

2 to 3 tablespoons red wine vinegar, or to taste

1 tablespoon chopped fresh oregano leaves

Sea salt and freshly ground black pepper

Place the potatoes in a large wide pot and add water to cover by 2 inches (5 cm). Bring to a boil. Season generously with salt. Reduce the heat to low and simmer for 20 to 25 minutes, until the potatoes are fork-tender. Remove from the heat and gently drain the potatoes in a colander set in the sink. Rinse under cold running water until cool enough to handle, then cut into large chunks.

Transfer the potatoes to a large bowl. Add the tomatoes, onions, and cucumber. Chop the sardine fillets and add them to the salad.

Make the dressing: Whisk together the olive oil, vinegar (use more or less to your liking), and oregano in a small bowl until well combined. Season to taste with salt and pepper.

When ready to serve, pour the dressing over the potato salad. Toss gently and transfer to a serving bowl or individual serving plates. Serve.

GREEK BETWEEN

THE

BREAD

Λεφτά αγοράζουνε ψωμί, μα όχι ευγνωμοσύνη.

Lefta agorazoune psomi, ma ohi evgonomosyni.

"Money buys bread, but it doesn't buy gratitude."

Sandwiches are not historically a Greek snack or quick meal. But bread is by far the most popular manifestation of carbs in the Greek diet, so it stands to reason that the sandwich and all its variations have long been a part of the culinary landscape in Greece.

My oldest memories of anything remotely resembling a sandwich emporium were the *tost* shops, selling the local equivalent of panini, that used to dot Athens and other places around the country, especially appealing to this nation of fierce individualists who could make their own from a large choice of everything from tomatoes and cheeses to cooked omelets, Greek meatballs, and myriad spreads.

The last few years have seen a sandwich renaissance in Athens, with a handful of shops brimming with gourmet flair, a range of ingredients from all over Greece and the wider Mediterranean, and sandwich meisters who take the job pretty seriously, putting together combinations that push the envelope on this once humble handheld food.

If the expression "between the bread" is a straightforward metaphor for the sandwich in its most classic shape and form, what to make, then, of the wrap, a long-standing Greek tradition if one considers the classic pita bread wraps stuffed with shavings or chunks of grilled lamb, chicken, or pork and all the fixings: tzatziki, tomatoes, lettuce, and spices? These, too, have gotten a modern face-lift, with everything from vegetable fritters to fried fish rolled into a handheld snack for on-the-go practitioners of the Greek Mediterranean Diet.

In the following chapter, wraps, layered and open sandwiches, and a few Greek heros are all reinterpretations of the classics, lighthearted and fun, healthy but also indulgent. Some are handheld and mobile, while others need a plate and a few minutes to savor.

SPANAKOPITA GRILLED CHEESE

serves 4

The best things in life—and at the table—are sometimes born by total chance. Spanakopita, one of the best-known Greek dishes, is something I make pretty often at home. A little leftover filling and a eureka moment led me to spread a few heaping tablespoons of the filling between some bread and to grill it the old-fashioned way, in a skillet with a little olive oil. The result is this recipe, and at my Greek table, it's become a classic in its own right.

3 tablespoons extra-virgin Greek olive oil or unsalted butter, plus more as needed

1 large onion, 4 scallions, or 1 leek, chopped (and washed well, if using leek)

8 cups (160 g) chopped fresh spinach

1 cup (50 g) mixed chopped fresh dill, parsley, and/or fennel fronds

Pinch of freshly grated nutmeg

Salt and freshly ground black pepper

2 cups (300 g) large chunks Greek feta

8 (¼-inch-thick / 6 mm) slices good bread, preferably sourdough

In a large skillet, heat 1½ tablespoons of the olive oil or butter over medium heat. Add the onion and cook, stirring, until soft and lightly golden. Add the spinach and cook until wilted. Remove the mixture with a slotted spoon and drain well in a colander. Let cool.

Combine the spinach mixture with the fresh herbs. Season with the nutmeg and salt and pepper to taste. Mix in the feta.

Divide the mixture over 4 slices of the bread. Place the remaining 4 slices of bread on top.

In a large cast-iron or nonstick skillet, heat the remaining 1½ tablespoons olive oil or butter (or use both together over medium heat). Add the sandwiches, one or two at a time, and cook until golden on one side. Flip carefully and press down on the sandwich with a spatula to flatten slightly. Cover the pan and cook for a few minutes to help the feta melt more easily. Repeat with remaining sandwiches, adding more olive oil and/or butter to the pan as needed. Serve immediately.

Yeeros me Manitari

PORTOBELLO MUSHROOM GYRO

serves 4

Everyone loves a down 'n' dirty gyro, the thin slices of pork or chicken (not lamb, as many people believe) shaved off a layered stack that grills slowly on an upright rotisserie. It's classic Greek street food. But most of us feel a little guilty when indulging in it because in most cases the meat is processed and unhealthy, Mushrooms save the day! They contain many of the same nutritional qualities as meat, with none of the fat or cholesterol. Here's a healthy gyro that doesn't skimp on the indulgence scale but is full of healthy Greek spirit!

4 garlic cloves: 2 finely chopped, 2 thinly sliced

2 tablespoons finely chopped fresh dill or parsley

1 cup (240 ml) Greek yogurt

2 tablespoons extra-virgin Greek olive oil, plus more for brushing

Salt

1 pound (450 g) portobello mushrooms, trimmed and sliced

Scant 1 teaspoon dried Greek oregano

Freshly ground black pepper

4 to 6 pita bread rounds

2 ripe but firm tomatoes, halved, cored, and sliced

1 red onion, halved and thinly sliced

Cayenne pepper or paprika

Combine the finely chopped garlic, dill, yogurt, 1 tablespoon of the olive oil, and salt to taste in a small bowl. Cover and refrigerate until ready to use.

In a large nonstick or cast-iron skillet, heat the remaining 1 tablespoon olive oil over medium heat. Add the mushrooms and cook, stirring often, until wilted but still al dente. Add the sliced garlic and oregano, season with salt and pepper to taste, and cook, stirring, for a minute or so. Transfer the mushrooms to a bowl and cover to keep warm.

Wipe the skillet clean and set it over low heat. Warm the pita bread rounds one or two at a time, brushing each with a little olive oil.

To assemble the mushroom gyros, set each pita on a plate and top each with equal quantities of the mushrooms, tomatoes, onion, and the yogurt mixture. Season to taste with salt, pepper, and cayenne or paprika, and roll up like a wrap.

Avgosalata me Feta

EGG-AND-FETA-SALAD PITA POCKETS

serves 4

In the Greek countryside at Easter time, there are more eggs around than most people can imagine. We don't keep a chicken coop, but all our neighbors do, and we usually wake up to find fresh eggs outside our front door, way more than a family of four can manage. Tradition dictates that we boil and dye eggs red for the Easter table, but even so, there are usually lots of leftovers. Here's one of my favorite ways to use hard-boiled eggs, with a nod to the diner-noshes of my New York roots combined with a Greek touch: a little feta and oregano added to an otherwise classic egg salad sandwich.

6 hard-boiled eggs

¼ cup (40 g) crumbled Greek feta

3 scallions, finely chopped

3 tablespoons finely chopped fresh parsley

1 teaspoon dried Greek oregano, or 1 tablespoon chopped fresh oregano

¼ cup (60 ml) Greek yogurt, plus more if needed

2 tablespoons extra-virgin Greek olive oil, plus more if needed

½ teaspoon cayenne pepper or *boukovo* (Greek red pepper flakes), or more to taste

1 teaspoon Dijon mustard

Salt and freshly ground black pepper

4 mini pita pocket breads, halved and split open

Peel the hard-boiled eggs and mash them in a medium bowl with a fork. Add the feta, scallions, parsley, oregano, yogurt, olive oil, cayenne, and mustard and season to taste with salt and black pepper. Mash all together until very well combined. Add more yogurt or olive oil if you want a looser egg salad.

Spoon equal amounts of the egg salad into each of the pita halves. Serve immediately.

Lavraki Tiganito se Pita

SEA BASS WRAP
with greek yogurt tartar sauce

serves 6

Fried fish is a much-loved treat all over Greece, and many different types of fish, from cod to anchovies, are fried. To achieve crunch, sometimes nothing more than a light dredging in flour is needed; larger pieces of fish, such as cod or, as in this recipe, fresh sea bass, are often dipped in batter.

1 cup (135 g) coarse cornmeal

1 cup (125 g) all-purpose flour

1 tablespoon baking powder

1 tablespoon kosher salt

1 (12-ounce / 350 ml) bottle amber beer

2 teaspoons hot sauce

1 pound (450 g) Greek, Mediterranean, or other sea bass fillets, cut lengthwise into 1-inch-wide (2.5 cm) strips

Vegetable or olive oil, for frying

½ recipe Greek Yogurt Tartar Sauce (page 10)

6 soft, high-quality bread rolls, about 5 inches (12.5 cm) in diameter, 12 slices good sourdough bread, or 6 pita wraps

12 Bibb or other tender lettuce leaves

2 ripe but firm medium tomatoes, cored and sliced

In a large stainless steel bowl, whisk together the cornmeal, flour, baking powder, and salt. Pour in the beer and hot sauce and whisk the batter until smooth.

Place the fish strips in the batter, cover, and refrigerate for 15 minutes.

In a deep skillet or wide pot, heat 2 inches (5 cm) of vegetable oil over medium-high heat until it registers 375°F (190°C) on an instant-read or deep-fry thermometer. Using a slotted spoon or fork, carefully lift one strip of fish at a time from the batter and let the excess batter drain back into the bowl. Place the fish gently in the hot oil, then add a few more strips, being careful not to crowd the pan. Fry for about 3 minutes per side, until the fish is golden brown and crisp. Remove with kitchen tongs or a slotted spoon and drain on paper towels. Repeat with the remaining fish, skimming any burnt bits from the oil between batches, if necessary.

To assemble the sandwiches: Smear a little tartar sauce on your bread of choice. Place a few pieces of lettuce and tomato on one side of the bread or roll or on the surface of the pita and place the fish on top. Cover with another piece of bread or, if using pita, wrap and serve.

Tiganito Santwits me Tono, Kasseri kai Elies

GREEK-STYLE TUNA MELT
with kasseri cheese and olives

serves 6

This open-faced sandwich was born a few years ago, when I first discovered the delicious local tuna of Alonissos, an island in the Sporades in the western Aegean. Although most of the catch is shipped directly to Japan to be used for sushi, a few local fishermen banded together to form a cooperative, and now the brined or oil-preserved tuna is available all over Greece. At least one Greek food company, Ergon, exports the tuna to the United Kingdom and other places.

To make this Greek-inspired tuna melt, you can use any great-quality tuna, preferably packed in water.

1 teaspoon store-bought or homemade *taramosalata* (page 55) or avocado *taramosalata* (page 53)

6 tablespoons (90 ml) extra-virgin Greek olive oil

⅓ cup (50 g) chopped pitted green or kalamata olives

½ small red onion, minced

2 celery stalks, minced

1 (12-ounce / 350 g) can or jar of tuna Alonissou or other good-quality bonito or albacore tuna packed in water, drained and flaked

Juice of 1 lemon, strained

Freshly ground black pepper

6 thick slices country bread, trimmed to a square, with crusts

8 ounces (225 g) kasseri or other mild yellow sheep's-milk cheese, thinly sliced or shredded

Preheat the broiler.

In a large bowl, combine the *taramosalata* and 4 tablespoons (60 ml) of the olive oil. Add the olives, onion, celery, tuna, lemon juice, and pepper to taste and toss to combine.

Arrange the bread on a baking sheet and lightly brush one side of each slice with the remaining 2 tablespoons olive oil. Toast under the broiler, watching closely to avoid burning, until toasted on the first side, then flip to toast the second side. Divide the tuna mixture evenly among the slices of bread, spread the tuna to cover them, and top evenly with the cheese. Return the baking sheet to the oven and broil until the cheese melts. Transfer each sandwich to a plate and serve.

Garides Saganaki se Psomi

SHRIMP SAGANAKI HERO

serves 2

Shrimp saganaki, *that luscious combination of shrimp, tomatoes, feta, and various other ingredients, depending on the recipe, is a Greek icon. The dish appears on Greek restaurant and taverna menus all over the world. One of the best moments is the end, when there's nothing but bread on the table and sauce in which to dip it left in the dish. Here's a transformation that combines the best of the recipe with its penultimate moment of enjoyment!*

4 tablespoons (60 ml) extra-virgin Greek olive oil

1 red onion, finely chopped

2 scallions, finely chopped

1 garlic clove, minced

1 cup (180 g) finely chopped tomatoes (preferably fresh, but drained canned tomatoes are fine, too)

2 tablespoons ouzo

1 star anise pod

1 teaspoon Dijon or Greek mustard

1 pound (450 g) small shrimp, preferably fresh, peeled and deveined

2 tablespoons chopped pitted kalamata olives

⅔ cup (100 g) crumbled Greek feta

½ teaspoon grated lemon zest

Salt and freshly ground black pepper

Red pepper flakes (optional)

2 tablespoons finely chopped fresh parsley

2 whole-grain hero rolls, 2 (5- to 6-inch / 10 to 14 cm) pieces of baguette, or any other bread or pita-type wrap of your choice

In a large deep skillet or shallow, heavy, wide pot, heat 2 tablespoons of the olive oil over medium heat. Add the onion and scallions and cook, stirring, until soft and glistening, about 8 minutes. Add the garlic and cook, stirring, until softened, about 5 minutes.

Add the tomatoes, ouzo, star anise, and mustard. Stir to combine. Cook until the alcohol in the ouzo has burned off and most of the liquid from the tomatoes has evaporated, 6 to 8 minutes.

Add the shrimp, raise the heat a bit, and cook until the shrimp are bright pink and cooked through, 3 to 4 minutes. Add the olives and feta and cook all together for about a minute, or until the feta just begins to melt. Season with the lemon zest and salt, black pepper, and red pepper flakes (if using) to taste, then stir in the parsley. Remove the star anise.

Place a heavy skillet or griddle over medium-high heat. Brush the rolls with the remaining 2 tablespoons olive oil and sear lightly in the hot skillet. Fill with the shrimp *saganaki* mixture and serve.

Spartiatiko Kotopoulo Sandwits me Liomeno Tyri

SPARTAN CHICKEN MELT

serves 4

Spartan chicken, also known as chicken Bardouniotiko, after a group of mountain villages near the famous ancient city of Sparta, is a rich but simple combination of slow-cooked onion, chicken, and feta cheese. Some renditions, including the one in this book, call for the addition of olives and tomatoes. It so happens that the combination also makes a great sandwich, albeit with a bit of poetic license added to the recipe.

FOR THE MARINADE

3 tablespoons extra-virgin Greek olive oil

1 tablespoon mild mustard

2 tablespoons chopped fresh oregano

½ teaspoon tomato paste

½ teaspoon kalamata olive paste

1 tablespoon Greek or other balsamic vinegar

Freshly ground black pepper

2 large boneless, skinless chicken breasts, trimmed of excess fat and halved lengthwise

Extra-virgin Greek olive oil

2 large red onions, halved and sliced

1 tablespoon Greek or other balsamic vinegar

Whole-grain baguettes, ciabatta, or other good bread of choice, butterflied open

1 tablespoon mild mustard

1 small bunch arugula

1 cup (150 g) crumbled Greek feta

Make the marinade: In a large stainless steel bowl, whisk together the olive oil, mustard, oregano, tomato paste, olive paste, vinegar, and pepper to taste.

Place the chicken breast halves on a clean cutting board and place a piece of plastic wrap on top. Using a meat pounder or mallet, pound the breasts lightly to flatten to a thickness of about ½ inch (1.5 cm). Add the chicken to the bowl with the marinade, toss or stir to coat, cover, and refrigerate for at least 15 minutes or up to 3 hours.

In a nonstick skillet, heat 1 tablespoon olive oil over medium-low heat. Add the onions, reduce the heat to low and cook, stirring occasionally for about 20 minutes until golden. Add the vinegar to the onions about halfway through the cooking time. The onions can be prepared up to 1 day in advance and stored in the refrigerator.

Preheat the broiler with a rack positioned 8 inches (20 cm) from the heat source. Lightly oil a shallow baking pan.

Place the chicken in the pan and broil, turning once, until lightly golden. Remove from the oven (keep the broiler on) and set aside, tented with aluminum foil to keep warm.

Put the bread on a baking sheet and brush with olive oil. Broil for a few seconds until

lightly browned (or toast the bread in a skillet on the stovetop). Remove from the oven (keep the broiler on).

Spread a little of the mustard over the cut sides of the bread. Top with the arugula, then the chicken, onions, and feta. Place the sandwiches, open-faced, under the broiler for a few seconds, just until the feta begins to melt. Remove from the oven, close the sandwiches with their top halves, and serve.

NOTE: You can also cook the chicken breasts on the stovetop instead of broiling: In a sauté pan or nonstick skillet, heat 1 tablespoon olive oil over medium heat. Add the chicken and cook, turning once, until golden on all sides and cooked through, about 25 minutes.

O Akatastatos Yianis

SLOPPY YIANNI

serves 6

Taking the idea of a sloppy joe, giving it a Greek flavor palette, and making it a little healthier in the process by replacing half the meat with finely chopped mushrooms, I created this fun recipe. Serve this on nice sourdough buns with a salad on the side, and sip a Greek beer to wash it all down.

3 tablespoons extra-virgin Greek olive oil

1 large onion, very finely chopped

3 garlic cloves, minced

¾ pound (340 g) lean ground beef

1 pound (450 g) button mushrooms, chopped

2 tablespoons tomato paste

1 cinnamon stick

Scant 1 teaspoon ground allspice

2 bay leaves

1 cup (240 ml) dry red wine

Scant 1 teaspoon brown sugar, or 2 tablespoons *petimezi* (grape molasses)

Salt and freshly ground black pepper

2 teaspoons dried Greek oregano

6 (4- to 5-inch / 10 to 12 cm) pieces regular or sourdough baguette, split lengthwise, or 6 buns

In a large deep skillet or wide pot, heat the olive oil over medium heat. Add the onion and cook for about 5 minutes to soften. Reduce the heat to low and cook for 15 to 20 minutes more, until golden. Stir in the garlic.

Add the ground meat to the pan and cook, stirring and breaking it up with a wooden spoon as it cooks, until browned, about 10 minutes. Add the mushrooms and stir well to combine. Add the tomato paste and stir to distribute evenly. Add the cinnamon, allspice, and bay leaves. Pour in the wine, add the sugar, and cook over low heat, stirring every few minutes, until the mixture is dense and almost dry and the meat is thoroughly cooked, 45 to 50 minutes. The mixture should be moist but not runny, so simmer until all the liquid has cooked off and the mixture holds its shape when scooped with a spoon. Taste and season with salt and pepper then stir in the oregano. Remove the bay leaves and cinnamon stick.

Lightly toast the baguette pieces or buns. Spoon the meat mixture onto the bottom half of each, dividing it evenly. Cover with the top half and serve.

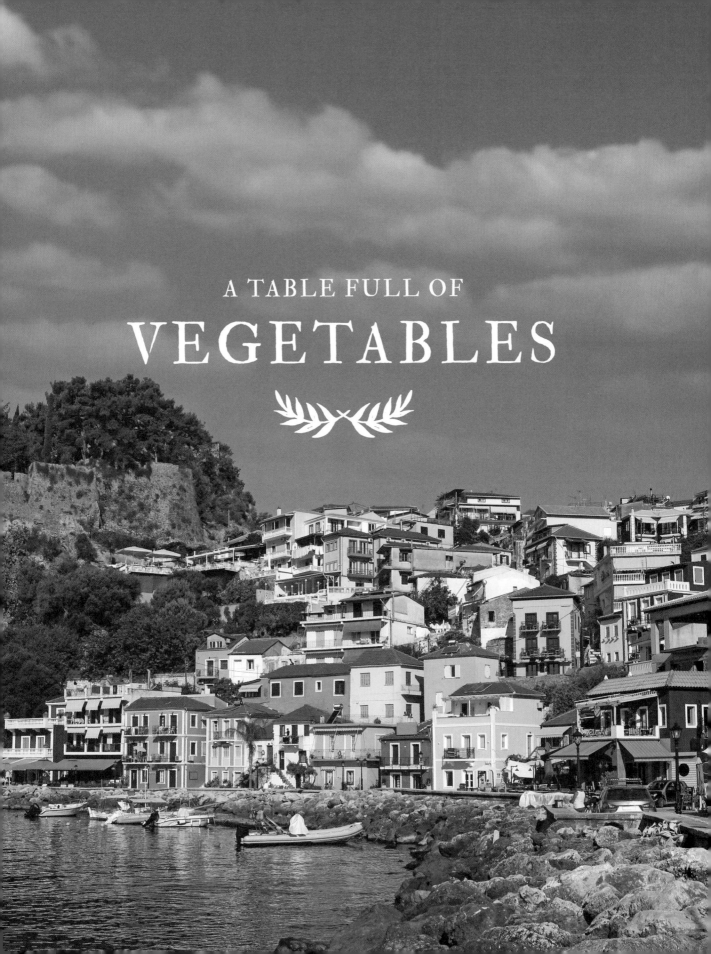

A TABLE FULL OF
VEGETABLES

Το λάδι κι η αλήθεια πάντα βγαίνουν από πάνω

To ladi kai y alitheia panta vgainoun apo pano

"Oil and truth always rise to the top."

My favorite aspect of the Greek table is by far the enormous breadth of vegetable- and other plant-based dishes that run the gamut from *meze* to main courses. To my mind, these dishes—varied from region to region yet consistent in approach, technique, and seasonality; in their often profuse use of olive oil; and in their embrace of herbs more than spices to flavor the pot—are the heart and soul of the Greek kitchen.

The variety and, in many cases, ingenuity of vegetable-based dishes tap into the deep connection Greeks still have to the land, even now, in the twenty-first century. Indeed, in these times, faced with national economic ruin and increasingly more strained urban life, many young people have returned to the land, bringing a little marketing know-how and sophisticated aesthetics to a whole new world of Greek farm products.

I can speak from my own experiences and from my observations over twenty-five years in Greece, connected to my own village and to the farm life that hums gently everywhere, regardless of the season. In spring, on Ikaria, a small island in the northeastern Aegean where we have a summer house and a little land, my husband plants the garden. Talk of tomato varieties seeps into house, hybrids vs. older types, thick-skinned vs. juicy. Seedlings line our patio: a handful of varieties of peppers, tomatoes, eggplants, cucumbers, zucchini. Onion bulbs and knobby potato seedlings sit in burlap bags waiting to be pressed into the earth. It takes a few days to turn the soil and clear the land of weeds, but even that has its delicious rewards in the reams of wild edible greens we collect and cook: wild sorrel, fennel, lemon balm, mallow, reichardia, poppy leaves, shepherd's needles, salsify, a range of wild chicories and dandelions, mustard greens, golden fleece, prickly lettuce—the list goes on and on, expanding and contracting as much by what has sprung from the soil as by one's knowledge and ability to recognize which weeds are actually edible.

The spring planting season is also the best time to forage for dozens of wild shoots, herbs, and slender wild roots and bulbs. We do. It's great fun, provides a gentle workout, and offers the most daring array of plant-based foods imaginable: dewy and refreshingly sour green almonds, pistachio tree shoots and vine tendrils to put up in brine, slender crisp stalks of wild asparagus that hide among the brambles and are excellent in omelets, wild carrot tops and their pouch-shaped meshy buds, which are nothing more than Queen Anne's lace before it opens into the flower. We dig for wild hyacinth bulbs to pickle. I go in search of borage flowers to add to tender salads, and scramble up the rocks along the beach to collect the succulent tiny leaves of sea fennel to pickle, and also to dry and grind, as its proximity to the water makes it a one-stop shop of seasoned salt. Summer is the time to reap, of course, but also to plan for winter by slicing, stringing, salting, sun-drying, or preserving in syrup almost everything the garden gives.

Even for me, by all measures an urban cook, this connection to the land has given a deep sense of appreciation for what grows naturally, and a deepening sense of shame at our own hubris in destroying so much of the planet's life. These natural cycles are not limited to the simplified, pared-down life in the Greek countryside. Even in cities, the seasons are apparent at the markets, something we Americans have long since lost and lamented all too little. End-of-summer tomatoes that are overripe and bruised sell for a fraction of the price that near perfect specimens bring in, and people scoop them up to put them up as sauce. Eggplants—a whole extended family in hues of regal purple and gentle white, long, short, round, thin, and flask-shaped—beckon, with the possibility of endless recipes for this most versatile of all vegetables. Peppers state their purpose by shape: bells for stuffing, bonnets and horns for pickling or putting up in olive oil.

Winter is comforting, too, in a Greek city farmers' market. Stalls stretch out along two sides, and a landscape of hard winter roots undulates in the soft colors of twilight: the purple of turnips and rutabagas, the gold and browns of various potato varieties, the scratchy ecru of parsnips, the deep tenor of blood-dark beets, and the orange optimism of carrots, all tempered by the craggy waves of greens, from common spinach to obscure chicories, that brim with minerals and vitamins and the promise of edible strength to ward off the dangers of the cold.

Plant-based cooking, which includes, of course, the beautiful bounty of beans, touches every part of a meal but is not necessarily vegetarian (as in, meatless) cooking. Many traditional plant-based Greek dishes incorporate meat, fish, or seafood, too. In this chapter, I've included a few such dishes and organized the recipes from small to large—that is, from plant-based side dishes to more substantial main courses. The handful of dishes we call *ladera*, or "olive oil–based," make an important component of the kitchen and are always purely vegetarian, and oftentimes vegan.

If I were to impart one solid rule when it comes to Greek vegetable cookery, it would be to ignore the embarrassment of often tasteless riches in American supermarkets and focus on what's in season wherever you happen to be. The dishes that follow are all easy enough to be flexible, and that's an important lesson. Use them more as a compass. Let the seasons be your guide.

Patates Psites stin Katsarola me xinomavro

SEARED STOVETOP FINGERLINGS
with xinomavro wine and sage

serves 4 to 6 as a side dish

There is something about the slick, crinkled skin, garlic-infused red wine tannins, and musky sage and rosemary that renders these potatoes irresistible. This also happens to be one of the easiest ways to prepare great potatoes with no muss, no fuss, and no hot oven, with results that coming strikingly close to the best "roasted" potatoes you've ever had. These are a frequent dish on my Greek table!

⅓ cup (80 ml) extra-virgin Greek olive oil

1 pound (450 g) fingerling potatoes, preferably organic, scrubbed

Coarse sea salt and freshly ground black pepper

4 to 6 garlic cloves, cut into paper-thin slivers

2 teaspoons whole dried sage leaves

3 fresh rosemary sprigs, broken into 2-inch (5 cm) pieces

⅔ cup (160 ml) Greek xinomavro or other dry, tannic red wine

In a large deep skillet or wide pot, heat the olive oil over medium heat. Add the potatoes, cover with a tight-fitting lid, and reduce the heat to medium-low. Let the potatoes steam in the olive oil for 5 minutes.

Uncover and sprinkle the potatoes with salt and pepper. Cover the pan and shake the potatoes a few times back and forth over the heat. Cook for 5 minutes more, then add the garlic, sage, and rosemary. Reduce the heat to low and cook for 10 minutes, shaking the pan back and forth a few times to keep the potatoes from burning. Pour in the wine, cover, and cook until the potatoes are fork-tender, about 20 minutes more. Taste and adjust the seasoning with salt and pepper. Serve hot.

Oi Agapimenes mou Patates Fournou

MY FAVORITE ROASTED GREEK POTATOES

serves 6 to 8 as a side dish

Roasted potatoes are the ultimate comfort food. This recipe isn't exactly my Greek grandma's recipe, but a modern take on a classic. Honey, mustard, citrus juices, and fresh herbs make these potatoes really irresistible.

4 pounds (1.8 kg) russet or other all-purpose potatoes

Salt

3 tablespoons Dijon or Greek mustard

3 tablespoons Greek pine honey, blossom honey, or thyme honey

Juice of 1 orange, strained

Juice of 1 lemon, strained

⅔ cup (160 ml) extra-virgin Greek olive oil

8 garlic cloves, chopped

4 fresh rosemary sprigs, broken into 2-inch (5 cm) pieces

10 fresh thyme sprigs

10 fresh oregano sprigs

Freshly ground black pepper

Preheat the oven to 375°F (175°C).

If your potatoes are organic, scrub them but leave the skins on. If not, peel them. Cut the potatoes into quarters lengthwise. Place the potatoes in a large pot, add water to cover, and bring to a rolling boil over medium-high heat. Add 1 tablespoon salt to the water. Reduce the heat to maintain a simmer and cook the potatoes for exactly 8 minutes. Drain the potatoes and place them in a baking pan large enough to hold them in one layer.

In a medium bowl, whisk together the mustard, honey, orange juice, lemon juice, and olive oil. Stir in the garlic, rosemary, thyme, and oregano. Pour this mixture over the potatoes and toss gently with a large spoon or spatula. Season the potatoes generously with salt and pepper. Cover the baking pan with parchment paper, then with aluminum foil, and roast for 35 minutes, checking the potatoes as they bake and turning them if they start to stick to the bottom of the pan. Remove the parchment and foil and roast until the potatoes start to crisp and brown lightly. Roast for 10 to 15 minutes more, until the potatoes are crusty but tender, turning them as needed.

Remove from the oven, let cool slightly, and serve.

Tiganites Patates opos tiw kanoun stin Avli

AVLI'S FRIES
with spicy whipped feta

serves 4

My friend Katerina was a pioneer, bursting onto the restaurant scene in Rethymnon, Crete, when she was just about twenty years old. She has built her restaurant Avli into a beautiful space, housed in an old Venetian building in the old town of this quaint port city. One of the best things on her delicious Cretan menu is also one of the simplest: fried potatoes, arguably the best I've ever had at a restaurant anywhere in Greece. The dollop of spicy whipped feta she plops on top of the fries is a stroke of culinary genius! She serves them up in an old-fashioned cesulus, *a stout metal scoop that was a measuring tool of yore.*

6 large, preferably organic russet potatoes, scrubbed

Corn or sunflower oil, for frying

Extra-virgin Greek olive oil, for frying

Coarse sea salt

Dried Greek oregano

1 recipe for Feta Fire (page 57)

Cut each potato into 6 or 8 long, finger-thick wedges. Place them in a bowl of cold water and refrigerate for 2 hours. Drain and pat dry thoroughly.

Fill a large deep skillet or wide pot with 2 inches (5 cm) of oil, using 3 parts corn oil to 1 part olive oil (the olive oil lends flavor). Heat the oil over medium-high heat until it registers 300°F (150°C) on an instant-read or deep-fry thermometer. Working in batches, add the potato wedges to the hot oil, being careful not to crowd the pan. Fry for about 5 minutes, just until the potatoes are softened but before they start to brown. Use a slotted spoon to transfer the potatoes to paper towels to drain. Repeat with the remaining wedges.

Raise the heat under the oil to high and bring it to 400°F (200°C). Again working in batches, add the par-cooked potatoes and fry until they are golden brown, with crisp, crinkly skin. Remove with a slotted spoon and drain on paper towels. Repeat with the remaining wedges.

Transfer the potato wedges to a serving bowl, sprinkle with salt and oregano to taste, and toss. Dollop a generous scoop of the whipped feta on top and serve.

Krema Kalambokiou me Feta

FRESH CORN AND FETA POLENTA

serves 4 to 6, as a side dish

New World corn laid down roots in Greece hundreds of years ago, mainly in the north, where it is still an important crop. This recipe is inspired by the old polenta-type dishes traditionally made in the northwestern mountain reaches of the Greek mainland. I transformed it into something a little more contemporary by using fresh corn instead of cornmeal. It pairs beautifully with vegetable casseroles such as Eleni's Ikarian Skillet Soufico (page 163), as well as with meat dishes such as My Son's Favorite Beef Stew (page 312). You can also make the polenta with frozen corn on the cob, thawed to room temperature, of course.

6 fresh ears corn, husked, silks removed (see Note)

3 tablespoons butter, plus more as needed

⅔ cup (100 g) crumbled Greek feta

Salt and freshly ground black pepper

Set a box grater directly in a medium saucepan or deep skillet. Grate the corn on the large holes of the grater into the pan (you want to capture all the corn milk, which is very sweet and starchy and will help the polenta thicken nicely).

Cover and cook over low heat for about 5 minutes, until the mixture becomes thick and creamy. Whisk in the butter, feta, a pinch of salt, if desired, and a little black pepper. Cook, whisking, until the mixture is very creamy, another 5 to 7 minutes. Remove and serve.

NOTE: You can save the corn silk, dry it on a plate in the kitchen, and submerge it in boiling water for a few minutes, then strain and discard, to make a natural infusion said to be very beneficial for many ailments, from kidney stones and bladder infections to high blood pressure and cholesterol.

Kalamboki stin Schara me Elaiovoutiro

GRILLED CORN ON THE COB
with kalamata olive butter

serves 8

"Awesome" is the only way to describe this delicious grilled corn recipe, a paean to my Greek American roots. Enjoy!

1 cup (2 sticks / 225 g) salted butter, at room temperature

2 tablespoons chopped fresh chives

2 tablespoons chopped pitted kalamata olives, well drained

1 garlic clove, minced

1 teaspoon grated lemon zest

8 fresh ears corn, with husks intact

Using a fork, whip the butter, chives, olives, garlic, and lemon zest in a small bowl until just combined. (Alternatively, you can do this in the bowl of a small food processor.)

Arrange a piece of sturdy plastic wrap, about 12 inches (30 cm) long, horizontally in front of you on a clean work surface.

Scoop the kalamata butter out of the bowl and onto the plastic wrap. Use the plastic to help loosely shape the butter into a rough cylinder about 6 inches (15 cm) long. Roll the plastic wrap up around the butter, twisting the ends and patting down, until the cylinder is about 8 inches (20 cm) in length. Refrigerate for several hours or freeze for about 1 hour, until solid.

Heat a grill to medium. Place 2 dabs of the kalamata butter inside each corn husk, close the husk, and wrap the corn in aluminum foil. Grill the corn for about 30 minutes, until tender. Remove and serve immediately, with the rest of the kalamata butter as an accompaniment.

Kastana Stifado

WINE-BRAISED CHESTNUTS AND SHALLOTS

serves 4

Chestnuts, one of the oldest foods in the eastern Mediterranean, known to the ancient and modern Greeks alike by the same name, kastano, *have always been an important food. They flourish in mountainous areas—and 80 percent of the Greek land mass is mountains. So important a food and ubiquitous a tree is the chestnut that all over Greece, from islands to mainland, there are countless villages actually named for this hearty, nutritious nut.*

I like to look at chestnuts from a chef's perspective and am enamored of the many recipes, from dips to main courses to desserts, of course, which call for it. Candied chestnuts and chestnut spoon sweets (whole chestnuts preserved in sugar syrup) abound in Mount Pelion and other parts of the Greek mainland. But it's the savory preparations that win my heart most, and this recipe is one of my favorites. It is an old country dish from Arcadia in the Peloponnese. Serve it with Greek or other noodles, or on its own.

¼ cup (60 ml) extra-virgin Greek olive oil	⅔ cup (160 ml) dry red wine
10 small shallots	2 to 3 tablespoons Greek balsamic vinegar
3 garlic cloves, chopped	5 or 6 fresh thyme sprigs
1 cup (180 g) coarsely chopped fresh or canned tomatoes	1 bay leaf
	1 cinnamon stick
3 cups peeled defrosted frozen or vacuum-packed chestnuts	4 allspice berries

In a wide, shallow medium pot, heat the olive oil over medium-low heat. Add the whole shallots and cook until lightly caramelized, about 20 minutes. Stir in the garlic. Add the tomatoes. Bring to a boil, reduce the heat to medium-low, and simmer for 15 minutes to thicken slightly.

Add the chestnuts, wine, vinegar, thyme, bay leaf, cinnamon, and allspice and cook until the chestnuts are tender and the pot juices are dense and thick. Remove and discard the thyme, bay leaf, cinnamon, and allspice. Serve.

NOTE: This is great on the Thanksgiving table and makes a wonderful alternative if you have any vegan guests. Serve it over mashed sweet potatoes!

Keil Sigomageiremeno me Ladi, Portokali kai Skordo

SLOW-COOKED KALE
with greek olive oil, oranges, and garlic

serves 6

Many years ago, I came across a recipe for slow-cooked spinach and oranges from the Mani, the bone-dry southern tip of the Peloponnese, where little else beyond orange and olive trees flourish. This is a variation on that, with kale, a relative newcomer to the long-standing members of the Brassica family that are mainstays of the Greek traditional table. You can also make this dish with any variety of sweet greens, such as Swiss chard or beet greens. It stands on its own with a little feta and good bread, but also makes a great side to any number of fish, seafood, and chicken recipes.

2 pounds (900 g) kale

⅔ cup (160 ml) extra-virgin Greek olive oil

6 garlic cloves, thinly sliced

2 oranges, peel on, cut into 8 wedges each

Salt and freshly ground black pepper

Remove and discard the kale stems and rinse the leaves well. Dry thoroughly in a salad spinner.

In a large wide pot, heat ⅓ cup (80 ml) of the olive oil over medium heat. Add the garlic and cook until soft. Stir in the orange wedges and cook for 1 minute.

Add the kale, in batches if necessary, and stir so the garlic and orange wedges are distributed evenly among the kale leaves. As the kale wilts, add more, stirring again, until all the kale is in the pot. Cover and cook for 20 to 25 minutes, until the kale is very tender. Season to taste with salt and pepper.

Remove from the heat and drizzle in the remaining ⅓ cup (80 ml) olive oil. Serve hot, warm, or at room temperature.

Ladera

OLIVE OIL NATION

It's impossible to talk about the vegetable- and other plant-based dishes of Greece without touching on the role of olive oil in Greek cooking. Although per capita consumption has decreased in the last few years, probably another "victim" of the Greek economic crisis, Greeks in Greece still consume more olive oil than anyone else on the planet, at approximately 15 quarts per person annually. The country is the third largest producer of olive oil.

Much of it is consumed as the de facto cooking fat and flavoring agent in a whole category of recipes called *ladera*, after *ladi*, the Greek word for "oil." These are by and large vegetable and bean stews or baked vegetable and bean casseroles. Many are vegan and tied to the long periods of fasting on the Greek Orthodox calendar; many are seasonal, such as the luscious eggplant dishes of a Greek summer and the hearty baked bean dishes from all over the country.

Home cooks of a few generations ago knew that a *ladero* dish was done when the only liquid left in the pot was the olive oil, infused, of course, with the sweet flavors of slow-cooked tomatoes, garlic, onions, and herbs, as if to describe a kind of stovetop emulsion, a unifying and softening of ingredients and flavors with olive oil as the silky conduit. Indeed, slow-cooked vegetables and beans impart their natural sugars, making everything from leafy greens to chickpeas to eggplant more palatable. Greek vegetable cookery is rich with a great variety of comfort foods as a result. Their underlying natural sweetness and soft textures are soothing balms for the palate and the body. It's no wonder that even kids learn to eat and love vegetables on the Greek table!

For the most part, *ladera* dishes are cooked in very little liquid, but with a copious amount of olive oil, not uncommonly up to 1 cup (240 ml) for 2 pounds (900 g) of vegetables. By simmering over a few hours, bean and vegetable dishes caramelize slowly; their inherent softness makes them easier to digest. And, perhaps most important of all, that olive oil left in the bottom of the pot is where all the nutrients reside.

Many nutrients, especially beta-carotene, an antioxidant, are fat-soluble, not water-soluble, so we don't absorb them simply by chewing and swallowing foods containing them. Cooking in olive oil allows us to extract and absorb these nutrients more efficiently.

The sweet, unctuous taste and texture of *ladera* vegetables and beans are almost always balanced with a little acid: lemon juice and vinegar are close at hand in most Greek kitchens. Feta, the briny Greek cheese, and even Greek yogurt provide a beautiful counterpoint to the comforting unctuousness of most of Greece's *ladera* dishes.

Prasa Psita me Ksismeno Tyri kai Tzanera

GRILLED OR SEARED LEEKS
with shaved sheep's-milk cheese and prunes

serves 4

Both island and mainland cooks have an affinity for all things in the onion family, from wild leeks and wild onions to scallions, shallots, onion stalks, and a host of purple and yellow onions of every shape and size. There are lots of dishes in the Greek kitchen, such as pies, stews, and roasted salads, that call for the onion as a main ingredient. This recipe is an adaptation of an old Macedonian dish that called for wild onion or leek stalks.

6 large leeks, white and light green parts only

6 tablespoons (90 ml) extra-virgin Greek olive oil, plus more for brushing

Sea salt and freshly ground black pepper

2 tablespoons Greek or other balsamic vinegar

1 tablespoon strained fresh lemon juice

4 pitted prunes, finely chopped

Grated zest of 1 lemon

5 ounces (140 g) kasseri, Kefalotyri, or aged myzithra cheese, or any sharp sheep's-milk cheese, such as pecorino, shaved

Cut the leeks in half lengthwise and rinse thoroughly under cold water to wash away any grit.

Bring 1 inch (2.5 cm) of water to a boil in the bottom of a pot fitted with a steamer basket. Place the leeks in the steamer basket, cover, and steam for 10 minutes. Transfer to a bowl, toss with 3 tablespoons of the olive oil, and season to taste with salt and pepper.

Whisk together the remaining 3 tablespoons olive oil, the vinegar, lemon juice, prunes, and lemon zest in a small bowl and season to taste with salt and pepper.

Heat a grill to medium or heat a grill pan over medium heat. Brush the grill grates or pan lightly with a little olive oil. Grill or sear the steamed leeks, turning them often with tongs, for 5 to 8 minutes, just until grill marks appear. Remove from the heat and place on a serving platter. Drizzle the leeks with the prune dressing and garnish with the shaved cheese. Serve.

LESVOS-STYLE GARLICKY WHOLE EGGPLANTS
in tomato sauce

serves 4 to 6

No other place in Greece boasts as many eggplant recipes as the island of Lesvos in the northeastern Aegean. Most, if not all, of these dishes arrived on the island with the wave of Greek refugees from Asia Minor in 1922, who brought with them a sophisticated, aromatic cuisine that transformed the rural cooking of the country.

8 small Japanese or other thin eggplants, such as Antigua or Fond May, each about 6 inches (15 cm) long, trimmed

4 large garlic cloves, cut into very thin slivers

½ cup (120 ml) extra-virgin Greek olive oil, plus more for drizzling, if desired

Salt and freshly ground black pepper

½ cup (120 ml) dry white wine

4 ripe large tomatoes, chopped or grated, or 2 cups (330 g) chopped canned tomatoes

2 tablespoons dried Greek oregano or savory

½ cup (25 g) chopped fresh parsley

⅔ cup (100 g) crumbled Greek feta

Peel the eggplants lengthwise at ¼-inch (6 mm) intervals so the exterior has alternating peeled and unpeeled stripes. Using a sharp paring knife, make four small (½-inch / 1.5 cm) lengthwise incisions in each eggplant and stuff each with a sliver of garlic.

In a large wide pot, heat the olive oil over medium heat. Add the eggplants and cook, turning occasionally, until lightly browned and softened on all sides, for about 10 minutes. Season lightly with salt and pepper. Gently stir in the remaining garlic slivers, being careful not to burn them. Add the wine and as soon as it steams up, add the tomatoes. Season to taste with salt and pepper, cover, reduce the heat to low, and simmer until the eggplants are tender, about 35 minutes.

Add the oregano, parsley, and feta and cook for a few minutes more, just until the feta starts to melt. Remove from the heat and serve, drizzled with additional olive oil if desired.

ELENI'S IKARIAN SKILLET SOUFICO

serves 6 to 8

Soufico is one of the "national" dishes of Ikaria, an island (not a nation!) in the northeastern Aegean that also happens to be where my family roots are. It is one of many dishes throughout Greece, and throughout the Mediterranean at large, that calls for the same medley of summer vegetables, anchored by eggplant, the fleshiest and most filling of all of them. This is my friend Eleni's version. It is one of the simplest and most delicious I've ever tried.

2 medium eggplants, about 8 inches (20 cm) long, trimmed

3 medium potatoes, peeled

3 large zucchini, about 8 inches (20 cm) long, trimmed

2 large onions, coarsely chopped

Sea salt

½ cup (120 ml) extra-virgin Greek olive oil, plus more as needed

4 garlic cloves, chopped

3 green bell peppers, cut into 1-inch-wide (2.5 cm) strips

Freshly ground black pepper

4 large fresh tomatoes, peeled

1 cup (240 ml) dry white wine

3 fresh bay leaves

2 tablespoons *petimezi* (grape molasses; optional)

6 to 8 large fresh basil leaves, coarsely chopped

⅔ cup (35 g) chopped fresh parsley

5 fresh oregano sprigs

3 or 4 fresh thyme sprigs

Cut the eggplants in half crosswise, then cut each half into rectangular pieces, about ¾ inch (2 cm) wide and 2½ inches (6.25 cm) long. Set aside. Cut the potatoes and zucchini into rectangles of the same size.

In a wide shallow pot or deep skillet, cook the onions over low heat, with no oil, sprinkled with a little salt, until they begin to soften. Add the olive oil and cook the onions until translucent, about 8 minutes. Stir in the garlic. Add the eggplant and stir gently. Add the potatoes and stir. Next, add the bell peppers and stir. Finally, gently stir in the zucchini pieces. Season lightly with salt and black pepper.

Working with one at a time, hold a tomato over the pot in one hand and use a sharp paring knife to cut it into small chunks and drop them into the vegetables. Add the wine. When it begins to evaporate, stir in the bay leaves.

Reduce the heat to low, cover the pot, and simmer for about 25 minutes, or until the vegetables are tender. Stir in the *petimezi*, if using. Add the basil, parsley, oregano, and thyme, cover, and cook for 10 minutes more. Taste and adjust the seasoning with salt and black pepper. Remove the bay leaves and herb sprigs. Serve hot, warm, or at room temperature.

Mantza

NAOUSSA SUMMER STEW
with fried cheese

serves 4 to 6

Salt

2 large eggplants, trimmed and cut into 1-inch (2.5 cm) cubes

2 or 3 medium zucchini, trimmed and cut into 1-inch (2.5 cm) cubes

½ cup (120 ml) extra-virgin Greek olive oil

1 large onion, finely chopped

3 red bell peppers, cut into 1-inch (2.5 cm) chunks

2 sweet long fleshy red peppers, cut into 1-inch (2.5 cm) chunks

2 large tomatoes, grated (1½ to 2 cups / 360 to 480 ml); see Note, page 92)

8 ounces (225 g) Kefalotyri or Greek feta cheese, cut into 1-inch (2.5 cm) cubes

1 teaspoon sweet paprika

¼ teaspoon cayenne pepper, or to taste

3 to 4 tablespoons finely chopped fresh parsley, for garnish

Lightly salt the eggplant and zucchini cubes in a colander and let stand in the sink for about 30 minutes to drain. Do not rinse.

In a large deep skillet or wide pot, heat 2 tablespoons of the olive oil over high heat. Add the onion and all the peppers and cook, stirring, for a few minutes to soften. Remove with a slotted spoon and set aside on a plate.

Add 3 tablespoons of the olive oil to the skillet, then add the eggplant and zucchini and cook over high heat, stirring occasionally, until the vegetables are lightly browned and crisp around the edges. Add more olive oil if necessary. Return the onion-pepper mixture to the pan. Pour in the tomatoes and ½ cup (120 ml) water. Cover the pan with the lid ajar and cook over low heat until the vegetables are tender and the pan juices are thick.

Just before removing the vegetables from the heat, toss the cheese cubes into the pot. Season with the paprika and cayenne and salt to taste. Remove from the heat and serve on a platter or on individual plates, drizzled with any remaining olive oil and garnished with the parsley.

Spetzofai me Agria Manitaria

WILD MUSHROOM AND ONION STEW

serves 6

Spetzofai, *a dish native to the Mount Pelion region of central Greece, is traditionally a stew of sausages and peppers cooked in a tomato-based sauce. Indeed, its name comes from the Italian* spezzatino *("red sauce") and* fai, *the Greek word for food—literally, "red food"! There are variations for pescatarians and vegetarians alike, with shrimp or small fish, such as mullets, and peppers giant beans and peppers—and this hearty rendition of mushrooms and peppers.*

½ cup (120 ml) extra-virgin Greek olive oil

3 large red onions, halved and sliced

6 green or red bell peppers, cut into 1-inch-wide (2.5 cm) strips

4 garlic cloves, minced

1 pound (450 g) oyster mushrooms, wiped clean and trimmed

1 pound (450 g) portobello mushrooms, wiped clean and trimmed

1 cup (35 g) dried porcini mushrooms, soaked in 1½ cups (360 ml) warm water for 15 minutes, or ¼ pound (115 g) fresh, wiped clean and trimmed

1 cup (240 ml) dry white wine

2 bay leaves

1 tablespoon tomato paste, diluted in ½ cup (120 ml) water

10 fresh thyme sprigs

2 fresh rosemary sprigs

1 to 2 tablespoons Greek balsamic vinegar, as needed

Salt and freshly ground black pepper

½ cup (25 g) finely chopped fresh parsley

¼ cup (13 g) chopped fresh oregano

In a large wide pot or saucepan, heat ¼ cup (60 ml) of the olive oil over medium heat. Add the onions and bell peppers and cook, stirring gently, until wilted, 8 to 10 minutes. Stir in the garlic.

Cut any overly large oyster mushrooms in half vertically and cut the portobellos into 3 or 4 slices each. If using dried porcinis, drain them, reserving their soaking liquid, and set aside until ready to use. Strain the soaking liquid through a coffee filter or fine-mesh sieve and set aside.

Add the oyster, portobello, and fresh or dried porcini mushrooms to the pan. Raise the heat to medium-high and pour in the wine. As soon as the alcohol cooks off, add the porcini soaking liquid, if you used dried porcinis, the diluted tomato paste, bay leaves, thyme, and rosemary. Season to taste with salt and black pepper. Cover with the lid ajar and simmer for about 20 minutes, or until the mushrooms are tender but not overcooked.

Remove the thyme and rosemary sprigs and bay leaves. Taste and season with the vinegar (using more or less to your liking) and salt and black pepper to taste. Gently stir in the parsley and oregano. Remove from the heat, drizzle with the remaining ¼ cup (60 ml) olive oil, and serve.

MY FAVORITE STUFFED VEGETABLE DISHES

I am a great fan of stuffed vegetables and have always been surprised by the range and ingenuity of these simple, seasonal dishes throughout Greece. Most people know the classics like rice-and-herb-stuffed tomatoes and bell peppers; ground meat–filled zucchini tubes; and *imam bayildi*, an onion-rich vegetarian stuffed eggplant. But the variations, even on the classics, are endless and speak tomes about the way country cooks take basic ingredients to create lasting traditions with regional distinctions.

In northern Greece, for example, a stuffed pepper might not be the classic green bell variety but a fleshy, horn-shaped sweet red pepper called a Florina. Up north, rice and herbs are typically enhanced with raisins and pine nuts, an influence that traces its roots to the cooking of the Anatolian Greek settlers who arrived en masse from Asia Minor (modern-day Turkey) almost a hundred years ago, bringing with them an urbane, aromatic cuisine. Another classic of Thessaloniki is a roasted feta-stuffed Florina pepper, one of the most popular taverna dishes.

Eggplants have inspired home cooks with stuffings that range from a whole quail—an old dish from the Aegean islands—to spiced ground meat, octopus and rice (as in the recipe from Lesvos on page 170), cheeses, seafood, and more. In this chapter, I have a few stuffed eggplant recipes, one for a not-so-classic *papoutsaki*, which means "shoe" in Greek, a creative reference to how these eggplant boats look when baked, and one for my rendition of *imam bayildi*, with grape molasses and raisins.

The grains used in traditional stuffed vegetable recipes, especially for stuffed tomatoes, peppers, zucchini, and eggplant, run the gamut from rice, which is cultivated in Greece, to bulgur, *trahana* (see page 214), and, nowadays, quinoa and buckwheat. There is a special short-grain stuffing rice grown, like the other varieties, in Chalastra, just south of Thessaloniki, on the delta of the Axios River. Its proximity to the sea while growing gives Greek rice a particularly delicious flavor.

Papoutsakia apo tin Lesvo

LESVOS-STYLE EGGPLANT "SHOES"

serves 4 or 8

One more of the many delicious eggplant dishes from the island of Lesvos.

4 medium eggplants, stems intact

½ cup (120 ml) extra-virgin Greek olive oil, plus more as needed

6 red onions, coarsely chopped

4 garlic cloves, minced

5 fresh tomatoes, chopped

1 cup (100 g) coarsely grated graviera or other mild sheep's-milk cheese

½ cup (50 g) grated Kefalotyri, Parmesan, or other sharp sheep's-milk cheese

½ cup (75 g) crumbled Greek feta

1 cup (50 g) chopped fresh mint

1 cup (50 g) chopped fresh parsley

Salt and freshly ground black pepper

2 large eggs, lightly beaten

Preheat the broiler with a rack positioned 8 inches (20 cm) from the heat source. Line a baking sheet with parchment paper.

Cut the eggplant down the middle lengthwise, keeping the stems intact. Using a sharp paring knife, score the flesh of each eggplant half in a crosshatch pattern, being careful not to draw the knife completely through the flesh into the skin or to puncture the skin in any way. Lavishly brush the eggplant skin and flesh with olive oil. Place the eggplant halves skin-side down on the prepared baking sheet. Broil for 5 to 7 minutes, until the skin starts to char lightly, then turn using kitchen tongs and broil until the flesh is tender but still al dente, 6 to 7 minutes.

Remove from the oven and set aside to cool. Switch the oven to bake at 350°F (175°C). Oil a glass or ceramic baking dish just big enough to hold the eggplant halves snugly.

In a deep skillet or wide pot, heat 3 tablespoons of the olive oil over medium heat. Add the onions and cook until wilted and just starting to brown, 10 to 12 minutes. Stir in the garlic. Stir in the tomatoes. Raise the heat to medium-high and cook for about 5 minutes, until most of the liquid from the tomatoes has cooked off. Set aside to cool.

Using a tablespoon, carefully scoop out most of the flesh from the eggplant halves, leaving enough against the skin to keep it firm enough to hold up to the filling. Coarsely chop the eggplant flesh and stir it into the onion-tomato mixture. Combine the cheeses in one bowl, stirring with a fork. Add half the cheese mixture, the mint, and the parsley to the bowl with the eggplant. Season to taste with salt and pepper. Stir in the beaten eggs.

Place the eggplant halves in the prepared baking dish. Spoon equal amounts of the onion-tomato mixture into the eggplant halves. Bake for 30 minutes, or until the filling is set and the onions are soft. Sprinkle the remaining cheese mixture over the top of each eggplant half and bake for a few minutes more, until the cheeses melt and start to bubble. Remove from the oven, let cool slightly, and serve.

Imam Bayildi me Stafides kai Petimezi

EGGPLANTS
stuffed with onions, raisins, and grape molasses

serves 4 to 8

These deliciously sweet, vegan stuffed eggplants are a riff on a classic dish, imam bayldi, *eggplants stuffed with onions and tomatoes. It's one of the great* ladera *(olive oil–based) dishes of Greece.*

½ cup (120 ml) extra-virgin Greek olive oil, plus more as needed

6 red onions, coarsely chopped

4 garlic cloves, minced

5 fresh tomatoes, coarsely chopped

¼ cup (35 g) Greek or other seedless raisins

3 tablespoons *petimezi* (grape molasses)

1 to 2 tablespoons Greek balsamic vinegar

4 medium eggplants, stems attached

1 cup (50 g) chopped fresh mint

1 cup (50 g) chopped fresh parsley

Salt and freshly ground black pepper

Preheat the broiler with a rack 8 inches (20 cm) from the heat source. Line a baking sheet or shallow roasting pan with parchment paper.

In a deep skillet or wide pot, heat 3 tablespoons of the olive oil over medium heat. Add the onions and cook until wilted and just starting to brown, 12 to 15 minutes. Stir in the garlic and tomatoes. Raise the heat to medium-high and cook for 10 to 15 minutes, until most of the liquid from the tomatoes has cooked off. Stir in the raisins, *petimezi*, and vinegar. Set aside to cool.

Cut the eggplants in half lengthwise, keeping the stems intact. Using a sharp paring knife, score the flesh of each eggplant half in a crosshatch pattern, being careful not to draw the knife completely through the flesh into the skin or to puncture the skin in any way. Lavishly brush the eggplant skin and flesh with olive oil. Place the eggplant halves flesh-side down on the prepared pan. Broil for 5 to 7 minutes, until the skin starts to char lightly, then turn using kitchen tongs and broil until the flesh is tender but still al dente, 6 to 7 minutes.

Remove from the oven and set aside to cool. Switch the oven to bake at 350°F (175°C). Oil a glass or ceramic baking dish just big enough to hold the eggplant halves snugly.

Using a tablespoon, carefully scoop out most of the flesh from the eggplant halves, leaving enough against the skin to keep it firm enough to hold up to the filling.

Coarsely chop the eggplant flesh and stir it into the onion-tomato mixture. Mix in the mint and parsley and season to taste with salt and pepper. Place the eggplant halves in the prepared baking dish. Spoon equal amounts of the onion-tomato mixture into the eggplant halves. Bake for 30 minutes, or until the filling is set and the onions are soft. Remove from the oven, let cool slightly and serve, drizzled with additional olive oil, if desired.

Melitzanes Yemistes me Ktapodi kai Ryzi

EGGPLANT BOATS
stuffed with octopus and rice

serves 4 or 8

Here is another beautiful eggplant dish from the rich repertoire of Lesvos, shared with me by Maria Koutsoumbis from the town of Molyvos. She and her sister, Dora Parisi, are something of a local legend. Dora wrote the book on the island's cuisine, documenting dozens of recipes that speak tomes about Lesvos's complicated history and the historical events that have shaped the island's culture and cuisine. This recipe, according to Maria, is best made with a Greek island classic, sun-dried octopus, which is all but impossible to find stateside. Cooked octopus works almost as well. The dish is exotic but light, and very delicious! Note that if you're using frozen octopus for this recipe, you'll need to let it defrost in the refrigerator overnight, so plan accordingly.

2 pounds (900 g) fresh or frozen octopus

½ cup (120 ml) extra-virgin Greek olive oil, plus more as needed

6 red onions, finely chopped

4 garlic cloves, minced

½ cup (120 ml) dry white wine

2 tablespoons red wine vinegar

4 Italian or Sicilian eggplants, about 6 inches (15 cm) long, trimmed

2 ripe tomatoes, cored and squeezed into chunks by hand, or 4 to 6 tablespoons (40 to 65 g) good-quality chopped canned tomatoes

⅔ cup medium-grain white rice

1 cup chopped fresh parsley

Salt and freshly ground black pepper

If using frozen octopus, defrost it overnight in the refrigerator.

When ready to cook the octopus, preheat the oven to 375°F (190°C). Line a baking sheet with parchment paper.

Using a sharp paring knife, trim the octopus, cutting away its head sac and removing its beak and the cartilage on the underside of the beak. Discard the sac, beak, and cartilage. Cut the octopus into 8 pieces along the tentacles.

In a large deep skillet or wide pot, heat the olive oil over medium heat. Add the onions and cook, stirring occasionally, until soft and lightly browned, about 15 minutes. Stir in the garlic. Add the tentacles, reduce the heat to low, cover the pan with the lid slightly ajar, and cook until the tentacles exude their pink musky juices, about 15 minutes. Raise the heat a little and add the wine and vinegar. Reduce the heat to maintain a slow simmer, cover again with the lid ajar, and cook until the tentacles are tender but al dente, 35 to 45 minutes.

While the octopus is simmering, halve the eggplants lengthwise. Using a sharp paring knife, score the flesh of each eggplant half in a crosshatch pattern, being careful not to draw the knife completely through the flesh into the skin or to puncture the skin in anyway. Brush with olive oil and place cut-side down on the prepared baking sheet. Brush the skin with a little olive oil. Bake for 25 to 20 minutes, until the flesh is easy to pierce with a fork but the eggplant is still al dente. Remove from the oven and let cool slightly. Reduce the oven temperature to 350°F (175°C). Lightly oil a glass or ceramic baking dish just big enough to hold the eggplant halves snugly.

Strew the tomatoes over the bottom of the prepared pan and set aside.

Remove the octopus tentacles from the skillet and transfer them to a cutting board. Measure out the pot liquid; there should be about 2 cups (480 ml). Discard any excess. Return the reserved 2 cups (480 ml) liquid to the pan and bring to a simmer over medium-low heat. Add the rice, reduce the heat to low, cover, and cook until about two-thirds of the way done, about 15 minutes. Remove from the heat. Coarsely chop the tentacles and stir them into the rice, together with the parsley.

Using a tablespoon, carefully scoop out most of the flesh from the eggplant halves, leaving enough against the skin to keep it firm enough to hold up to the filling (I usually leave about ⅛ inch / 3 mm).

Chop the eggplant flesh and add it to the octopus-rice mixture. Season to taste with salt and pepper. Place the eggplant halves in the prepared baking dish, over the tomatoes. Divide the octopus-rice mixture evenly among the eggplant shells. Pour ½ cup (120 ml) water into the baking dish. Cover with parchment paper, then aluminum foil, and bake for 30 to 40 minutes, until the rice and octopus are tender. Remove from the oven, let cool slightly, and serve.

Melitzanodolmades Gemistoi me Tyri

EGGPLANT ROLLS
stuffed with cheese

serves 6

This is another one of the great eggplant dishes of Lesvos, and one of several that combine the "world's most versatile vegetable," as eggplant is called in Greece, with some rich cheeses and tomato sauce.

3 tablespoons plus ½ cup (120 ml) extra-virgin Greek olive oil, plus more as needed

3 garlic cloves, chopped

8 large tomatoes, cored and chopped, or 2 cups (330 g) good-quality chopped canned tomatoes

Pinch of sugar

Salt and freshly ground black pepper

1 cup chopped fresh basil leaves

4 medium (7- to 8-inch-long / 18 to 21 cm) Sicilian or Italian eggplants, trimmed

1½ cups (225 g) crumbled Greek feta

1½ cups (360 ml) well-drained fresh anthotyro, farmer cheese, or good-quality fresh ricotta cheese

1½ cups (150 g) grated Lesvos Ladotyri (olive oil cheese), Kefalograviera, or other mild, nutty, semihard, yellow sheep's-milk cheese

1 large egg, lightly beaten

Preheat the oven to 350°F (175°C). Line two baking sheets with parchment paper.

In a medium saucepan, heat 3 tablespoons of the olive oil over low heat. Add the garlic and cook, stirring, for a minute or two to soften. Add the tomatoes. Raise the heat to bring the mixture to a simmer. Cover and cook until the sauce has reduced by about one-third and thickened, about 25 minutes. Season with the sugar and salt and pepper to taste.

Puree the sauce directly in the pot using an immersion blender, or carefully transfer it to the bowl of a food processor or a blender (work in batches, if necessary) and puree, then return it to the pot. Stir in the basil. Set aside.

While the sauce is simmering, one at a time, stand the eggplants upright on a cutting board and, using a sharp chef's knife, cut them into long, wide slices about ⅛ inch (3 mm) thick. Place in a large bowl and toss with the remaining ½ cup (120 ml) olive oil. Place the eggplant slices in a single layer on the prepared baking sheets. Brush with additional olive oil and season lightly with salt and pepper. Bake for 10 to 12 minutes, turning once, until the slices are soft but not disintegrating. Remove from the oven and let cool.

Mix all the cheeses together in a medium bowl and stir in the egg.

Brush a 9 x 13-inch (23 x 33 cm) glass baking dish with a little olive oil. Spoon a ladleful of the sauce into the dish and spread it over the bottom.

Working on a clean work surface or large plate, place a scant teaspoon of the cheese mixture on one end of an eggplant slice. Roll up the eggplant into a small cylinder and place it seam-side down in the baking dish. Repeat until you run out of eggplant slices or filling, arranging the rolls in the baking dish in three snug rows.

Spoon the remaining sauce on top. Cover the baking dish with parchment paper, then with aluminum foil. Bake for about 20 minutes, until the eggplant slices are completely cooked through and the sauce has thickened even further. Remove from the oven, let cool slightly, and serve.

CAULIFLOWER BAKED
with three greek cheeses

serves 6

Cauliflower is an often maligned vegetable in Greek homes. Too many people have memories of overboiled cauliflower drizzled with nothing but olive oil and lemon juice. Here I take a cue from a classic summer dish, melitzanes me tyri (eggplant baked with cheese), and use seasonal, wintry cauliflower instead. My sixteen-year-old carnivore devours it!

⅔ cup (160 ml) extra-virgin Greek olive oil, plus more for greasing

2 cups (250 g) all-purpose flour

Salt and freshly ground black pepper

3 large eggs

1½ cups (150 g) plain dried bread crumbs

1 large cauliflower head, trimmed and cut into roughly equal-size florets

1 large onion, finely chopped

3 garlic cloves, minced

2½ cups (450 g) canned chopped tomatoes

3 or 4 pinches of ground cinnamon

1 teaspoon dried Greek oregano

1 cup (150 g) crumbled Greek feta

1 cup (240 ml) fresh anthotyro or ricotta cheese, drained

1½ cups (150 g) grated graviera, Kefalograviera, or Kefalotyri cheese, or other hard, piquant sheep's-milk cheese

⅓ cup (17 g) chopped fresh parsley

Preheat the oven to 375°F (190°C). Line a baking sheet with parchment paper and drizzle generously with olive oil.

Place the flour in a wide, shallow bowl and season it with salt and pepper. Whisk the eggs with ⅔ cup (160 ml) water in a medium bowl. Spread the bread crumbs over another shallow bowl or plate.

Toss the florets, a handful or two at a time, in the seasoned flour, then dip a few pieces at a time into the eggs. From there, roll them in the bread crumbs. Place the florets on the prepared baking sheet. Continue until all the florets are coated. Place them snugly in a single layer on the baking sheet and drizzle with 2 tablespoons of the olive oil, or more to taste. Bake for about 20 minutes, turning once, to lightly brown the florets on all sides. Remove from the oven and let cool.

While the cauliflower is crisping in the oven, in a medium skillet, heat the remaining olive oil over medium heat. Add the onion and cook until wilted and glistening, about 8 minutes. Add the garlic and cook, stirring, for a minute to soften. Add the tomatoes, season to taste with salt and pepper, and simmer until thickened.

Assemble the casserole: Spread 3 to 4 tablespoons of the tomato sauce over the bottom of a large ovenproof glass or ceramic casserole dish. Drizzle some olive oil on the bottom as well, if desired. Place a layer of the breaded, baked cauliflower over the tomato sauce. Spoon over about a third of the sauce. Sprinkle with a pinch of cinnamon and some of the oregano. Dot the surface with one-third of the cheeses. Repeat two more times, to get three layers of cauliflower, finishing with the remaining tomato sauce, cinnamon, oregano, and cheeses.

Cover with parchment paper, then aluminum foil (or with the casserole's top, if it has one), and bake for 25 to 30 minutes, or until the cheeses melt, the sauce is bubbling, and the cauliflower is tender. Remove from the oven, sprinkle with the parsley, let cool slightly, and serve.

Kounoupidi Olokliro Psito me Meli kai Feta

WHOLE ROASTED CAULIFLOWER
slathered with feta and greek honey

serves 4 to 6

This is divine. And dramatic. And easy. This dish is a thoroughly modern take on an oft misunderstood vegetable, and calls into action two beloved Greek ingredients, feta and honey.

1 large head cauliflower	1 tablespoon Greek balsamic vinegar
4 garlic cloves, cut into slivers	Salt and freshly ground black pepper
½ cup (120 ml) extra-virgin Greek olive oil	½ cup (25 g) chopped fresh parsley leaves
4 tablespoons (60 ml) Dijon mustard	½ cup (75 g) crumbled Greek feta
2 teaspoons Greek honey	Lemon wedges, for serving

Preheat the oven to 450°F (230°C). Line a baking sheet with parchment paper.

Remove the leaves from the cauliflower and cut off enough of the stem so that it is level with the bottom of the head, enabling the cauliflower to stand upright on the baking sheet.

Gently stuff the garlic slivers between the florets all around the cauliflower head.

Whisk together the olive oil, 2 tablespoons of the mustard, the honey, and the vinegar in a small bowl and season to taste with salt and pepper.

Put the cauliflower on the prepared baking sheet and brush the entire surface with the olive oil mixture. Roast the cauliflower until beautifully browned and tender, 50 minutes to 1 hour. You can insert a long skewer into the cauliflower to see if it's done. It should pass through smoothly. Keep the oven on.

Meanwhile, combine the parsley and feta in a small bowl. Brush the remaining 2 tablespoons mustard all over the surface of the roasted cauliflower and rub with the parsley-feta mixture. Roast for 5 minutes more, or until the feta melts. Remove from the oven and serve with lemon wedges.

Anginaropita Tinou

ARTICHOKE BREAD PUDDING

serves 6

Artichokes are an ancient food in Greece, and today a few places around the country are renowned for their cultivation. Tinos, an island in the Cyclades that has seen a mini food renaissance in the last few years, is one of them. This recipe is inspired by a similar dish that was born in local tavernas on the island.

6 tablespoons (¾ stick / 85 g) unsalted butter, plus 1 tablespoon for the baking dish

3 tablespoons all-purpose flour

3 cups (720 ml) warm milk

½ teaspoon freshly grated nutmeg

Salt and freshly ground black pepper

16 large fresh or thawed frozen artichoke hearts

¼ cup (60 ml) extra-virgin Greek olive oil

2 large red onions, very finely chopped

3 garlic cloves, minced

1½ pounds (680 g) country bread, crusts removed, cut into ½-inch-thick (1.5 cm) slices

1½ cups (150 g) grated graviera or other mild, yellow sheep's-milk cheese

1 tablespoon chopped fresh thyme

In a medium saucepan, melt 3 tablespoons of the butter over medium heat until bubbling. Add the flour and whisk for about 5 minutes, until the mixture turns lightly golden. Pour in the milk and whisk continuously over medium heat until the mixture thickens. Season with the nutmeg and salt and pepper to taste. Remove the béchamel from the heat, cover with a cloth to keep warm, and set aside.

Bring a medium pot of salted water to a rolling boil. Add the artichoke hearts and blanch for 3 to 4 minutes, until soft. Remove with a slotted spoon and set aside. When cool enough to handle, coarsely chop the artichokes.

In a heavy medium skillet, heat the remaining 3 tablespoons butter with the olive oil over medium heat. Add the onion and cook until wilted and lightly colored, about 12 minutes. Stir in the garlic and cook all together, stirring, for about 1 minute.

Preheat the oven to 400°F (200°C). Butter a 9 x 13-inch (23 x 32 cm) baking dish.

Place as many slices of bread as will fit in one layer in the buttered baking dish. Spoon half the onions evenly over the bread. Sprinkle with 3 tablespoons of the cheese, a little thyme, and salt and pepper. Spread half the artichokes on top and sprinkle with half the remaining cheese. Gently press the remaining bread slices over the artichokes in one layer. Spread the remaining onions, cheese, thyme, and artichokes, in the same order, over the top, finishing with a layer of artichokes and cheese. Pour the béchamel over everything, spreading it evenly. Bake until the béchamel is set and golden, about 40 minutes. Remove from the oven, let cool slightly, and serve.

HOW TO CLEAN FRESH ARTICHOKES

Most Greek recipes call for just the artichoke heart. Greeks generally don't eat the leaves.

Squeeze the juice of 1 lemon into a bowl filled with 3 cups (720 ml) water; reserve the squeezed lemon rinds. Snap off the tough leaves around the base and up through the middle of the artichoke. Trim off any remaining tough leaves. Place the artichoke on its side and, using a sharp serrated knife, cut through the artichoke right where the leaves indent slightly and the base and inner "heart" begin. Use a teaspoon to scrape out the purple, fuzzy choke. Rub the artichoke with a reserved lemon rind and place it in the acidulated water.

To blanch, of needed: Bring a large pot of salted water to a rolling boil. Fill a large bowl with ice and water. Use a slotted spoon to transfer the artichokes to the boiling water and blanch for 1 minute. Remove and drop immediately into the ice water to stop the cooking.

Mousakas me Kolokytha kai Glykopatates

BUTTERNUT SQUASH– SWEET POTATO MOUSSAKA

serves 8 to 10

This is a recipe I love and first published in a slightly different rendition in my book The Country Cooking of Greece, *which has long been out of print. It's a great addition to a festive meal.*

FOR THE CHEESE BÉCHAMEL

4 tablespoons (½ stick / 55 g) unsalted butter

¼ cup (30 g) all-purpose flour

1 quart (1 L) whole milk, at room temperature

2 large eggs, lightly beaten

1 cup (150 g) grated or crumbled Greek feta

½ cup (50 g) Kefalotyri or pecorino cheese

½ teaspoon freshly grated nutmeg

Salt and freshly ground black pepper

FOR THE VEGETABLES

1 tablespoon butter

1 cup (240 ml) extra-virgin Greek olive oil

4 large red onions, coarsely chopped

3 pounds (1.4 kg) butternut or calabaza squash, peeled, seeded, and cut into ¼-inch-thick (6 mm) slices

Salt

1½ pounds (680 g) sweet potatoes or yams, peeled and cut lengthwise into ¼-inch-thick (6 mm) slices

TO ASSEMBLE

Olive oil

Salt and freshly ground black pepper

1 cup (50 g) chopped fresh mint

½ cup (25 g) chopped fresh parsley

Make the béchamel: In a large pot, melt the butter over medium heat. When it has completely melted and stopped bubbling, but before it turns brown, add the flour and whisk to incorporate. Cook, whisking, until the mixture is lightly colored, about 5 minutes. While whisking, slowly pour in the milk and continue whisking until the sauce thickens, 10 to 12 minutes total. Remove from the heat. While whisking vigorously, pour in the eggs and whisk until incorporated. Stir in the cheeses. Season with the nutmeg and salt and pepper to taste. Set aside, covered with a kitchen towel.

Cook the vegetables: In a large wide pot or deep skillet, heat the butter and 1 tablespoon of the olive oil together over medium heat until the mixture begins to bubble softly. Add the onions, reduce the heat to low, and cook for about 20 minutes, until the onions are lightly golden.

Preheat the oven to 350°F (175°C). Line two baking sheets with parchment paper.

In a large basin or bowl, toss the squash with ½ cup (120 ml) of the olive oil. Spread the pieces in one layer on the baking sheets and sprinkle lightly with a little salt. Bake for 10 to 12 minutes, turning once, until softened but not thoroughly cooked. Remove from the oven and transfer the squash to a large plate; set aside. Keep the oven on.

To assemble the moussaka: Lightly oil a large baking pan. Layer the sweet potatoes in the bottom of the pan. Season with salt and pepper and sprinkle with ⅓ cup (17 g) of the mint. Sprinkle with a little of the parsley. Spread a scant layer of the caramelized onions on top. Pour about one-third of the béchamel over the onions, spreading it out evenly with a spatula. Repeat with a layer of butternut squash, salt and pepper, mint, parsley, onions, and a little béchamel. Repeat once more with more squash, topping that, too, with salt and pepper, mint, parsley, onions, and a final coating of béchamel. Bake for 35 to 40 minutes, until the béchamel is puffed and golden and the vegetables are tender. Remove from the oven and let rest for 15 to 20 minutes before serving.

Anginares Mousaka

ARTICHOKE MOUSSAKA
with caramelized onions and feta

serves 8 to 10

This recipe has become a classic of sorts. I've reinterpreted it over the years for various restaurants where I've worked or worked with, and it's always a bestseller. An early version was originally published in my book The Country Cooking of Greece. *I hope you make it one of your family favorites, too!*

2 tablespoons unsalted butter

½ cup (120 ml) plus 1 tablespoon extra-virgin Greek olive oil

8 onions, coarsely chopped

3 medium potatoes, peeled and sliced lengthwise into ⅛-inch-thick (3 mm) pieces

Salt

2 large lemons, halved (optional, if using fresh artichokes)

14 large globe artichokes, prepped (see page 179), 14 thawed frozen artichoke hearts, or 3 cups drained sliced artichokes in olive oil

FOR THE BÉCHAMEL

6 tablespoons (¾ stick / 85 g) unsalted butter

6 tablespoons (45 g) all-purpose flour

5 cups (1.2 L) milk

1 cup (240 ml) light cream

2 large eggs, lightly beaten

⅓ cup (50 g) crumbled Greek feta

¼ cup (25 g) grated Kefalotyri or Parmesan cheese

½ cup (120 ml) fresh anthotyro or ricotta cheese

Salt and freshly ground black pepper

TO ASSEMBLE

Olive oil, for greasing

¼ cup (13 g) chopped fresh thyme

¼ cup (13 g) chopped fresh basil

½ cup (25 g) chopped fresh parsley

¼ cup (13 g) chopped fresh oregano

½ cup (25 g) chopped fresh mint

1 cup (100 g) plain dried bread crumbs

Salt and freshly ground black pepper

1 cup (150 g) crumbled Greek feta

Preheat the oven to 350°F (175°C). Line two baking sheets with parchment paper.

In a large wide pot or deep skillet, heat the butter and 1 tablespoon of the olive oil over medium heat until the mixture begins to bubble softly. Add the onions, reduce the heat to low, and cook for about 20 minutes, until the onions turn lightly golden.

Meanwhile, in a large basin or bowl, toss the potato slices with the remaining ½ cup (120 ml) olive oil. Season lightly with salt. Arrange the potato slices in neat rows on the prepared baking sheets. Bake for about 15 minutes, until softened but not cooked through, turning once. Remove from the oven and let cool.

If using frozen artichokes, blanch them in a pot of salted boiling water for 3 minutes, then drain and rinse in a colander under cold running water and thinly slice. If using canned or jarred, drain them very well and coarsely chop them if the pieces are large. Set aside.

Make the béchamel: In a medium pot, melt the butter over medium heat. When it has completely melted and the bubbling subsides, add the flour and whisk to incorporate. Cook, stirring, for about 5 minutes, until the mixture is golden. Pour in the milk and cream and cook, whisking, until thick, 10 to 12 minutes. Remove from the heat. While whisking vigorously, pour in the eggs and whisk to incorporate. Mix in the cheeses. Season to taste with salt and pepper. Set aside.

To assemble the moussaka: Preheat the oven to 350°F (175°C). Oil a 9 x 13-inch (23 x 33 cm) glass baking dish or ceramic casserole.

Toss the thyme, basil, parsley, oregano, and mint together in a small bowl. Sprinkle a handful of the bread crumbs over the bottom of the prepared baking dish. Add half the potatoes in one layer. Season with salt and pepper. Sprinkle with a handful of the bread crumbs. Add about one-third of the onions and one-third of the herb mixture. Layer half the artichokes evenly over the surface. Season with salt and pepper and sprinkle with another handful of the bread crumbs. Sprinkle with half the feta, one-third of the herbs, and a third of the onions. Repeat the layering process, in the same order, one more time.

Pour the béchamel over the surface and spread it evenly with a spatula. Bake until lightly golden, 55 minutes to 1 hour. Remove from the oven, let cool slightly, cut into squares, and serve.

GREAT
BEANS

Φασούλι, φασούλι γεμίζεις το σακούλι.

Fasouli, fasouli gemizeis to sakouli.

"Bean by bean, you fill the bag."
(Meaning: Saving a little each day will result in a bounty.)

Beans and legumes, called *ospria* in Greek, are one of the most ancient and important staples in the cuisine. They are also one of my favorite foods.

Porridges of *koukia* (broad beans), lupins, lentils, peas, and chickpeas were the food of the poor, as well as the favorite food of Hercules, according to the ancient Greek comic writer Aristophanes, who mentions that in his renowned work, *The Frogs*. (Indeed, ancient Greek literature is filled with references to this humble foodstuff.) The ancient Greeks consumed beans and pulses in various forms, not all that different from what we still find in the Greek kitchen today: as porridges, mentioned above; fresh (tender green broad beans, pea and chickpea shoots, green beans, and fresh black-eyed peas are still loved in Greek cooking today); dried like nuts, as in the ancient *trogalia*, roasted chickpeas, which continue to be a favorite snack called and are called *stragalia* today; and, of course, cooked into stews and soups.

The importance of beans and pulses in the ancient diet has long been corroborated by physical evidence, as remnants of these seminal foods have been found at many archeological sites, some dating to the early Bronze Age.

The range of beans and pulses cultivated in Greece has grown, with white beans, native to the New World, now the most important, so much so that Greeks consider one of their national dishes to be *fasolada*, or white bean soup (page 247). Small and medium white beans, as well as giant beans, known as *gigantes* (YEE-ghan-dess), are cultivated in the fertile, damp terrain of northern Greece, namely in the areas around Kozani and Kastoria. Santorini, with its unique volcanic soil, is renowned for its yellow split peas, an ancient, seminal food on the island. The islands of Limnos and Amorgos, as well as Feneos in Arcadia, the Peloponnese, also produce split peas highly esteemed by Greek connoisseurs. The best Greek lentils are said to be from Englouvi in the highlands of Lefkada, one of the Ionian islands, and the best broad bean is from Lasithi in Crete.

Beans and pulses have nourished and inspired Greek cooks from the most ancient times to the present. The country wouldn't have have made it through wars, famine, or the Axis occupation during World War II without beans and pulses. The long fasting periods of the Greek Orthodox calendar, which amount to about half the year, would be a nutritional desert without the myriad bean dishes that provide an excellent source of plant protein, and whole protein when combined with grains or other vegetables.

In this chapter, I've offered up a few of my favorite dishes—some traditional, some contemporary—to show the range, imagination, and traditions of Greek bean cuisine.

Minoikes Fakes

CLAY-BAKED MINOAN LENTILS

serves 6

The idea for this dish came after a conversation with Jerolyn Morrison, an American anthropologist living in Crete, who has studied and re-created recipes from the Minoan era. One of the most fascinating aspects of Greek cuisine is the continuity of use of so many ingredients from prehistoric times to the present. Among the oldest ingredients still revered today are honey, olive oil, herbs, and native pulses, first among which is the humble lentil. Honey, together with spices and herbs, was often used to flavor savory dishes in antiquity as well. The recipe that follows is my adaptation, with a fair amount of poetic license!

⅔ cup (160 ml) extra-virgin Greek olive oil, plus more if needed

2 large leeks, trimmed, washed well, and chopped

4 garlic cloves, chopped

1 pound (450 g) dried small green or brown lentils, picked over for debris and rinsed

2 bay leaves

4 dried Greek oregano sprigs

1 tablespoon coriander seeds, crushed in a mortar with a pestle or in a spice grinder

1½ teaspoons cumin seeds, crushed in a mortar with a pestle or in a spice grinder

¼ cup (60 ml) Greek thyme honey, pine honey, or blossom honey

2 tablespoons red wine vinegar

Sea salt

Water or vegetable broth

In a large wide saucepan or flameproof clay casserole, heat 3 tablespoons of the olive oil over medium heat. Add the leeks and cook, stirring, for about 8 minutes to soften. Stir in the garlic. Add the lentils and stir to coat with the oil. Pour in enough water to cover the lentils by 2 inches (5 cm). Add the bay leaves and oregano sprigs, raise the heat slightly, and bring to a boil. Cover, reduce the heat to medium-low, and simmer for about 30 minutes, until the lentils are al dente but not completely cooked. The lentils will have absorbed almost all the water by the time they are ready to come off the stove. Discard the oregano sprigs and bay leaves.

Preheat the oven to 375°F (190°C).

If you were using a metal pan, empty the lentils into a clay or glass baking dish with a lid. Toss the lentils with the remaining olive oil, the coriander, cumin, honey, vinegar, and salt to taste. Add enough water or vegetable broth to cover the lentils by about ½ inch (1.5 cm). Cover and bake for 45 minutes to 1 hour, until the lentils are tender but still retain their shape. Check on the liquid content during baking and add additional water or broth as needed. The end result should not be soupy or too wet, but rather the lentils should have absorbed all the liquid in the pan, expanded nicely, and not disintegrated or dried out. Serve with good crusty bread, preferably whole-grain or sourdough.

A QUICK WORD ON GIANT BEANS

One of my favorite bean stories involves a New York restaurant and a Greek American New Yorker friend with enough moxie to get up and walk out when the server pronounced the *gigantes* appetizer *"jee-GON-tez."* They may as well have served *moo-SA-ka*, my incensed pal Valerie joked.

Truth be told, Greek cooks are partial to their *gigántes* (pronounced *YEE-ghan-dess*) and have a trick or two for cooking them. The beans always need to be soaked overnight or for at least 8 hours and up to 12 hours, enough for them to swell and soften to the touch just a little. Then, before being baked, giant beans need to be boiled. I do this by draining them and placing them in a pot with enough fresh cold tap water to cover. It's hard to advise on the exact simmering time, which can be anywhere from 1 to 2½ hours depending on the age and condition of the beans (buy them from a Greek store, either brick-and-mortar or online) and the alkalinity of the water. Soft water, like my favorite New York tap, is best for cooking beans. If you live in a place with hard water, add a pinch of baking soda to the pot when simmering the beans. Do not salt them.

You will know the giant beans are done to the point of being ready to drain and bake when they are still al dente but soft enough to eat in, say, a salad. Their skins might be cracking or peeling off, which is natural.

When you do bake them, as in the recipes on pages 193 and 196, what you are looking for is a finished dish in which the beans are on that magical verge of disintegrating, still holding their shape, but buttery and soft on the inside. It's not by chance that the closest thing to a Greek giant bean stateside is, indeed, the butter bean. You can substitute those, but cooking times will vary, and butter beans are a little smaller and softer.

Gigantes Ston Fourno me Psimenos Skordo kai Ntomates

GIANT BEANS BAKED
with roasted garlic and tomatoes

serves 6 to 8

There are lots of different ways to prepare giant beans, called gigantes *(and pronounced YEE-ghan-dess) all around Greece. The beans, which are similar to what we in American call butter beans but firmer and a tad larger, are a staple on both restaurant and home menus. The beans always have to be soaked for at least 8 hours (be sure to plan ahead), then boiled before being baked into any number of hearty casseroles. They are sometimes baked with greens, or with sausages or other meats, with tomatoes, spices and herbs, and even mixed with seafood or vibrant dressings in salads that are hearty enough to be a main course.*

1 pound (450 g) dried Greek *gigantes* beans, picked over for debris and rinsed

⅔ cup (160 ml) extra-virgin Greek olive oil, plus more for drizzling, if desired

2 teaspoons sugar, or 2 tablespoons honey or *petimezi* (grape molasses)

4 tablespoons (60 ml) Greek or other balsamic vinegar

20 plum tomatoes, halved lengthwise

1 whole head of garlic

2 large red onions, finely chopped

1 large leek, trimmed, washed well, and chopped

4 garlic cloves, minced

3 fresh rosemary sprigs

½ cup (25 g) chopped fresh oregano leaves

Put the beans in a large bowl, add cool water to cover, and set aside to soak for at least 8 hours or up to overnight. Drain and place in a large pot. Add cold water to cover by 3 inches (7.5 cm). Bring to a boil over high heat, reduce the heat to medium-low, cover with the lid slightly ajar, and simmer for about 1½ hours, or until the beans are tender but firm to the touch.

While the beans are simmering, preheat the oven to 350°F (175°C). Line a baking sheet with parchment paper.

In a large stainless steel bowl, whisk together 3 tablespoons of the olive oil, the sugar, and 2 tablespoons of the vinegar. Add the tomatoes and, using your hands or a large spoon, gently toss to coat in the olive oil mixture. Arrange the tomatoes cut-side down on the prepared baking sheet.

Using a sharp knife, cut off the top of the garlic head to expose the cloves. Wrap the garlic head in aluminum foil and place it on one end of the baking sheet or on another rack in the oven.

(CONTINUED)

Roast the tomatoes and the head of garlic for 1 to 1½ hours, turning the tomatoes as they shrink and being careful not to over-char them. The tomatoes should be wrinkled, lightly charred, and intensely flavored. Remove the tomatoes and the roasted garlic head from the oven and set aside. Keep the oven on.

While the beans are simmering and the tomatoes roasting, in a large skillet, heat 2 tablespoons of the olive oil over medium heat. Add the onions, leek, and minced raw garlic and cook, stirring, for 12 to 15 minutes, until the vegetables begin to brown lightly. Set aside.

When the beans are done, reserve 4 cups (1 L) of their cooking liquid and drain the rest. Place the drained beans, roasted tomatoes, and onion-leek mixture in a glass or ceramic baking dish. Unwrap the roasted garlic and squeeze the creamy roasted cloves out of the papery skins directly into the beans. Add enough of the bean cooking liquid to come just above the surface of the beans. Stir in the remaining olive oil and place the rosemary sprigs on top. Cover with parchment paper, then with aluminum foil, and bake for 45 minutes to 1 hour, until the beans are very tender.

Season with salt and pepper immediately after removing from the oven. Remove and discard the rosemary. Gently stir in the oregano. Serve, drizzled with additional olive oil, if desired.

NORTHERN GREEK GIANT BEANS BAKED
with red peppers and feta

serves 6 to 8

So many giant bean casseroles are basically beans cooked in tomato sauce with varying additions of vegetables, herbs, and spices. I love this dish from the Prespes Lakes region because it speaks to the regional importance of Florina peppers and to the importance of peppers in general up there. In the early fall, to this day, gardeners and farmers thread the range of peppers they grow on strings and hang them to dry like garlands outside their homes. You can use Florina peppers in brine for this dish, which are available in Greek shops, but you can also use any one of a number of fleshy sweet red peppers or bell peppers and roast them yourself before adding them to the beans. As for the feta . . . it makes everything taste better! Note that the beans need to soak for at least 8 hours, so plan ahead.

1 pound (450 g) dried Greek *gigantes* beans, picked over for debris and rinsed

8 roasted red Florina peppers in brine, drained, or 8 red bell or sweet pimiento peppers, roasted, peeled, and seeded

2 large red onions, chopped

6 garlic cloves, chopped

3 large bay leaves

4 fresh rosemary sprigs

3 tablespoons balsamic vinegar, plus more to taste

⅔ cup (160 ml) extra-virgin Greek olive oil, plus more for drizzling, if desired

Salt and freshly ground black pepper

½ cup (25 g) chopped fresh oregano

1½ cups (225 g) crumbled Greek feta

Put the beans in a large bowl, add cold water to cover, and set aside at room temperature to soak for at least 8 hours or up to overnight. Drain and place in a large pot. Add cold water to cover by 3 inches (7.5 cm). Bring to a boil over high heat, reduce the heat to low, and simmer for about 1½ hours, or until the beans are tender but al dente. Remove from the heat. With a slotted spoon, transfer the beans from their cooking liquid to a 9 x 13-inch (23 x 33 cm) glass or ceramic baking dish, reserving the cooking liquid, which will be needed for baking the beans.

Preheat the oven to 350°F (175°C).

Coarsely chop the roasted red peppers and add them to the baking dish, along with the onions, garlic, bay leaves, rosemary, vinegar, and olive oil. Stir to combine. Add enough of the bean cooking liquid to come just flush with the surface of the ingredients. Cover with parchment paper, then with aluminum foil (or with the lid, if the baking dish has one), and bake for about 50 minutes, or until the beans are tender.

Remove the cover, season to taste with salt and pepper, and gently stir in the oregano and feta. (If there is a lot of excess liquid in the pan when you uncover it, you can remove some with a ladle or cook the beans until most of the liquid has evaporated. Add the salt, pepper, oregano and feta after the liquid has either been spooned or cooked off.) Return to the oven and bake, uncovered, until the feta has melted, about 10 minutes.

Let the beans cool slightly before serving. Taste and adjust the seasoning with additional vinegar, if needed, drizzle with olive oil as desired, and serve.

Gigantes me Saltsa Pesto apo Ambelofylla

GIANT BEANS
with grape leaf pesto

serves 4 to 6

Giant beans, the big, buttery white beans that flourish in various parts of northern Greece and are generally baked into savory casseroles. But in the traditional kitchen, one salad, called piaz, *simply dressed with onions, parsley, and olive oil, sometimes calls for giant beans. The beans are great in salad because they are so filling and substantial. This could easily be a main course. As for the grape leaf pesto, it's a playful way to rethink one of the most iconic ingredients in the Greek kitchen. The soft, buttery quality of the beans is nicely countered by the briny, pleasantly acidic flavor of the pesto. Note that the beans need to soak for at least 8 hours, so plan ahead.*

2 cups (390 g) dried Greek *gigantes* beans, picked over for debris and rinsed

FOR THE PESTO

12 grape leaves in brine, drained, blanched, and trimmed (see page 73)

1 cup (50 g) fresh mint leaves

4 garlic cloves, chopped

⅔ cup (90 g) pine nuts or blanched almonds, toasted

⅔ cup (160 ml) extra-virgin Greek olive oil, plus more as needed

Salt and freshly ground black pepper

FOR THE SALAD

2 cups (40 g) baby arugula

½ cup (25 g) chopped fresh parsley

4 scallions, chopped

Grated zest of 1 lemon

⅔ cup (100 g) crumbled Greek feta

Put the beans in a large bowl, add cold water to cover, and set aside at room temperature to soak for at least 8 hours or up to overnight. Drain and place in a large pot. Add cold water to cover by 3 inches (7.5 cm). Bring to a boil over high heat, reduce the heat to maintain a simmer, and cook the beans until tender, 1 to 1½ hours. Drain.

Make the pesto: Coarsely chop the grape leaves and put them in the bowl of a food processor. Add the mint, garlic, and nuts and pulse until the mixture is a dense paste. With the motor running, gradually add the olive oil, until the resulting sauce is thick but liquid. Season to taste with salt and pepper.

Make the salad: Combine the beans, arugula, parsley, scallions, and lemon zest in a serving bowl. Pour in the pesto and toss. Top with the feta and serve hot or at room temperature.

Mavromatika Ston Fourno me Kafteres Piperies

BLACK-EYED PEAS BAKED
with sweet and hot peppers

serves 6 to 8

All over Greece, black-eyed peas are made into an easy salad for all seasons. In a few parts of the country, they are also part of the local range of stews and casseroles: in Rhodes and other islands in the Dodecanese, they're cooked with olive oil and served with a generous heaping of caramelized onions; in the Peloponnese, they are stewed with sweet greens and tomatoes. This recipe is also from the Peloponnese, from the region around Arcadia, home to some of Greece's finest white wines.

1 pound (450 g) dried black-eyed peas, picked over for debris and rinsed

¾ cup (180 ml) extra-virgin Greek olive oil

2 large red onions, finely chopped

1 or 2 fresh green or red chiles, seeded and finely chopped

3 green bell peppers, chopped

4 garlic cloves, minced

¼ cup (60 ml) ouzo

3 roasted red bell peppers, finely chopped

3 cups chopped fresh or canned plum tomatoes

3 to 4 tablespoons sherry vinegar or balsamic vinegar

Salt and freshly ground black pepper

Finely grated zest of 1 lemon

½ cup (25 g) chopped fresh oregano

Place the black-eyed peas in a large pot and add water to cover by 2 inches (5 cm). Bring to a boil and drain in a colander without rinsing. Fill the pot with water and bring to a boil again. Add the hot black-eyed peas and bring the water back to a boil. Reduce the heat to medium-low and simmer the black-eyed peas for about 25 minutes, until al dente.

Preheat the oven to 350°F (175°C).

While the black-eyed peas cook, in a large skillet, heat 3 tablespoons of the olive oil over medium heat. Add the onions, chile(s), and bell peppers and cook until soft and translucent, about 10 minutes. Stir in the garlic. Carefully pour in the ouzo and stir to deglaze the pan. Cook, stirring, until the alcohol burns off, a few minutes more.

Using a slotted spoon, transfer the black-eyed peas to an earthenware or glass baking dish, reserving their cooking liquid. Add the onion–bell pepper mixture, the roasted red peppers, tomatoes, 3 tablespoons of the vinegar, all but 3 tablespoons of the olive oil, and salt and black pepper to taste. Add enough reserved cooking liquid to come just to the surface of the black-eyed peas.

Cover and bake for 35 to 40 minutes, until the black-eyed peas are tender. If there is too much liquid in the dish, remove the cover and bake for 10 to 15 minutes more to evaporate the excess liquid. Adjust the seasoning with salt, pepper, and vinegar, and gently stir in the lemon zest, oregano, and remaining 3 tablespoons olive oil. Serve warm or at room temperature.

CHICKPEAS
baked with squid, *petimezi,* and nigella

serves 4 to 6

Chickpeas are paired with seafood in a few traditional recipes from around Greece, mainly in the islands. This is a contemporary rendition of an old Cretan stew. The nigella seeds, called mavrosousamo in Greek, add a wonderful smoky undertone. Note that the chickpeas need to soak overnight and the squid, if frozen, needs to thaw overnight in the refrigerator, so plan ahead.

1 pound (450 g) dried chickpeas, picked over for debris and rinsed (see Note)

½ cup (120 ml) extra-virgin Greek olive oil, plus more for drizzling

2 large red onions, finely chopped

1 leek, trimmed, washed well, and finely chopped

3 garlic cloves, finely chopped

2 pounds (900 g) fresh or frozen squid, cleaned, bodies cut into ¼-inch-thick (6 mm) rings, tentacles halved lengthwise

1 tablespoon smoked paprika

⅔ cup (160 ml) dry white wine

4 ripe tomatoes, peeled and coarsely chopped, any juices reserved

3 tablespoons *petimezi* (grape molasses)

1 cup (50 g) chopped fresh parsley

Salt and freshly ground black pepper

1 tablespoon nigella seeds

Put the chickpeas in a large bowl, add cold water to cover, and set aside at room temperature to soak overnight. Drain and transfer to a large pot. Add cold water to cover by 3 inches (7.5 cm). Bring to a boil over medium-high heat, reduce the heat to maintain a simmer, and cook, skimming off any foam from the top as they cook, for about 1½ hours, or until the chickpeas are tender.

While the chickpeas cook, in a large wide pot, heat 3 tablespoons of the olive oil over medium heat. Add the onions and leek and cook, stirring, until wilted and lightly browned, 12 to 15 minutes. Stir in the garlic.

Stir in the squid and cook, stirring, until its flesh goes from translucent to opaque white. Add the paprika and stir for a minute.

Pour in the wine and stir to deglaze the pan, letting the alcohol cook off. Add the tomatoes and enough water so the squid is covered by about 2 inches (5 cm). Simmer the squid for about 30 minutes, until the squid is about halfway cooked.

Preheat the oven to 375°F (190°C).

When the chickpeas are done, reserve 4 cups (1 L) of their cooking liquid and drain the rest. Transfer the chickpeas to a glass or ceramic baking pan. Add the squid mixture and gently stir in the *petimezi* and remaining olive oil. Add enough of the reserved chickpea cooking liquid to

come just to the surface of the chickpeas. Season with salt and pepper. Cover with parchment paper, then aluminum foil, and bake for 30 to 45 minutes, until the chickpeas and squid are very tender. Stir in the parsley. Drizzle with additional olive oil, and garnish with a sprinkling of nigella seeds just before serving.

NOTE: You can use 6 cups (996 g) of good-quality canned chickpeas for this dish and bypass the soaking and boiling steps.

Soutzoukakia Smyrneika me Revithia

SERIFOS CHICKPEA "SAUSAGES"
cooked in tomato sauce

serves 6

Chickpeas, one of the most ancient pulses in Greece, are an important staple food in several of the Cyclades and Dodecanese islands. There are many recipes for chickpea soups and stews, for chickpea fritters, and for these mock sausages, a local adaptation of the classic soutzoukakia Smyrneika, *a luscious mixture of ground meat and cumin shaped into small sausages that are part of the cooking traditions of the Anatolian Greeks.*

There is one secret here: You must use soaked dried chickpeas for the best result. Think falafel. You want the chickpea sausages to be crispy and not at all pasty, which means you need to use dried chickpeas that have been soaked; their starch content will still be intact, which will help retain the shape of the mock sausages, as opposed to cooked or canned chickpeas, in which the starch has been boiled out, requiring the addition of flour. Note that the chickpeas need to soak overnight, so plan ahead.

1 pound (450 g) dried chickpeas, picked over for debris and rinsed

2 teaspoons ground cumin, plus a pinch

4 large red onions, finely chopped

4 garlic cloves, minced

1 cup (50 g) finely chopped fresh parsley

Salt and freshly ground black pepper

1½ cups (190 g) all-purpose flour, for dredging, plus more for dusting

⅔ cup (160 ml) extra-virgin Greek olive oil

3 cups (720 ml) crushed or chopped canned tomatoes

1 bay leaf

½ cup (120 ml) white wine

Olive or other oil, for frying

Put the chickpeas in a large bowl, add cold water to cover, and set aside at room temperature to soak overnight or in the refrigerator for up to 24 hours. Drain and rinse the chickpeas.

Transfer one-third of the chickpeas to the bowl of a food processor. Add one-third each of the cumin, onions, and garlic. Pulse until the mixture is mealy. Add one-third of the parsley and pulse to combine. Season to taste with salt and pepper and pulse to combine. Transfer the mixture to a bowl. Repeat in two batches with the remaining chickpeas, cumin, onions, garlic, and parsley, seasoning each batch with salt and pepper before transferring to the bowl.

Lightly dust a baking sheet with flour. Take a heaping tablespoon of the chickpea mixture and shape it into an oblong little sausage. Place it on the baking sheet and repeat with the remaining chickpea mixture. Cover lightly with plastic wrap and refrigerate for at least 30 minutes and up to 2 hours to firm up a little.

While the sausages are in the fridge, in a large wide pot, heat the olive oil and tomatoes together over medium heat. Season with the pinch of cumin and salt and pepper to taste. Add the bay leaf. Add the wine and 1 cup (240 ml) water and bring to a simmer. Cover and simmer for 15 minutes. Remove from the heat and set aside, covered to keep warm.

In a large deep skillet, heat ½ inch (1.25 cm) olive or other oil over medium-high heat. Spread the flour over a plate or platter. Dredge the chickpea sausages lightly in the flour, shaking off the excess. Working in batches, fry the sausages in the hot oil until golden brown and crisp on all sides. Remove with a slotted spoon and drain on paper towels.

Add the chickpea sausages to the pan with the tomato sauce, arranging them in one or two layers. Add enough water to come about two-thirds of the way up the contents of the pan. Cover and bring to a simmer over medium-low heat. Simmer for 30 minutes, or until the sausages are tender and the sauce is thick. Remove the bay leaf.

Remove from the heat and serve hot.

ANCIENT GRAINS,
MODERN COMFORTS

Kai oi dyo petres alethoun t'alevri

"It takes two stones to grind flour."
(Meaning: Cooperation bears results.)

Grains are integral to the Greek Mediterranean diet. While bread is by far the most popular manifestation of grains (carbs) on the Greek table—indeed, even as the fear of gluten takes hold of some of the most traditional Greek home cooks—almost no meal is complete without a few slices of good, and real, bread.

With the exception of the recipe for Cretan mixed-grain rusks (page 209), a very ancient food on Crete and around Greece, all the recipes in this chapter are for easy main courses in which various grains, from bulgur to quinoa, rice, and pasta, are the main ingredient.

Wheat, whether in the form of pasta, bulgur, or *trahana* (see page 214), soothes the Greek soul and has always been a highly symbolic food in Greece. The Eleusinian Mysteries, devoted to Demeter, goddess of the grain and agriculture, were the most important ancient religious rites. Demeter's daughter, Persephone, was abducted by Hades, god of the underworld, and released back to earth for eight months a year, roughly corresponding to the harvest cycle. To this day, wheat in Greece symbolizes rebirth. Wheat-based dishes, such as *kolyva*, boiled whole wheat kernels mixed with dried fruits, pomegranates, nuts, and spices, is made and distributed at funeral and memorial services; an unusual sweet wheat porridge seasoned with cinnamon, nuts, and raisins called *varvara* is made to commemorate Saint Barbara on her name day, December 4. *Keskeki*, another wheat-based porridge mixed with goat's meat, is a festive food at the *panygyria*, or village feasts, throughout the islands of the eastern Aegean. All over the country, to this day, there are local ritualistic preparations that involve wheat in some way.

I like to joke that I've never met a pasta dish I didn't like, and all the better if it derives from the traditions I hold dearest. Greece is, to the surprise of many a pasta aficionado, a country that boasts a long-standing, deep-rooted love affair with pasta, both fresh and dried. By some accounts, the ancient Greeks invented the world's most popular food, forebear of which was a grilled flat noodle-like preparation called *laganum*, the etymological forerunner of lasagna. There are dozens of regional pasta shapes, from small squares called *hilopites* made all over Greece to tongue-twisters like *schioufichta*, a twirled pasta shape specific to Crete.

Rice is another important grain, but it's a newcomer. Rice was known to the ancients and mentioned by Theophrastus, a contemporary of Aristotle who chronicled Greece's natural environment, but it took millennia for rice to move from the steppes and paddies of Asia to the tables of Greece. Even as recently as a hundred years ago, it was an expensive imported food, reserved either for holidays, weddings, and other major celebrations of life, or for the ill, served up in soups and rice pudding to soothe minor ailments.

It really wasn't until the middle of the last century that rice became a household item, and that thanks to the efforts of American agrarians working under the auspices of the U.S. Marshall Plan, who taught northern Greek farmers how to cultivate it. Today, Greece is the third most important rice-growing region in Europe, after Spain and Italy. Almost all of it is cultivated in the deltas of the Axios River, in the northern Greek region of Macedonia, around the town of Chalastra, just south of Thessaloniki. Because of its proximity to the Aegean, Greek rice is naturally flavorful, nurtured on the sea breeze. On the Greek table, rice appears in soups, pilafs, and traditional, comforting dishes that are akin to risotto, such as *tomatorizo* (page 226).

The Greek table has also seen an embrace of newer "ancient" grains, such as quinoa, one of my personal favorites and now widely available all over Greece; it's even sold in bulk in Athens's Central Market.

In thinking about ancient grains for modern cooks, I've tried to offer up accessible recipes for the most popular grain products, such as pasta, as well as for rice and the newcomer quinoa. Some recipes are a spin on tradition, such as the quinoa *spanakorizo* (page 219). All are totally Greek, whether by tradition or evolution.

Paximadia

TRADITIONAL CRETAN MIXED-GRAIN RUSKS

makes about 10 pounds (4.5 kg) rusks

Paximadia—*rusks*—*have a long and storied history in Greece.* Paximadia *more or less as we know them today derive from the ancient Greek* dipyros, *which means "twice-baked," and were essentially a savory biscuit. The rusks are called* paximadia *after a first-century-AD monk named Paximus, who improved on the ancient recipe, leaving a legacy that is a living tradition to this day. Rusks are made all over Greece and come in all manner of shapes and sizes; the dough can be made from wheat, rye, barley, corn, carob, or chickpea flour, or from various combinations thereof. This recipe is from a home baker in the town of Enagron, a mountain village between Rethymnon and Irakleion. Crete, perhaps more than anywhere else in Greece, is renowned for the variety of* paximadia, *both sweet and savory, traditionally made on the island.*

2 pounds (900 g) whole wheat flour

2 pounds (900 g) all-purpose flour

2 pounds (900 g) cornmeal

2 pounds (900 g) rye flour

2 pounds (900 g) barley flour

1 pound (450 g) sourdough starter (called *prozymi* in Greek and made by keeping 1 pound / 450 g of dough from previous breadmaking; see Note, page 210)

1½ quarts (1.5 L) lukewarm water

2 tablespoons sugar

2 cups (480 ml) extra-virgin Greek olive oil

3 tablespoons salt

18 lemon leaves, if you can get them

Fire up a wood-burning oven or preheat your oven to 450°F (230°C).

Sift all the flours together into a very large bowl. Form a well in the center.

Dilute the starter in the well with about a third of the lukewarm water. Add the sugar on top of starter (sugar will help the starter work better). Add 1 cup (240 ml) of the olive oil and and sprinkle the salt around the rim of the flour. Add a cup or two (240 to 480 ml) more of the water and start gradually kneading to form a dense dough mass that doesn't stick. (Local bread bakers, toward the end of the kneading process, dampen their hands with water, thus adding a little more moisture to the dough without adding so much that the dough will be sticky.)

Cover the dough with a folded white cotton bedsheet and cover that with a woolen blanket to contain the heat, which ultimately helps the dough rise. The ceramic bowl also retains heat. Let it rise for about an hour.

(CONTINUED)

Shape the dough into loaves about 3 inches (7.5 cm) wide and as long as your baking sheets can hold. Score the slices almost but not all the way to the bottom. This will help you separate the slices when the dough is baked.

Lay the loaves next to one another, a few inches apart, on the baking sheets. Brush them with olive oil and place the lemon leaves, if you can get them, in a few places under the loaves, which imparts a lovely aroma and is a traditional rusk-making technique on Crete.

Put the baking sheet into the oven and bake for 15 to 20 minutes.

Remove, cool slightly, and break off the scored slices. Remove the leaves and lay the rusks on a dry baking sheet.

Let the wood-fired oven die down, or reduce the temperature on a conventional oven to 130°F (54°C). Return the rusks to the oven to dehydrate overnight in the low heat.

Remove from the oven, let cool, and store in muslin bags at room temperature in a cool, dry place for up to 6 months.

NOTE: To make sourdough starter, or *prozymi*, as it is called in Greek, you either need to be a home bread baker or have access to dough from a home or commercial (preferably artisan) bread baker. Break off a fist-size piece of bread dough and place it in a tight-lidded container in the refrigerator. It will ferment and sour. Break it into small pieces and dilute with warm water before using to make bread or rusks. You can keep this indefinitely by breaking it into small chunks, "feeding" it by stirring in a few tablespoons of flour and water each week, and using it when needed. Keep refrigerated.

Pligouropilafo me Ouzo, Myrodika kai Tomata

BULGUR PILAF
with ouzo, herbs, and tomato

serves 4 to 6

Bulgur and cracked wheat are two of the most ancient grain products still used in the Greek kitchen. Made into salads and pilafs, used as the base for stuffings, added to soups and stews to make them more filling, tiny pebble-like bulgur or cracked wheat predates rice, which comes from the East, by many thousands of years. Bulgur is so nutty and easy to use, it's a mainstay in my personal larder, and this recipe makes for a great midweek pilaf or the base for something more festive, such as some grilled or baked fish.

1½ cups (210 g) coarse bulgur wheat

Salt

⅓ cup (80 ml) extra-virgin Greek olive oil

1 leek, trimmed, washed well, and chopped

1 large fennel bulb, chopped

2 garlic cloves, chopped

1 cup (145 g) cherry or teardrop tomatoes, halved

6 pitted green olives, chopped

3 tablespoons ouzo

½ cup (60 g) chopped walnuts

Grated zest of 1 lemon

⅔ cup (35 g) chopped fresh parsley

½ cup (25 g) chopped fresh dill

Freshly ground black pepper

Place the bulgur wheat in a bowl with 3 cups (720 ml) water and a pinch of salt. Cover and let stand for 2 hours, until the bulgur absorbs most of the water and is tender. Drain the bulgur in a fine-mesh sieve to remove any remaining water and set the bulgur aside.

In a deep skillet or wide pot, heat 2 tablespoons of the olive oil over medium heat. Add the leek and fennel and cook until softened but still al dente, about 5 minutes. Stir in the garlic. Raise the heat to high and add the tomatoes. Cook until they start to crinkle. Stir in the olives. Carefully pour in the ouzo. When the alcohol has evaporated, turn off the heat, add the walnuts and drained bulgur, and toss to combine. Stir in the lemon zest, parsley, and dill.

Taste and adjust the seasoning with salt and pepper. Stir in the remaining olive oil and fluff the bulgur. Serve warm or at room temperature.

TRAHANA
THE DAIRY-BASED GRAIN PRODUCTS OF GREECE

What's nutty, mild or sour, crunchy or creamy, slow but also fast food, ancient and also thoroughly contemporary? One Greek product fits all these descriptions: timeless *trahana*, a milk-based granular grain product, and its regional relatives, such as *xinohondros* from Crete and *hahles* from Lesvos.

Trahana is one of the oldest foods in the world. In Greece, it is still made at home but also in small workshops around the country, typically at the end of the summer, when it can be left to dry under the hot August sun. There are many regional variations. The basic recipe calls for cooking cracked wheat with milk or buttermilk until the mixture becomes a dense mass, almost like overcooked oatmeal. Once cooled down, this mass is broken up into chunks, which are laid out to dry on and under nets so that air circulates around the pieces and they dehydrate evenly.

Then they are either broken into small but still rather substantial pieces (as the Cretan variety, *xinohondros*) or pushed through a fine-mesh sieve to get granules that are larger than Moroccan couscous but smaller than pastina. On Lesvos, a large island in the northeastern Aegean, the local *trahana* is called *hahles* or *koupes*, and is shaped into small cups. One of the most delicious, if simple, Greek country *mezedes* are these *koupes* lightly roasted in a fireplace and washed down with a stinging, delicious glass of ouzo, the national drink of Greece, some of the best of which is produced on Lesvos as well.

Trahana and its cousins are cooked into soups and stews (page 251), adding a complex, deliciously sour, milky note that is surprisingly satisfying. It's one of my all-time favorite Greek foods.

Melitzana me xinohontro

EGGPLANT BRAISED
with cretan xinohontro

serves 4

Xinohondros *is the name of a local version of* trahana, *a deliciously sour milk-based grain product that is one of the oldest foods in Greece. I've known this dish in various renditions since first coming across it on Crete about thirty years ago. I was delighted to see it still appearing on restaurant menus even now, in this age of quick fixes and Westernized foods. I cooked it together with Eleftheria Vogiatsaki, the home cook who runs the kitchen at a busy meze restaurant called Raki Ba Raki in Rethymnon, Crete. This is her recipe, and it's surprisingly simple. One caveat: You've got to be a starch lover to appreciate it! You can find xinohondros online.*

½ cup (120 ml) extra-virgin Greek olive oil, plus more for drizzling

1 large onion, coarsely chopped

3 Italian or Sicilian eggplants, trimmed and cut into 1½-inch (4 cm) chunks or cubes

2 potatoes, peeled and cut into 1¼-inch (3 cm) cubes

⅔ cup (160 ml) dry white wine

3 garlic cloves, coarsely chopped

3 medium tomatoes, grated (see Note, page 92)

Salt

3 tablespoons chopped fresh thyme

2 tablespoons chopped fresh parsley

2 tablespoons chopped fresh mint

1 cup Cretan *xinohondros* or sour *trahana* (see page 214)

In a wide pot, heat the olive oil over medium heat. Add the onion and cook, stirring, until soft, about 10 minutes. Add the eggplant pieces and stir gently for 2 minutes, until slightly softened. Add the potatoes and stir.

Pour in the wine. As soon as it steams up, add the garlic and tomatoes. Season with salt, then add the thyme, parsley, and mint. Simmer for 10 to 15 minutes, until the vegetables are about halfway cooked.

Add the *xinohondros* and cook for 10 minutes or so more, until the *xinohondros* is tender. If the *xinohondros* needs to cook a bit longer, add an additional 1 cup (240 ml) water. Remove from the heat, drizzle with olive oil, and serve.

Pilafi me Kinoa, Ktapodi kai Revithia

QUINOA PILAF
with octopus and chickpeas

serves 4

Quinoa is a new grain in Greece, but one that people have embraced with open arms. It is now widely available throughout the country. There is at least one Greek company producing and packaging it.

1 small (1½- to 2-pound / 680 to 900 g) octopus or pulpo (see Note)

½ cup (120 ml) extra-virgin Greek olive oil

3 tablespoons balsamic vinegar

3 or 4 fresh oregano sprigs

2 bay leaves

10 whole black peppercorns

1 cup (170 g) dried quinoa, rinsed

Salt and freshly ground black pepper

1 red onion, diced

1 small fennel bulb, diced

1 garlic clove, minced

15 cherry or teardrop tomatoes, halved

1½ cups (240 g) cooked chickpeas (good-quality canned are fine)

½ cup (25 g) any chopped fresh herbs of your choice (basil, mint, oregano, parsley, cilantro, dill)

Grated zest of 1 lemon

To clean the octopus or pulpo, cut off and discard the sack just below the eyes. Cut out the beaklike mouth and discard. Cut the tentacles into individual pieces and place them in a medium saucepan with 2 tablespoons of the olive oil, 1 tablespoon of the vinegar, the oregano sprigs, bay leaves, and peppercorns. Cover and cook over very low heat until the tentacles are tender, 35 to 40 minutes. Set aside in the pot.

Place the quinoa in a medium saucepan and add water to cover by 3 inches (7.5 cm). Bring to a gentle boil, salt the water lightly, and cook, covered, for about 15 minutes, until tender and popped. Drain any excess liquid.

While the quinoa is cooking, in a medium skillet, heat 2 tablespoons of the olive oil over medium heat. Add the onion, fennel, and garlic and cook, stirring, until soft.

Drain the octopus and cut it into chunks. (If desired, you can add a little extra texture and flavor by searing it lightly on a nonstick grill pan before cutting it.)

Combine the quinoa, octopus, onion-fennel mixture, tomatoes, chickpeas, and herbs in a bowl. Season with the lemon zest and salt and pepper to taste. Toss with the remaining olive oil and vinegar and serve.

NOTE: You can swap out the octopus for about 2 cups (500 ml) of any seafood of your choice, such as calamari, shelled mussels, or shrimp, or any combination thereof.

"Politiki" Kinoa me Revithia, Portokali kai Stafides

AROMATIC QUINOA
with chickpeas, orange, and greek raisins

serves 4

There are a few highly aromatic rice-based pilafs that come from the heady, urbane cooking of the Greeks whose ancestry is in Asia Minor (present-day Turkey). I have taken a cue from those flavors to create a pilaf using the same spice palette. It's delicious with a little Greek yogurt on the side, too.

½ cup (120 ml) extra-virgin Greek olive oil

2 medium carrots, diced

1 small fennel bulb, diced

1 red onion, diced

Scant 1 teaspoon ground cumin

½ teaspoon ground cinnamon

1 star anise pod

1 garlic clove, chopped

Peel of 1 orange, peeled with a vegetable peeler into 1-inch-wide (2.5 cm) strips and julienned

2 tablespoons sugar

1 cup (170 g) dried quinoa, rinsed and cooked according to the package directions

2 cups (320 g) cooked or good-quality canned chickpeas

½ cup (75 g) golden raisins

½ cup (25 g) chopped fresh parsley

Salt and freshly ground black pepper

In a medium skillet, heat 2 tablespoons of the olive oil over medium heat. Add the carrots, fennel, and onion, cover, and cook until soft and glistening, about 8 minutes. Stir in the cumin, cinnamon, and star anise and cook all together for a minute. Add the garlic and cook, stirring, for a minute. Remove from the heat. Remove and discard the star anise.

Bring 1 cup (240 ml) water to a boil in a small pot. Add the orange peel and blanch for 1 minute. Drain in a fine-mesh sieve and repeat two more times to remove the bitterness from the peel. After the third round of blanching, leave the peel in the sieve and place the sugar and ½ cup (120 ml) water in the pot. Bring to a simmer and add the orange peel. Cook for 2 to 3 minutes, then drain.

In a bowl, combine the quinoa, onion-fennel mixture, orange peel, chickpeas, raisins, parsley, and remaining olive oil. Season to taste with salt and pepper. Serve warm or at room temperature.

Spanakorizo me Kinoa

QUINOA SPINACH PILAF

serves 4

The traditional Greek recipe for spanakorizo, *a spinach-rice pilaf, is transformed here with quinoa.*

Salt

1 cup (170 g) dried quinoa, rinsed

½ cup (120 ml) extra-virgin Greek olive oil

1 large red onion, chopped

½ leek, trimmed, washed well, and cut into thin rounds

10 cups (200 g) coarsely chopped fresh spinach

Freshly ground black pepper

2 garlic cloves

½ to ⅔ cup (75 to 100 g) crumbled Greek feta

In a small saucepan, bring 2 cups (480 ml) water to a boil, season with salt, and add the quinoa. Reduce the heat to low and simmer, uncovered, stirring frequently, until the quinoa has absorbed all the water, 15 to 20 minutes.

While the quinoa is cooking, in a large deep skillet or shallow pot, heat 2 tablespoons of the olive oil over medium heat. Add the onion and leek and cook, stirring, until wilted, about 8 minutes. Add the spinach and cook until wilted. Season to taste with salt and pepper. Cook off any excess liquid.

In a small skillet, heat 3 tablespoons of the olive oil over low heat. Add the garlic and cook, stirring, until crisp and very lightly colored. Remove from the heat as soon as the garlic starts to acquire a little color.

When the quinoa is ready, add it to the skillet with the spinach and stir to combine. Garnish with the crisped garlic and the feta (use more or less to your liking). Drizzle with the remaining olive oil and serve.

Pilafi me Kroko, Arakas, Fistikia kai Amygdala

OUZO SAFFRON RICE PILAF
with peas, pistachios, and almonds

serves 4

My favorite rice is, of course, Greek! It's more flavorful than other rices from around the world because it grows near the river deltas in northern Greece, where it's seasoned by the salty spray of the sea nearby. We cook rice for dinner in Greece, as a main course, not only as a side dish. This recipe calls for Greek saffron (known as krokos Kozanis) *and olive oil, too.*

6 tablespoons (90 ml) extra-virgin Greek olive oil

2 shallots, finely chopped

1 red onion, finely chopped

2 garlic cloves, finely chopped

1 star anise pod

2 cups (370 g) Greek Carolina rice or other long-grain rice

½ cup (120 ml) ouzo

3½ cups (840 ml) vegetable broth or water, or a combination

Salt and freshly ground black pepper

½ teaspoon Greek red saffron (*krokos Kozanis*)

1 cup (145 g) shelled fresh or thawed frozen peas

½ cup (65 g) unsalted pistachios

½ cup (70 g) blanched almonds

1 tablespoon Greek honey

In a large heavy deep skillet, heat 4 tablespoons (60 ml) of the olive oil over medium heat. Add the shallots, onion, and garlic and cook for 5 minutes. Add the star anise and cook until the vegetables are softened and lightly browned, 5 to 7 minutes more.

Add the rice and stir to coat with the olive oil. Carefully pour in the ouzo and cook to evaporate the alcohol. Add the broth and reduce the heat to low. Season with salt and pepper. Combine the saffron and 2 tablespoons hot water in a small bowl. Let it sit for a minute, then stir the saffron water into the rice. Cover and simmer for 6 minutes. Gently stir the peas into the rice, cover again, and cook for 6 to 9 minutes more, until the rice is tender. Rice cools in 20 minutes tops, so we're good to go.

While the rice is cooking, in a medium skillet, heat the remaining 2 tablespoons olive oil. Add the nuts and toast until lightly browned. Stir in the honey and a pinch of salt. Cook until the honey starts to thicken. Remove from the heat and set aside.

Serve the pilaf hot or warm in individual cups or mounds, with the nuts on top.

Hortorizo

GREENS AND RICE PILAF

serves 4

One of the classic Greek rice dishes is spanakorizo, *a wonderful, comforting combination of onions, spinach, and a variety of Greek rice called Carolina, which is similar to Italian risotto rice. It's one of my family's favorite healthy meals. Here is a rendition that calls for greens beyond spinach, adding a slightly more complex flavor to this standard-bearer of Greek plant-based cooking.*

3 tablespoons extra-virgin Greek olive oil, plus more for drizzling

1 large onion, finely chopped

2 garlic cloves, finely chopped

1⅓ cups (245 g) Greek long-grain rice, preferably Carolina

1½ pounds (680 g) mixed non-bitter greens, such as spinach, Swiss chard, chervil, and sweet sorrel, trimmed, chopped, washed, and drained thoroughly

1 cup (240 ml) dry white wine (optional)

1 cup (240 ml) vegetable broth (optional)

Leaves from 1 bunch dill, chopped

Juice of ½ lemon, or more to taste, strained

Salt and freshly ground black pepper

In a wide deep pot, heat the olive oil over medium heat. Add the onion and cook until soft and very lightly browned, about 8 minutes. Add the garlic and cook, stirring, for about a minute to soften. Add the rice and stir to coat with the oil.

Add the greens to the pot, in increments if necessary to fit, and stir to combine with the rice-onion mixture as they wilt. When all the greens have been added and wilted, pour in 3 cups (720 ml) water (or 1 cup / 240 ml water, the wine, and the vegetable broth). Cover the pot, reduce the heat to low, and simmer for about 40 minutes, until everything is soft. Stir in the dill. Season with the lemon juice and salt and pepper to taste.

Serve alone, drizzled with the remaining olive oil and a little more lemon juice, or with one of the following accompaniments:

• Shaved Greek feta, crushed pink peppercorns, and lemon wedges
• A dusting of hot paprika and Greek yogurt
• Sunny-side-up eggs

Risotto me Gefsi Avgolemonou

AVGOLEMONO RISOTTO

serves 4

There is something deeply soothing about a bowl of Greek avgolemono soup, the lemony rice-based soup usually made with chicken or fish broth. The basic idea here is to replicate both the comfort level and the flavor palette of avgolemono soup in a creamy risotto.

5 to 7 cups (1.2 to 1.7 L) hot vegetable broth or chicken broth

2 large egg yolks

⅓ cup (80 ml) strained fresh lemon juice, or more to taste

2 tablespoons unsalted butter

1 tablespoon extra-virgin Greek olive oil

4 scallions, cut into thin rings

1 garlic clove, minced

1¼ cups (230 g) Greek Carolina rice or Italian risotto rice, such as Arborio or Carnaroli

¾ cup (100 g) frozen peas

Salt and freshly ground black pepper

In a medium pot, bring the broth to a simmer.

In a medium stainless steel bowl, vigorously whisk the egg yolks until frothy. While whisking, slowly add the lemon juice and whisk until creamy. Whisking all the while, add 2 cups (480 ml) of the hot broth to the egg-lemon mixture in a slow, steady stream and whisk until completely incorporated. Set aside, uncovered, until ready to use.

In a wide pot or deep skillet, heat the butter and olive oil together over medium heat. Add the scallions and cook, stirring, until soft and translucent, 4 to 6 minutes. Stir in the garlic. Add the rice and stir to coat with the butter and oil. Reduce the heat to medium-low.

Add a ladleful of the hot broth and stir until the rice has absorbed the broth. Stir in the peas. Continue to add the broth, a ladle at a time, waiting until the liquid has been absorbed after each addition before adding the next, until the rice is cooked to al dente, 12 to 15 minutes. Season to taste with salt and pepper.

Over very gentle heat, reheat the egg-lemon mixture, whisking all the while to keep it from curdling. While stirring, slowly add the egg-lemon mixture to the risotto. The rice will be dense and creamy as the egg-lemon mixture thickens slightly. Remove from the heat, taste, and adjust the seasoning with salt and pepper. Serve immediately.

Mydopilafo me Melani

"DIRTY" MUSSEL RICE

serves 6 to 8

Mussel pilaf is one of the great rice dishes of Greece. Originally a transplant, tucked into the handwritten recipe books and memories of the million or so Greeks who emigrated to the motherland as refugees from Asia Minor (modern-day Turkey) in 1922, a time of political upheaval in the region, and changed the face and flavor of the Greek table. Their cuisine was, and still is, aromatic, sophisticated, and more complex than the traditional agrarian fare found throughout the country on islands and mainland alike. This dish has a few modern twists, the culmination in some ways of all my own time spent in restaurant kitchens.

50 in-shell or shelled mussels

½ cup (240 ml) white wine, plus more as needed for steaming the mussels

12 cups (2.9 L) shrimp broth, fish broth, or seafood broth

½ cup (120 ml) extra-virgin Greek olive oil

1 large leek, trimmed, washed well, and chopped

2 scallions, chopped

1 large red onion, chopped

1 fennel bulb, chopped

3 garlic cloves, chopped

2 cups (370 g) Greek Carolina or Italian risotto rice, such as Arborio or Carnaroli

1 sachet of squid ink (see Note)

½ cup (120 ml) ouzo

Sea salt and freshly ground black pepper

⅔ cup (35 g) chopped fresh dill

Grated zest of 1 lemon

Crushed pink peppercorns, for garnish

If using whole, in-shell mussels, rinse them under cold water and remove their beards and any debris on their shells. Fill a large, wide pot with wine to a depth of 2 inches (5 cm). Place the mussels in a steamer basket and place the basket in the pot. Cover, bring the wine to a simmer over medium-high heat, and steam until the mussels have opened, about 5 minutes. Discard any that haven't opened. Remove some (or all) of the mussels from their shells to make them easier to eat inside the rice. (I like to keep a few in their shells because it looks dramatic in the rice.)

In a medium saucepan, bring the broth to a simmer.

In a separate large deep skillet or wide pot, heat ¼ cup (60 ml) of the olive oil over medium heat. Add the leek, scallions, onion, and fennel. Cook, stirring, until soft and translucent, about 8 minutes. Stir in the garlic.

Add the rice to the pan and stir to coat with the oil. While stirring, add two ladles of the hot broth to the pot and cook, stirring, until the rice has absorbed most of the liquid. Add the squid ink and stir to distribute it evenly. Add two more ladles of hot broth and stir until they have been absorbed. Carefully pour in the ouzo and ½ cup (120 ml) wine and cook until the alcohol has evaporated. Continue adding the hot broth, letting the rice absorb each addition before adding the next, until the rice is almost cooked through. Season to taste with salt and black pepper.

Add the mussels to the rice and stir gently. Stir in the dill, lemon zest, and pink peppercorns. Serve.

NOTE: Squid ink is available online and at brick-and-mortar specialty stores.

Tomatorizo me Pinelia Moderna

TOMATO RICE
with a modern twist

serves 4

The range of Greek vegetable-rice dishes covers all manner of seasonal ingredients, from greens and spinach in the spring to fresh tomatoes in the summer to leeks, winter squash, and cabbage in the winter. These recipes are in a category all their own, more similar in texture to Italian risotti than to the pilafs (pilafi in Greek) of the East. This is one of my favorite go-to recipes when I want to create something that harks back to tradition but is modern, easy, and elegant.

4 to 5 cups (1 to 1.2 L) vegetable broth

2 tablespoons butter

2 tablespoons extra-virgin Greek olive oil

1 medium red onion, finely chopped

2 garlic cloves, finely chopped

1 cup (185 g) Greek Carolina rice or Italian risotto rice, such as Arborio or Carnaroli

⅓ cup (80 ml) ouzo

1⅓ cups (320 ml) grated ripe tomatoes (see Note, page 92)

1 star anise pod

⅔ cup (100 g) crumbled Greek feta

2 tablespoons finely chopped fresh oregano leaves

Grated zest of 1 lemon

Salt and freshly ground black pepper

In a small saucepan, bring the broth to a simmer.

In a large deep skillet, heat 1 tablespoon butter and the olive oil together over medium heat. When the butter has completely melted and starts to foam, add the onion and cook, stirring, until soft, about 5 minutes. Stir in the garlic, giving it a swirl in the pan to soften.

Add the rice to the skillet and stir until it is well coated with the butter and oil and glistening. Add 1 cup (240 ml) of the hot broth and cook, stirring gently, until the rice has absorbed the broth. Carefully pour in the ouzo and stir until it has been absorbed and the alcohol has cooked off, a minute or two. Add the tomato and star anise and cook, stirring gently, until the mixture is thick, 3 to 4 minutes.

Add most of the remaining broth in 1-cup (240 ml) increments, stirring after each addition until the rice has absorbed the broth before adding the next, and cook until the rice is creamy but al dente. Add the feta and stir until it has melted. Add the oregano and lemon zest and stir to combine. Season to taste with salt and pepper. Remove the star anise. Remove from the heat, stir in the remaining 1 tablespoon butter, and serve immediately.

Grigora Raviolia me Anthotyro kai Saltsa apo Syka kai Kremmydia

QUICK ANTHOTYRO RAVIOLI
with fig-onion sauce

makes about 96 small ravioli, to serve 8 to 10

Ravioli has a unique place on the Greek table, as both a savory and a sweet dish. The dish, obviously, has Italian roots, despite the fact that we find traditional Greek recipes for ravioli (or rafioli) on various islands, mainly those whose history includes a long period of rule by either the Venetians or the Genoese. Among these are the various Cyclades islands and the Eptanisa, or seven islands of the Ionian, among them.

This recipe is inspired by that tradition, but is a long way from anything one might encounter in a traditional Greek island kitchen. For one thing, I cheat! After getting past the notion that everything has to be made totally by hand, and finding myself never really having time to make my own pasta, I now use a wheat-based wonton wrapper for this and a few other recipes. Grand-mothers of Greece . . . forgive me!

1 cup (240 ml) fresh anthotyro or ricotta cheese, drained

½ cup (75 g) crumbled Greek feta

Salt and freshly ground black pepper

48 wheat-based wonton wrappers

1 large egg, lightly beaten

FOR THE SAUCE

⅓ cup (80 ml) extra-virgin Greek olive oil, plus more for drizzling

4 large red onions, halved and thinly sliced

Pinch of salt

10 dried Greek figs, stemmed, soaked in 1 cup (240 ml) warm water

2 tablespoons Greek balsamic vinegar

2 tablespoons *petimezi* (grape molasses)

½ cup (120 ml) dry red wine

3 cups (60 g) chopped wild or baby arugula

Salt and freshly ground black pepper

Crushed pink peppercorns, for garnish

1 cup (100 g) grated Kefalotyri or dried myzithra cheese

Combine the anthotyro and feta together in a bowl and mash with a fork until smooth. Taste and season with a little salt, if needed, and black pepper to taste.

Line a baking sheet with parchment paper. Place 8 wonton wrappers in front of you on a clean work surface (keep the others covered with a damp paper towel so they don't dry out). Cut each in half to get 16 pieces total. Brush the edges of each piece lightly with the beaten egg. Place 1 teaspoon of the cheese filling in the center of each wonton piece. Fold over and press the edges together, using your fingers or the tines of a fork to seal the edges well. Place on the prepared baking sheet. Repeat to fill the remaining wonton wrappers, layering another sheet of

parchment on top of the ravioli if they don't all fit in one layer. At this point, the entire baking sheet can be wrapped tightly with plastic wrap and refrigerated for up to 2 days.

When ready to cook the ravioli, make the sauce: In a large, heavy skillet or wide, shallow pot, heat the olive oil over low to medium heat. Add the onions and sprinkle lightly with salt. Cook over low heat, stirring occasionally, until the onions are soft and lightly caramelized, about 20 minutes.

While the onions are cooking, drain the figs, reserving their soaking liquid. Chop or slice the figs.

Add the vinegar, *petimezi*, and wine to the pan with the onions. As soon as the wine begins to evaporate, add the figs and their soaking liquid. You can add a little warm water, if needed, to keep the sauce moist. Simmer the onion-fig mixture until thick, adding the arugula right at the end and tossing to wilt slightly. Remove from the heat. Season to taste with salt and black pepper. Set the sauce aside, covered.

Cook the ravioli: Bring a large pot of water to a boil and add a generous amount of salt. Reduce the heat to maintain a simmer and stir the water in one direction with a long spoon to form a whirlpool in the center. Quickly add the ravioli, 24 at a time, stirring gently to separate them as they touch the water. Simmer gently for about 2 minutes, or until they rise to the surface and are slightly translucent. Remove the ravioli with a slotted spoon and place on a serving platter. Spoon some of the sauce over the first layer. Drizzle with a little olive oil; crush some pink peppercorns between your fingers and sprinkle them over the top. Sprinkle with some of the grated cheese. Cook the remaining ravioli in batches of 24, removing them with a slotted spoon and placing them on the platter on top of the previous layer. Spoon the remaining sauce on top and drizzle with olive oil. Garnish with more crushed pink peppercorns and the remaining grated cheese. Serve immediately.

Grigora Raviolia me Yemisi apo Pastitsio

QUICK PASTITSIO RAVIOLI

makes 24 ravioli, to serve 4 to 6

When a home cook like me works side by side with the chefs de cuisine at various Greek restaurants, all sorts of ideas germinate. Pastitsio, conspicuously absent in its most traditional (and cliché) form from these pages, gets a breath of fresh air in this fun and easy recipe. I took the basic components of a classic pastitsio *and turned them into these elegant ravioli. They're perfect for a dinner party entrée.*

FOR THE FILLING

1 large bay leaf

1 small cinnamon stick

3 allspice berries

3 whole cloves

3 tablespoons extra-virgin olive oil

1 small red onion, chopped

1 garlic clove, chopped

¾ pound (340 g) ground beef

2 tablespoons tomato paste

1 cup (240 ml) white wine

Salt and freshly ground black pepper

48 wheat-based wonton wrappers

1 large egg, lightly beaten

FOR THE BÉCHAMEL

2 tablespoons olive oil

Scant 2 tablespoons all-purpose flour

1½ cups (360 ml) milk

½ cup (120 ml) light cream

Salt and freshly ground white pepper

Freshly grated nutmeg

Salt

10 fresh chives, finely chopped, for garnish

¼ cup (40 g) crumbled Greek feta, for garnish

Make the filling: Put the bay leaf, cinnamon stick, allspice, and cloves on a square of cheesecloth and tie it into a bundle. Set aside.

In a medium saucepan, heat the olive oil over medium heat. Add the onion and cook until soft and lightly colored, about 12 minutes. Add the garlic and cook, stirring, for about a minute. Add the ground meat and cook, stirring, until it turns from pink to grayish brown. Add the tomato paste and stir to combine. Add the wine and spice bundle and season with salt and black pepper to taste. Cover and simmer over low heat until the filling is thick and all the liquid has cooked off. Set aside to cool completely, then drain off excess fat, if necessary. The filling can be prepared up to 1 day ahead and stored in an airtight container in the refrigerator. Bring it to room temperature before using.

When you're ready to make the ravioli, line a baking sheet with parchment paper. Place 8 wonton wrappers in front of you on a clean work surface. Brush the edges lightly with the beaten egg. Place 1 tablespoon of the filling in the center of each wrapper. Top each with a second wonton wrapper to cover the filling, aligning the edges of the wrappers. Use your fingers or the tines of a fork to seal the edges well. Place the ravioli on the prepared baking sheet. Repeat to fill the remaining wonton wrappers, layering another sheet of parchment on top of the ravioli if they don't all fit in one layer. At this point, the entire baking sheet can be wrapped tightly with plastic wrap and refrigerated for 1 to 2 days.

Thirty minutes before you want to serve the ravioli, make the béchamel: In a medium saucepan, heat the olive oil over medium-high heat. Add the flour and stir briskly with a wire whisk to incorporate. Cook, stirring, for 4 to 5 minutes, until the mixture starts to turn blond. Pour in the milk and cream and season to taste with salt, white pepper, and nutmeg. Reduce the heat to medium and cook, stirring continuously with the whisk, until the béchamel thickens but not so much that it becomes pasty. This béchamel should be loose, like a cream sauce. Cover with a kitchen towel to keep warm.

Cook the ravioli: Bring a large pot of water to a rolling boil and add 2 tablespoons salt. Add about half the ravioli and boil for about 3 minutes. Remove with a slotted spoon and transfer immediately to a platter or individual serving plates. Repeat to cook the remaining ravioli.

Spoon some of the béchamel over the ravioli, sprinkle with the chopped chives, and garnish with the crumbled feta. Serve immediately.

Makaronia Psita me Yemisi apo Spanakopita

SPANAKOPITA MAC 'N' CHEESE
with olive oil béchamel

serves 6

Luscious. Delicious. A great way to get kids to eat their spinach. That's what my spanakopita mac 'n' cheese with olive oil béchamel is all about!

FOR THE BÉCHAMEL

3 cups (720 ml) milk (see Note, page 234)

3 tablespoons extra-virgin Greek olive oil

3 tablespoons all-purpose flour

½ teaspoon freshly grated nutmeg

Salt and freshly ground black pepper

1 large egg, lightly beaten

½ cup (50 g) grated Kefalotyri, Kefalograviera, Parmesan, or Pecorino Romano cheese

FOR THE PASTA

Salt

1 pound (450 g) elbow pasta or Greek *hilopites* (egg noodles)

2 tablespoons extra-virgin Greek olive oil

FOR THE FILLING

2 tablespoons extra-virgin Greek olive oil

2 leeks, trimmed, washed well, and chopped

1 garlic clove, chopped

1 pound (450 g) pre-cut fresh spinach

Leaves from 1 bunch dill, snipped

1½ cups (225 g) crumbled Greek feta

1 cup (240 ml) fresh anthotyro or ricotta cheese, drained

½ teaspoon freshly grated nutmeg, or more to taste

Salt and freshly ground black pepper

TO ASSEMBLE

Olive oil, for greasing

¼ cup (25 g) plain dried bread crumbs

Grated Kefalotyri, Kefalograviera, Parmesan, or Pecorino Romano cheese, for sprinkling (optional)

Preheat the oven to 375°F (190°C).

Make the béchamel: Warm the milk in a medium saucepan over medium heat and set aside.

In a separate medium saucepan, heat the olive oil over medium heat. As soon as it starts to shimmer a little, add the flour and whisk to incorporate. Cook, whisking continuously, for 3 to 5 minutes, but do not allow the mixture to brown. While whisking, slowly add the warm milk and whisk the béchamel until it thickens but is still liquid, with the consistency of pancake batter.

(CONTINUED)

Season with the nutmeg and salt and pepper to taste. While whisking vigorously, pour in the egg in a fast, steady stream. Stir in the grated cheese. Remove from the heat, cover with a kitchen towel, and set aside.

Cook the pasta: Bring a large pot of water to a rolling boil and salt it generously. Add the pasta and cook according to the package directions until a little less done than al dente. Drain immediately, return it to the pot, and toss with the olive oil. Set aside.

Make the filling: In a large, deep skillet, heat the olive oil over medium heat. Add the leeks and cook, stirring, until translucent. Add the garlic and cook, stirring, for a minute to soften. Add the spinach, in increments if necessary to fit, and cook until the leaves are wilted and most of the liquid they have released has cooked off. Remove from the heat. Stir in the dill, feta, and anthotyro and season with the nutmeg and salt and pepper to taste.

Assemble the mac 'n' cheese: Oil a large casserole or baking dish.

In a large bowl, stir together the pasta, spinach mixture, and béchamel. Spoon the mixture into the prepared casserole and sprinkle the top evenly with the bread crumbs and grated cheese, if desired. Bake for 30 minutes, or until set and golden.

Remove from the oven, let cool slightly, and serve.

NOTE: You can use skim, whole, or even goat's milk to make the béchamel, and you can make the béchamel and the filling a day or two ahead of time and assemble the mac 'n' cheese the day you plan to cook it.

Kalokairini Makaronada apo tin Ikaria me Agria Horta

IKARIAN SUMMER PASTA
with wild greens pesto

serves 4 to 6

You can find the original rendition of this dish at Mary Mary, a small, popular tavern in the seaside village of Armenistis, on the north side of Ikaria. The restaurant's chef-owner, Nikos Politis, takes local traditions and transforms them into modern cuisine with a local twist.

⅓ cup (80 ml) Greek pikramigdalo (bitter almond liqueur) or amaretto liqueur

½ cup (120 ml) extra-virgin Greek olive oil, plus more as needed

1 large zucchini, trimmed, halved lengthwise, and cut into ⅛-inch-thick (3 mm) slices

4 garlic cloves, chopped

2 tablespoons brined capers, drained, rinsed, and patted dry

2 pounds (900 g) mixed non-bitter greens, such as spinach, chard, sorrel—anything, really, that you can access that is a sweet green

½ cup (65 g) pine nuts

½ cup (70 g) almonds

⅔ cup (65 g) grated Kefalograviera, Kefalotyri, or Parmesan cheese

Salt and freshly ground black pepper

1 pound (450 g) Greek *hilopites* (egg noodles), fettucine, or tagliatelle noodles

1 cup (240 ml) fresh anthotyro or full-fat ricotta cheese

Place the liqueur in a small saucepan and heat over medium heat for a few minutes to cook off the alcohol. Remove from the heat

In a medium skillet, heat 2 tablespoons of the olive oil over medium heat. Add the zucchini and one-quarter of the garlic and cook until the zucchini is slightly softened but still al dente. Transfer the zucchini mixture to a bowl and set aside, covered to keep warm.

In the same skillet, heat 1 teaspoon of the olive oil over high heat. Add the capers and fry for a few minutes, until crispy. Set aside on a plate.

Working in batches, in the bowl of a food processor, combine the greens, remaining garlic, the pine nuts, almonds, and cheese and process until pureed. Season to taste with salt and pepper. With the motor running, add enough of the olive oil and liqueur to make a spreadable, pesto. Use a spatula to scrape the pesto into a large bowl, and repeat with the remaining batches.

Bring a large pot of water to a rolling boil and season with salt. Add the pasta and cook according to the package directions. Drain, reserving 1 cup (240 ml) of the pasta cooking liquid. Immediately add the pasta to the bowl with the pesto and toss to combine. Add the anthotyro, zucchini, and enough of the reserved pasta cooking liquid to make the mixture creamy and toss to combine. Season to taste with pepper, top with the fried capers, and serve.

Kypriaki Mountzentra

LENTIL-PASTA TERRINE
with cumin and prunes

serves 4 to 6

Here is a twist on a very old and traditional Greek and Cypriot dish. Lentils are cooked with pasta, bulgur, or rice in the Greek country kitchen. This dish is spruced up with a tiny Greek pasta called couskousaki, *and spiced with prunes or other dried fruit, cumin, and more.*

1½ cups (300 g) dried small lentils, picked over for debris and rinsed

1 bay leaf

Salt

¾ cup (135 g) Greek *couskousaki* or small orzo pasta

½ cup (120 ml) extra-virgin Greek olive oil

1 small red onion, finely chopped

1 garlic clove, minced

Scant 1 teaspoon ground cumin

½ teaspoon ground coriander

½ teaspoon ground turmeric

½ cup (25 g) chopped or julienned fresh mint leaves

6 pitted large prunes, chopped

1 tablespoon Greek balsamic vinegar

Freshly ground black pepper

4 to 6 teaspoons prepared balsamic syrup, for serving

Place the lentils and bay leaf in a medium pot and add water to cover by at least 2 inches (5 cm). Bring to a boil, reduce the heat to low, and simmer for 20 to 25 minutes, until the lentils are tender but still al dente.

While the lentils are boiling, bring a medium pot of water to a rolling boil and season with salt. Add the pasta and cook according to the package directions. Drain the pasta, return it to the pot, and toss with 1 tablespoon of the olive oil.

In a nonstick medium skillet, heat 2 tablespoons of the olive oil over medium heat. Add the onion and cook, stirring, until soft and lightly caramelized, 12 to 15 minutes. Add the garlic, cumin, coriander, and turmeric and cook, stirring, for 30 seconds. Remove from the heat.

Drain the lentils and transfer to a large bowl. Add the pasta, spiced onion mixture, mint, and prunes and toss to combine. Add the remaining olive oil and the vinegar. Season to taste with salt and pepper. Let stand for 20 minutes before serving.

To serve, set a ring mold on a plate and fill it with the lentil mixture, or pack the lentil mixture into a cup and invert it onto a plate. Repeat to plate the remaining servings. Drizzle with the balsamic syrup and serve.

SOUPS
FOR EVERY SEASON

Vrazei sto zoumi tou

"He boils in his own broth."
(Meaning: He's angry.)

I love soup. It's my go-to meal for everything from weeknights in winter to elegant dinner parties. But the irony is that temperate Greece is not a country of die-hard soup slurpers. Sure, there are a few classic soups, among them avgolemono, the rich egg-lemon soup that can be as pedestrian or sophisticated as the cook who makes it; bean soups, a winter staple; a few vegetable soups; and a handful of regional fish and meat soups. But my take on Greek soups spans a wider range, to include soups inspired by some of my most beloved Greek ingredients. I also have a special fondness for the immersion blender, and I love silky veloutés of just about anything, and often spike them with Greek ingredients, from ouzo to feta cheese.

A few "foreign" soups have taken hold in Greece, inserting themselves into the mindsets and palates of younger generations than mine. Carrot, pumpkin, and sweet potato soups, often garnished with Greek yogurt or sweetened with a touch of honey, are now pretty popular among home cooks and are often on restaurant menus, too.

On my Greek table, soup is reason to experiment, and so I have in the following recipes. Some are recognizably traditional but with a twist, such as the avgolemono with saffron and orzo on page 254. Others are my own creations, inspired by Greek flavors or Greek traditional dishes, such as the fava (yellow split pea) soup with bits of pork, a liquid version of the very traditional way in which the classic puree of yellow split peas is served on Santorini.

Whatever is simmering in a Greek soup pot, one thing is for sure: Like all Greek food, so, too, with soups—the flavors are simple and robust and the soups based on the freshest seasonal ingredients available.

Selinoriza Soupa me Ouzo, Syka kai Feta

CELERY ROOT SOUP
with a splash of ouzo and fig-feta pesto

serves 6

A totally gluten-free soup that's so luscious and filling! The fig-feta pesto adds an amazing dimension to the flavor profile.

1 large or 2 medium celery roots (celeriac), about 4 pounds (1.8 kg) total

⅔ cup (160 ml) extra-virgin Greek olive oil

1 fennel bulb, chopped

2 leeks, trimmed, washed well, and chopped

Salt and freshly ground black pepper

2 garlic cloves, minced

½ cup (120 ml) ouzo

1 cup (240 ml) dry white wine

1½ quarts (1.5 L) vegetable broth or water, plus more as needed

4 dried Greek figs, stemmed

¼ cup (40 g) crumbled Greek feta

¼ cup (13 g) chopped fresh parsley or cilantro

2 to 3 tablespoons Greek balsamic vinegar

1 tablespoon Greek honey or *petimezi* (grape molasses)

2 tablespoons pomegranate seeds

Cut the celery root(s) in half and, using a sharp chef's knife, slice off the woody peel. Cut the root(s) into 1-inch (2.5 cm) cubes.

In a soup pot, heat ¼ cup (60 ml) of the olive oil over medium heat. Add the fennel, leeks, and celery root and season with salt and pepper. Cover and sweat the vegetables over low heat for 10 to 12 minutes, checking them occasionally and turning them in the oil to keep them from burning. Stir in the garlic.

Carefully pour in the ouzo and wine. Cover and cook for 5 minutes. Add the broth, raise the heat to high, and bring the liquid to a boil. Reduce the heat to medium-low, cover with the lid ajar, and simmer the soup for 35 to 40 minutes, until the vegetables are very tender.

While the soup is simmering, in the bowl of a food processor, combine the figs, feta, parsley, a little pepper, and 2 to 3 tablespoons of the olive oil. Pulse on and off until broken down into a chunky paste. Set aside.

Remove the soup from the heat and puree it directly in the pot with an immersion blender. Taste and adjust the seasoning with the vinegar, honey, and salt and pepper to taste.

Ladle into bowls, garnish each with some fig-feta pesto, a few pomegranate seeds, and a drizzle of the remaining olive oil, and serve.

Kastanosoupa

MODERN GREEK CHRISTMAS CHESTNUT SOUP

serves 8

Chestnut trees grow all over Greece. They are one of the traditional ingredients in the rice stuffing for the Christmas or New Year's turkey. They stud wine-braised pork. Chestnut spoon sweets, chestnut puree, and chestnut flour are all beloved artisanal foods in many parts of the country.

58 vacuum-packed or fresh chestnuts

4 tablespoons (½ stick / 55 g) unsalted butter

2 tablespoons extra-virgin Greek olive oil, plus more for serving

1 large fennel bulb, finely chopped

3 leeks, white parts only, washed well and finely chopped

2 garlic cloves, minced

1 large potato, peeled and diced

1 cup (240 ml) ouzo

3 quarts (3 L) chicken broth or vegetable broth

Salt and freshly ground black pepper

½ cup (120 ml) light cream

½ cup (120 ml) Greek yogurt, for serving

Fresh chives or fennel fronds, for garnish

Crushed pink peppercorns

If using vacuum-packed chestnuts, follow the package directions for cooking them in the bag in boiling water, then transfer to a bowl and set aside. If using raw chestnuts, place them in a large pot and add cold water to cover. Bring the water to a boil, then reduce the heat to medium and simmer for 3 minutes. Remove from the heat. Working in batches and keeping the rest of the chestnuts in the water so their skins stay soft enough to score open, remove a few of the chestnuts and use a sharp paring knife to peel them. Set aside in a bowl until ready to use.

In a large soup pot, heat 2 tablespoons of the butter and the olive oil together over medium heat. Add the fennel, leeks, and garlic and cook, stirring, until soft and glistening, about 10 minutes. Add the potato and 50 of the peeled chestnuts (reserve 8) and stir to coat with the oil.

Carefully pour in the ouzo. As soon as the alcohol cooks off, add the broth. Bring the soup to a simmer, cover, and cook for about 40 minutes. Puree the soup directly in the pot with an immersion blender, or carefully transfer the soup in batches to the bowl of a food processor and puree until smooth, then return the pureed soup to the pot. (Although it isn't necessary, you can strain the pureed soup through a fine-mesh sieve or chinois for a silkier texture and more elegant result.) Taste and adjust the seasoning with salt and black pepper.

Bring the soup back to a simmer, add the cream, and stir. Taste and adjust the seasoning. Right before serving, stir in the remaining 2 tablespoons butter.

Ladle into individual bowls and top each with a dollop of Greek yogurt and a chive or fennel frond. Drizzle with extra-virgin olive oil and sprinkle with crushed pink peppercorns. Garnish each bowl with a chestnut and serve.

Soupa apo Fava me Pasto Hoirino

CREAMY YELLOW SPLIT PEA SOUP
with cured pork

serves 8

Taking a cue from the combination of yellow split pea puree and cured pork that is part of the old food traditions of Santorini and other Cyclades islands, I was inspired to make this chic but simple and inexpensive soup. You can switch out the pork for two grilled or sautéed portobello mushrooms, cut into slivers, to make it totally vegan or vegetarian, and you can spruce it up with a drizzle of truffle oil to give it a festive note.

3 tablespoons extra-virgin Greek olive oil, plus more if needed

1 large onion, finely chopped

1 pound (450 g) dried yellow split peas, preferably from Santorini, picked over for debris and rinsed

2 quarts (2 L) water or chicken broth, or a combination, plus more if needed

2 bay leaves

2 or 3 fresh thyme sprigs

Salt and freshly ground black pepper

Juice of ½ lemon, strained

Truffle oil, for garnish (optional)

Fresh thyme sprigs, fresh chives, and/ or crushed pink peppercorns, for garnish

4 ounces (115 g) cured Greek pork or other cured pork, such as smoked bacon or pancetta, cooked and finely chopped or crumbled

In a large pot, heat the olive oil over medium heat. Add the onion and cook, stirring occasionally, until softened, 8 to 10 minutes. Add the split peas and stir well to coat with the oil. Add the water or broth, raise the heat to high, and bring to a boil. Reduce the heat to maintain a simmer and add the bay leaves and thyme. Season with salt and black pepper. Simmer until the lentils are tender, 50 minutes to 1 hour, skimming off any foam from the surface as the soup simmers.

Remove the bay leaves and thyme sprigs. Carefully transfer the soup in batches to the bowl of a food processor and process until smooth, or puree the soup in the pot using an immersion blender until smooth. Taste and adjust the seasoning with salt and black pepper if needed. Stir in the lemon juice. Dilute the soup with additional water or broth, if necessary, and gently reheat.

To serve, ladle the soup into individual bowls and garnish each with a few drops of olive oil or truffle oil, fresh thyme sprigs, fresh chives, and/or crushed pink peppercorns, and a few pieces of the cured pork.

Mia Fasolada, Polles Ekdohes

TEMPLATE FOR A CLASSIC GREEK BEAN SOUP

serves 6

Fasolada, *the classic Greek bean soup, comes in many regional variations. In western Crete, for example, a few strips of orange zest are sometimes added to the soup as it simmers. In the north of Greece, where the palate is spicier, fasolada is often seasoned with* boukovo (*Greek red pepper flakes) or a couple of hot chiles. Mint and red pepper flakes together are another uniquely northern Greek addition to the soup. Greeks whose roots are in the Black Sea region add something called* korkota, *beautiful amber crystals of dried corn. A cup or two of browned, chopped sausage meat makes the soup heartier. Another option, and one I exercise quite a bit, is to run an immersion blender in the soup for a few seconds, pureeing just a bit of it to give the soup a creamy, dense texture. The choices are yours to make! Add a generous amount of additional olive oil when serving the soup, and accompany it with a side of feta and/or salted sardines. Note that the beans need to soak overnight, so plan ahead.*

1 pound (450 g) dried medium-size white beans, such as cannellini, picked over for debris and rinsed

⅔ cup (160 ml) extra-virgin Greek olive oil

3 large red onions, finely chopped (about 3 cups)

3 medium carrots, chopped

3 celery stalks, with leaves, chopped, or 1½ cups (150 g) chopped wild celery with leaves

3 garlic cloves, finely chopped

2 cups (330 g) chopped canned plum tomatoes and their juices

2 bay leaves

3 tablespoons Greek balsamic vinegar

½ cup (25 g) chopped fresh parsley

Salt and freshly ground black pepper

CHOICE OF ADDITIONS

2 (1-inch-wide / 2.5 cm) strips orange zest (peeled with a vegetable peeler), added with the vegetables

2 dried red chiles, added with the vegetables

½ cup (45 g) parched corn, added with the vegetables

½ cup (25 g) chopped fresh mint, added at the end

1 cup diced browned sausage meat, added about ¾ of the way through cooking

6 to 8 salted sardines, added to the individual soup bowls when served

4 to 6 ounces (115 to 170 g) Greek feta, crumbled, added as garnish

Put the beans in a bowl and add cold water to cover. Set aside at room temperature to soak overnight. Drain and rinse them; set aside.

In a large pot, heat ⅓ cup (80 ml) of the olive oil over low heat. Add the onions, carrots, and celery and cook until softened, about 12 minutes. Stir in the garlic. Add the beans and toss to coat with the oil. Pour in the tomatoes and 8 cups (2 L) water and bay leaves. Raise the heat to high and bring to a boil. Reduce the heat to low and simmer, skimming off any foam from the top as it cooks, for about 2 hours, or until the soup is thick and creamy and the beans and vegetables are very soft. About 10 minutes before removing from the heat, stir in the vinegar and parsley, taste, and season with salt and pepper.

As soon as you remove the soup from the heat, pour in the remaining ⅓ cup (80 ml) olive oil. Serve hot, garnished, if desired, with a couple of sardines and a little feta sprinkled over each bowl or served on the side.

Revithada Fournisto sto Pylino

CLAY-BAKED CHICKPEA SOUP

serves 6

Chickpeas, one of the oldest legumes found in the eastern Mediterranean, continue to be an important food in the Cyclades, especially on the island of Sifnos, where to this day a clay pot–baked chickpea soup is the Sunday meal. Home cooks fill their xespastaria—a unique clay pot with a wide bottom and narrow, tapered mouth—with the ingredients for a traditional revithada, or chickpea soup, and bring the pots to the local baker, who heats the vessels overnight in a hot, but not fully fired, wood-burning oven. The next day, usually after church, people pick up their blackened pots to take home for the family meal. Sometimes rice or dried corn is added to make the soup more filling. Note that the chickpeas need to soak overnight, so plan ahead.

1 teaspoon baking soda

1 pound (450 g) dried chickpeas, picked over for debris and rinsed

2 large red onions, coarsely chopped

6 garlic cloves, minced

2 large carrots, cut into ½-inch (1.5 cm) cubes

2 celery stalks, chopped

1 cup (240 ml) extra-virgin Greek olive oil, plus more for seasoning the finished soup

3 bay leaves

2 fresh rosemary sprigs

Salt

3 tablespoons strained fresh lemon juice or red wine vinegar

Dissolve the baking soda in a large bowl of cold water, add the chickpeas, and soak in the refrigerator overnight. Drain and rinse very well.

Place the chickpeas in a large pot and add cold water to cover by 3 inches (7.5cm). Bring to a boil over medium heat, then reduce the heat to maintain a simmer and cook the chickpeas until they are al dente, about 1 hour, skimming off any foam from the top as they cook.

Preheat the oven to 350°F (175°C).

Remove the pot of chickpeas from the heat. Using a slotted spoon, transfer the chickpeas to a large ovenproof clay or earthenware pot with a tight-fitting lid, reserving their cooking liquid. Add the onions, garlic, carrots, celery, olive oil, bay leaves, and rosemary, season with salt, and add enough of the reserved chickpea cooking liquid to cover the ingredients by 3 inches (7.5 cm). Cover the pot and transfer to the oven.

Bake for 2 hours, or until the chickpeas are very soft. Remove from the oven. Remove and discard the bay leaves and rosemary. Ladle 2 cups (480 ml) of the soup into the bowl of a food processor and puree until smooth, or ladle it into a medium bowl and puree with an immersion blender until smooth. Return the pureed soup to the pot. Season with salt, lemon juice or vinegar, and olive oil to taste. Stir well to combine.

Taste and adjust the seasoning with additional salt, additional lemon juice or vinegar, and olive oil. Serve hot.

Kokoras Protoyiahni

CHICKEN NOODLE SOUP
with fresh pasta, tomatoes, and grated cheese

serves 6 to 8

Almost every country in the world has its version of chicken noodle soup. In Greece, this comforting combination comes in many regional variations, one of my favorites being an old recipe from the Peloponnese called protoyiahni, *which is typically made with rooster, the dark meat of which lends a depth and richness to this simple country classic. I've adapted the recipe and call for chicken. But note: Roosters have a much richer flavor and darker flesh, which give the soup a fuller taste. So if it's possible for you to find a flavorful rooster for your pot, by all means, use it.*

½ cup (120 ml) extra-virgin Greek olive oil, plus more for garnish

1 large red onion, chopped

1 large carrot, chopped

6 garlic cloves, chopped

1 boiling chicken, about 3½ pounds (1.6 kg), cleaned

4 cups (660 g) chopped canned tomatoes and their juices

1 bay leaf

3 or 4 fresh thyme sprigs

3 or 4 fresh oregano sprigs

4 allspice berries

Salt and freshly ground black pepper

1 tablespoon tomato paste

1 heaping tablespoon Greek honey

1 pound (450 g) Greek *hilopites* (egg noodles) or other egg noodles

Grated myzithra or other hard sheep's-milk grating cheese, for serving

In a large deep pot, heat the olive oil over high heat. Add the onion and carrot and cook, stirring, until soft and translucent, 8 to 10 minutes. Stir in the garlic.

Add the chicken, tomatoes with their juices, bay leaf, thyme, oregano, and allspice to the pot. Add water to cover the chicken by 3 inches (7.5 cm). Bring to a boil, season generously with salt and pepper, reduce the heat to low, and simmer until the chicken is falling off the bone, about 1½ hours.

Using kitchen tongs or a slotted spoon, carefully remove the chicken from the pot and transfer it to a bowl. Let cool. When cool enough to handle, remove the meat from the bones, discarding the bones, and shred or chop the meat. Discard the skin, if desired.

Remove the herb sprigs, bay leaf, and allspice from the pot. Add enough water to the pot to make 3 quarts (3 L) of liquid total. Stir in the tomato paste and honey. Add the noodles and bring the liquid to a boil. Cook according to the package directions.

Stir the shredded chicken into the soup. Serve in soup bowls, garnished with a generous grating of cheese and additional olive oil, if desired.

Pikantiki Trahanosoupa me Thalassina

SPICY TRAHANA SOUP
with fresh seafood

serves 6 to 8

Seafood soups abound in Greece, and many call for the addition of some type of starch, typically either potatoes, rice, or trahana, *a dry, dairy-based, granular grain product that is one of the most ancient foods in the world (see page 214). I like to use the sour version of* trahana *in this rendition of a northern Greek classic recipe because it lends a delicious underlying tartness.*

4 pounds (1.8 kg) fresh mussels, scrubbed and beards removed, or 6 cups cleaned thawed frozen mussels

1 cup (240 ml) dry white wine, plus more for steaming mussels

½ cup (120 ml) extra-virgin Greek olive oil

1 pound (450 g) medium shrimp, peeled and deveined

½ cup (120 ml) sour *trahana* (see page 214), or bulgur wheat

3 garlic cloves, minced

¼ teaspoon red pepper flakes or *boukovo* (Greek red pepper flakes)

1 cup (240 ml) clam juice (optional, if using frozen mussels)

2 cups (480 ml) pureed fresh or finely chopped good-quality canned tomatoes

Salt and freshly ground white pepper

3 tablespoons strained fresh lemon juice

5 ounces (140 g) Greek feta, crumbled

1 tablespoon chopped fresh parsley (optional)

If using fresh mussels, fill a large wide pot with wine to a depth of 1 inch (2.5 cm). Place the mussels in a steamer basket and place the basket in the pot. Cover, bring the wine to a simmer over medium-high heat, and steam until the mussels have opened, about 5 minutes. Discard any that haven't opened. Strain the cooking liquid through a fine-mesh sieve or coffee filter and set aside. Remove the mussels from their shells, keeping a few in the shell as a garnish.

In a large skillet, heat 2 tablespoons of the olive oil over high heat. Add the shrimp and frozen, defrosted mussels, if using, and sear until the shrimp turn bright pink. Remove from the heat and set aside.

In a soup pot, heat the remaining 6 tablespoons (90 ml) olive oil over medium heat. Add the *trahana*, and stir to coat with the oil. Cook for 2 minutes. Stir in the garlic and red pepper flakes. Add 1 cup of wine and 1 cup of mussel steaming liquid or clam juice. As soon as it starts to evaporate, add 6 cups (1.4 L) water and the tomatoes and cook over medium heat until the soup starts to thicken and the *trahana* softens. Season to taste with salt and white pepper. Add the mussels, shrimp, and any juices that have collected in the bowl or skillet to the pot. Mix gently. Stir in the lemon juice, feta, and parsley, if using. Remove from the heat.

Garnish the soup with the steamed mussels in their shells, if you kept some aside, and serve.

Mageiritsa me Kotsi Arniou

GREEK EASTER SOUP
with lamb shank

serves 8 to 10

This is my gentrified version of the classic Greek Easter soup, which traditionally calls for all the viscera and head of the lamb. It doesn't have to be Easter to enjoy it!

4 lamb shanks

Salt and freshly ground black pepper

1 cup (240 ml) extra-virgin Greek olive oil

2 quarts (2 L) water, lamb broth or chicken broth

10 fresh thyme sprigs

10 fresh parsley sprigs

15 whole black peppercorns

3 bay leaves

2 onions

2 carrots

2 celery stalks

12 scallions, whites and tender upper greens finely chopped

2 cups (110 g) shredded romaine lettuce

1 cup (50 g) chopped fresh dill

1 cup (200 g) uncooked short-grain rice, such as Greek glacé (glazed rice)

FOR THE AVGOLEMONO

5 large eggs, at room temperature

Juice of 2 large lemons, or more to taste, strained

Season the shanks generously with salt and pepper. In a large soup pot, heat ½ cup (120 ml) of the olive oil over medium-high heat. Working in batches, add the shanks and sear, turning with kitchen tongs until the meat is deep brown on all sides. Replenish the olive oil if necessary and repeat with the remaining shanks.

Return the shanks to the pot. Pour in enough water or broth to cover the shanks by 3 inches (7.5 cm).

Tie up the thyme, parsley, peppercorns, and bay leaves in a small piece of cheesecloth. Add the herb bundle, onions, carrots, and celery to the pot. Bring to a boil, then reduce the heat to maintain a simmer. Cover and cook the shanks until the meat is falling off the bones, 3 to 4 hours.

Remove from the heat. Using a slotted spoon or kitchen tongs, carefully remove the shanks. Set aside in a bowl until cool enough to handle. Remove the herb bundle and vegetables with a slotted spoon and discard. Shred the meat from the shanks and return it to the pot; discard the bones.

Bring the soup to a boil, reduce the heat to maintain a simmer, and add the scallions. Cook for 10 minutes, until the scallions are soft. Add the shredded lettuce and dill and cook for a few more minutes, until the lettuce is soft. Add the rice and simmer until soft, about 20 minutes.

Meanwhile, make the avgolemono: In a medium bowl, whisk together the eggs and lemon juice until frothy. While whisking, very slowly add 2 to 3 cups (480 to 720 ml) of the hot soup to the egg mixture and whisk until the egg is tempered, beating vigorously to keep the egg from curdling. Pour the egg mixture into the pot with the soup and stir well with a wooden spoon. Taste and adjust the seasoning with salt, pepper, and lemon juice and serve right away, hot.

Avgolemono me Kroko kai Kritharaki

SAFFRON AVGOLEMONO SOUP
with orzo

serves 2 to 4

Avgolemono soup is Greek comfort food. Most recipes call for rice. I like to make mine with orzo, which gives the final soup a soothing but substantial and filling quality.

2 quarts (2 L) fish broth or chicken broth	6 Greek *krokos Kozanis* or red saffron threads
⅔ cup (150 g) orzo	2 whole large eggs or egg yolks
Salt and freshly ground black pepper	Juice of 1 lemon, or more to taste, strained

In a medium saucepan, bring the broth to a boil. Add the orzo and season with salt and pepper. Add the saffron threads. Cook for about 15 minutes, or until the orzo is tender.

While the orzo is cooking, whisk the eggs or egg yolks in a medium metal bowl until very frothy. Whisk in the lemon juice. Scoop off a ladleful of the broth from the top of the pot, so as not to get any orzo, and, while whisking vigorously, very slowly pour the broth into the egg-lemon mixture. Repeat with a second ladleful, then pour the egg-lemon mixture into the pot with the orzo, tilting the pot to it distribute evenly. Serve immediately.

LIFE OF
PIE

Pese pita na se fao

"Pita, fall so I can eat you."
(Meaning: I want something without too much effort.)

Spanakopita, the flaky, savory phyllo pie filled with spinach, herbs, and cheese, is to Greek cuisine what pizza or burritos are to Italian and Mexican, respectively: a traditional "peasant" dish that has conquered the world, crossed ethnic boundaries, and been embraced by and ensconced in the American food landscape.

I grew up with it in my Greek American home in Queens, New York, but also in the diners of my youth that were so much a part of my first dining experiences. My childhood friends did, too, and we even get together on occasion at our old diner haunts to enjoy some.

But every Greek recipe has a story, and even something as commonplace as spanakopita can trace its roots to the deepest Greek traditions, to the countryside, and the evolution of dishes that spring from the confluence of nature and need.

The earliest evidence of pita—what the Greeks call their beloved savory phyllo pies—dates to third-century Macedonia and the flat loaves of bread used as plates for meat. To this day, there are traditional recipes in the region that call for prebaking phyllo so it's almost like a large cracker.

Spanakopita is but one of an enormous range of Greek savory phyllo pies. This is Greek soul food—nourishing, comforting, and filling—and prepared traditionally with the seasonal ingredients that were, and still are, on hand or easy to access.

The tradition belongs to every part of Greece, but in some places, savory pies are a definitive local food. Macedonia, Thrace, Epirus, and Thessaly, where itinerant shepherds roamed until a generation ago, are the spiritual home of Greece's greatest savory pies, foods that evolved out of the roaming shepherd's tradition, when whole extended clans moved with their flocks from the lowlands to the highlands twice a year with the change of the seasons. The pies could be made with anything these families had on hand, most notably cheese and freshly foraged greens from near that day's camp.

Pies enclose a filling, and thereby made it less perishable in an age before refrigeration. *Pita*, the generic name for "pie" in Greek, is filling, an important thing when feeding a large family. It is inexpensive, also important in the economy of a country kitchen, and even more so in a mobile one. Pies are also something you can cut and hold in hand, a substantial food that's easy to carry to the field as a snack. In the traditions of the north and mainland Greece, pies were baked under a *sini*, a dome-shaped copper lid that became the family's moveable oven. By digging a shallow hole, placing charcoal or wood inside and a pan on top, and the *sini* over it all, anything could be baked.

On the mainland, phyllo pies tend to be made in whole pans, while on islands most phyllo specialties are small, individual pies that can be made in a skillet, because wood—fuel—for ovens was scarce.

The variety of Greek savory pies is enormous and differentiated by shape, size, filling, and phyllo variations. Some pies have no phyllo at all, but rather are thick batters baked with cheese or greens, and vegetable pies are topped with a layer of cornmeal that is either poured or patted on top and solidifies into a crust when baked. There are vegetable pies of every sort: zucchini, eggplant, tomatoes, cabbage, leeks, onions, peppers, and more; countless greens pies, including the classic spinach pie, but also pies filled at once with dozens of different greens and aromatic herbs. Leek pies alone number in the dozens all over Greece; so do cheese pies. Mushrooms make a filling in regions where they grow wild, especially Macedonia.

These pies were and still are a measure of the skillfulness of the cook, but they are also surprisingly easy and fun to make . . . as timely and creative today as they were more than a thousand years ago.

Spitiko Phyllo me Olikis Aleseos Alevri

HOMEMADE WHOLE WHEAT PHYLLO

enough for one 15-inch (37.5 cm) round pie or two 8-inch (20 cm) round pies

Over the many years I've been baking Greek pies and making my own phyllo, I've developed a few standard recipes that are easy to work with. This one, for whole wheat phyllo pastry, is especially earthy and goes beautifully with any of the fillings in this chapter. The addition of Greek yogurt gives the phyllo a springy, elastic texture that makes it very easy to work with.

3 cups (375 g) whole wheat flour

1 cup (125 g) all-purpose or fine semolina flour

1 teaspoon salt

½ cup (120 ml) extra-virgin Greek olive oil, plus more for greasing

½ cup (120 ml) Greek yogurt

1 tablespoon red wine vinegar, balsamic vinegar, or ouzo

Combine the flours in the bowl of a stand mixer fitted with the dough hook. Blend for a few seconds on medium speed.

In a medium bowl, dissolve the salt in ¾ cup (180 ml) water. Whisk in the olive oil, yogurt, and vinegar and add the olive oil mixture to the mixer bowl with the flours.

Mix at medium speed for a minute or two to combine, then raise the speed slightly and mix until the dough is soft and pliant but not sticky, 8 to 10 minutes. During the mixing process, add additional water if the dough seems too dry, or more semolina flour if it seems too wet and sticky.

Oil a large bowl. Remove the dough from the mixer, shape it into a ball, and place it in the oiled bowl. Cover with plastic wrap and set out at room temperature for at least 30 minutes and up to 6 hours before using as directed in the recipes that follow. You can also prepare the dough to this point, wrap it well, and refrigerate it for up to 3 days; bring it to room temperature before using.

Spanakopita me Spitiko Filo apo Mavro Alevri

SPINACH-CHEESE PIE
with homemade whole wheat phyllo

serves 8

Nothing speaks "Greek phyllo pie" more than a classic spanakopita. In this recipe, the whole wheat phyllo makes all the difference, because the spinach and whole wheat filling make for an incredibly earthy combination. Homemade phyllo is considerably different from the commercial variety, which is paper-thin and bakes up into a flaky, crispy final product. The homemade variety is more like a traditional pastry dough.

1 recipe Homemade Whole Wheat Phyllo (page 261)

3 tablespoons plus ½ cup (120 ml) extra-virgin Greek olive oil, plus more, as needed

2 large red or yellow onions, finely chopped

6 scallions, chopped

2 pounds (900 g) fresh spinach, trimmed, washed, and drained well

½ cup (25 g) chopped fresh dill

½ cup (25 g) chopped fresh mint

½ cup (25 g) chopped fresh parsley

2 cups (300 g) crumbled Greek feta

Salt and freshly ground black pepper

Freshly grated nutmeg

½ cup (70 g) bulgur, rice, or *trahana* (see page 214; optional)

Prepare the phyllo or bring it to room temperature, if chilled.

Preheat the oven to 350°F (175°C). Lightly oil a 15-inch (37.5 cm) round baking pan.

In a large deep skillet or wide pot, heat 3 tablespoons of the olive oil over medium heat. Add the onions and scallions and cook until soft and translucent, about 8 minutes. Transfer the mixture to a bowl.

In the same skillet, cook the chopped spinach, in batches if needed to fit, until most of the liquid it exudes cooks off. Drain the spinach very well in a colander and add it to the onion mixture.

Mix in the dill, mint, parsley, and feta. Season to taste with salt, pepper, and nutmeg. Let cool. If the filling is too wet or loose, mix in the bulgur, which will absorb excess liquid as the pie bakes.

Divide the phyllo into 4 equal balls. Roll out the first ball to a circle slightly larger than the circumference of the prepared pan, large enough so that a bit of the dough's edge hangs over the periphery. Fold the dough in half and then in half again so it looks like a rounded-off triangle.

Place the tip of the triangle in the middle of the prepared baking pan and unfold the phyllo to cover the surface of the pan and hang over the sides a bit. Brush the phyllo generously with some of the olive oil. Repeat with a second ball of phyllo, rolling it out, placing it in the pan over the first sheet, and brushing it generously with olive oil. Spread the filling over this phyllo layer. Roll out the third ball of phyllo, place it over the filling, and brush it generously with olive oil. Roll out the final ball of phyllo, but this time lay it down decoratively: Hold it over the top of your hands and wrists and place it gently over the pan, letting it fall in uneven folds over the surface. Using scissors or a knife, cut off the excess dough, leaving a 1-inch (2.5 cm) overhang, then join the excess dough hanging over the top and bottom together, turning in and pinching as you go, to form a rim around the inside periphery of the pie. Score the phyllo so that the pieces are either wedge-shaped or rectangular. Brush the top layer with olive oil and bake for 45 to 55 minutes, until the phyllo is firm, set, and beautifully browned. Remove and let cool for at least 30 minutes before serving.

NOTE: You can use 1 pound (450 g) of #4 or #7 commercial phyllo for the spinach pie, instead, of course. If using commercial phyllo, defrost it overnight in the refrigerator and bring to room temperature before using. Layer 8 sheets on the bottom of the pan, brushing each with olive oil. Spread the filling over the pastry, then layer on another 6 sheets of phyllo, brushing them with olive oil as well. Sprinkle the top sheet with a little water and score it into serving pieces. Bake as directed and serve. Seal any remaining phyllo in plastic wrap and store it in the refrigerator for up to a week to use in another recipe.

Kariotika Pitarakia tis Makrozoias

IKARIA'S LONGEVITY GREENS PHYLLO ROLLS

makes 20 to 30 pieces

These pies are one of the most beloved dishes on Ikaria, the Blue Zone island renowned for the longevity of its inhabitants. They are usually made with homemade phyllo, which is time-consuming to prepare, cut, and shape. Working with commercial phyllo makes it easy for anyone to assemble these. You can prepare then freeze them, and bake them off straight out of the freezer without defrosting them first.

¾ cup (180 ml) extra-virgin Greek olive oil, plus more as needed

1½ pounds (680 g) mixed non-bitter greens (any combination of spinach, sweet sorrel, sweet dandelion, Swiss chard, chervil)

Salt and freshly ground black pepper

1 fennel bulb, chopped

3 red onions, chopped

2 leeks, trimmed, washed well, and chopped

4 scallions, chopped

2 large carrots, grated, or 1½ cups (165 g) grated pumpkin or butternut squash (see Note)

1½ cups (75 g) mixed chopped fresh herbs (any combination of mint, parsley, oregano, marjoram, savory, dill, fennel fronds)

1 pound (450 g) commercial phyllo, at room temperature

Preheat the oven to 350°F (175°C). Lightly oil two baking sheets or line them with parchment paper.

In a large, deep skillet or wide pot, heat 2 tablespoons of the olive oil over medium heat. Working in batches, add the greens, season with a little salt and pepper, and cook, stirring, until the leaves are wilted and all the liquid they have released has cooked off, 10 to 15 minutes. Remove from the heat, transfer to a colander, and drain thoroughly. Transfer to a large bowl.

In the same skillet, heat 2 tablespoons of the olive oil over medium heat. Add the fennel, onions, leeks, and scallions and cook until wilted and translucent, about 10 minutes. Transfer to the bowl with the greens.

Add the grated carrot (or pumpkin or butternut squash) to the skillet and cook over medium heat to wilt, about 8 minutes. Transfer to the bowl. Mix in the herbs and season with salt and pepper.

On a clean work surface, roll out the phyllo in front of you horizontally. Cover it with a kitchen towel and then set a damp towel on top. You have to work fast, especially if the kitchen is hot. Take one sheet of the pastry out from under the towels, lay it horizontally in front of you, and brush it with olive oil. Take a second sheet and stack it on top, brushing that with olive oil, too.

Cut from top to bottom down the length of the stacked sheets to make 3 or 4 equal-size strips, 3 to 4 inches (7.5 to 10 cm) wide, as desired.

Take a heaping teaspoon of the filling and spread it across the bottom of each strip. Fold in the sides and roll up to form cylinders. Place the cylinders seam-side down on the prepared baking sheets. Continue until all the filling or phyllo has been used. (At this point, you can wrap the cylinders—or triangles, if you're making the variation—well and freeze them, then bake them directly from the freezer.)

Brush the surface of each cylinder with a little olive oil. Bake for about 20 minutes. Remove from the oven, let cool slightly, and serve.

NOTE: If using grated pumpkin or butternut squash, place it in a colander and salt it lightly. Knead it in the colander, squeezing out as much water as possible. Let stand for 1 hour to drain. You can opt to drain it even further by transferring it to a piece of cheesecloth and wringing out all the excess liquid.

VARIATION

Instead of rolling them, shape the *pitarakia* into triangles: Place one strip of phyllo on top of another, oiling both as above. Place a heaping teaspoon of the filling in the center bottom end of the double strip, about ½ inch (1.5 cm) from the edge. Take the right- or left-hand corner, whichever suits you more comfortably, and bring it up to the opposite side to form a triangle. Fold over across the width, then repeat in the opposite direction, continuing this way until you reach the top edge, the same way one folds a flag. Place the triangles seam-side down on the baking sheets, brush the tops with olive oil, and bake as directed.

Nisiotiki Kremmydopita

GREEK ISLAND ONION PIE

makes one 10-inch (25 cm) round pie or 20 to 30 crescents

Greek savory pies are the ultimate cucina povera, *hearty fare that can be filled with everything from leftovers to lentils to the finest meats and cheeses. Nothing I can imagine is simpler than a filling of onions, which are surprisingly versatile in the Greek kitchen. This onion pie is an amalgam of various recipes I've encountered in my travels through the Aegean islands over the years. You can bake the pie whole, or shape it into individual crescents for an easy make-ahead nosh or cocktail snack. If you're using frozen commercial phyllo for this pie, it needs to thaw overnight in the refrigerator, so plan ahead.*

1 recipe Homemade Whole Wheat Phyllo (page 261), or 1 pound (450 g) #4 frozen or chilled commercial phyllo

⅔ cup (160 ml) extra-virgin Greek olive oil

6 large red onions, chopped

1 pound (450 g) Kefalotyri cheese, grated

¼ cup (9 g) dried mint

Salt and freshly ground black pepper

If using homemade phyllo, prepare the dough or bring it to room temperature, if chilled.

In a large deep skillet, heat 3 tablespoons of the olive oil over medium heat. Add the onions and cook, stirring occasionally, until soft and glistening, 10 to 12 minutes. Transfer to a bowl and stir in the grated cheese, mint, and salt and pepper to taste.

To make a whole-pan pie with homemade phyllo: Lightly oil a 10 x 14-inch (25 x 35 cm) baking pan. Divide the phyllo into 4 equal balls. Roll out the first ball to a rectangle slightly larger than the area of the prepared pan and place it inside the pan so that a bit of the dough's edges hangs over the periphery. Brush generously with some of the olive oil. Repeat with a second ball of dough, rolling it out, placing it in the pan over the first, and brushing it with olive oil. Spread the filling over this phyllo layer. Roll out the third ball of phyllo, place it over the filling, and brush it generously with olive oil. Roll out the final ball of phyllo and place it over the third layer. Using scissors or a knife, cut off the excess dough, leaving a 1-inch (2.5 cm) overhang, then join the overhanging top and bottom layers together to form a rim around the inside periphery of the pie. Score the phyllo into serving pieces, without drawing the knife all the way through the bottom of the pie. Brush the top layer with olive oil and bake for 45 to 55 minutes, until the phyllo is golden and crisp. Remove and let cool for at least 30 minutes before serving.

If using commercial phyllo, defrost it overnight in the refrigerator and bring to room temperature before using. Layer 8 sheets on the bottom of the prepared baking pan, brushing each with some of the olive oil. Spread the filling over the pastry, then layer on another 6 sheets of phyllo, brushing them with olive oil as well. Sprinkle the top sheet with a little water and score it into serving pieces. Bake as above, let cool for 30 minutes, and serve.

To make fried individual crescents with homemade phyllo: Divide the dough into 5 equal pieces. With a rolling pin, roll out each piece to a large, thin sheet, sprinkling the dough with flour as you roll. Take a 4-inch (10 cm) round cookie cutter and cut circles out of the dough, or cut out circles with a paring knife using a saucer as your guide. Collect the dough scraps, reroll them, and cut out more circles.

Place 1 tablespoon of the filling in the middle of each circle. Using your fingers, dampen the edges with a little water, fold one side over to make a crescent, and press the edges together with a fork to seal.

In a deep skillet, heat 1 inch (2.5 cm) of olive oil over medium-high heat until it registers 370°F (188°C) on an instant-read or deep-fry thermometer. Working in batches, fry the small pies in the hot oil until golden on both sides. Remove with a slotted spoon and drain on paper towels. Let cool slightly and serve.

Kolokythopita me Yiaourti kai Dyosmo

ZUCCHINI PIE
with greek yogurt and fresh mint

serves 8

The tangle of zucchini that overflows in Greek summer gardens means that all over the country, the number of regional recipes incorporating it is mind-boggling. Savory pies filled with zucchini are just one category of dishes that call for this summer creeper! There are literally dozens of savory pies filled with zucchini, all slightly varied from place to place and cook to cook. This pie, with Greek yogurt, hails from the north.

4 pounds (1.8 kg) zucchini

Salt

½ cup (120 ml) extra-virgin Greek olive oil, plus more as needed

1 cup (240 ml) Greek yogurt

1 cup (100 g) grated Kefalotyri or other hard, sharp, yellow sheep's-milk cheese

3 large eggs, lightly beaten

½ cup (125 ml) rice, *trahana* (see page 214), bulgur, quinoa, or fine semolina

½ cup (25 g) chopped fresh mint

Freshly ground black pepper

1 recipe Homemade Whole Wheat Phyllo (page 261), or 1 (1-pound / 450 g) box #4 commercial phyllo

Trim off the stem and root ends of the zucchini. Wash and pat dry. Grate the zucchini on the large holes of a box grater or in a food processor with the grating attachment. Line a colander with cheesecloth. Place the zucchini in the lined colander, toss with 2 teaspoons salt, place a plate and a weight on top, and leave the grated zucchini to drain in the sink for 2 hours.

Pull up the ends of the cheesecloth, then squeeze and wring the zucchini to get out all the excess moisture. Transfer the drained zucchini into a clean bowl. Add the olive oil, yogurt, cheeses, eggs, rice, mint, and pepper to taste to the zucchini and mix well with a fork. Taste and adjust the seasoning with salt, as needed.

Preheat the oven to 350°F (175°C).

If using homemade phyllo, divide the dough into 3 balls, one slightly heavier than the others. Let rest, covered, for 10 minutes. Brush a 12-inch (30 cm) round baking pan with olive oil.

On a lightly floured surface, roll out the largest of the 3 dough balls to a 15-inch (37.5 cm) circle. Place in the oiled pan and brush the surface of the dough with 2 teaspoons olive oil. Spread the filling evenly over the dough. Pull the excess dough from around the rim over the edge of the filling, toward to center. Roll out the next dough ball to a 12-inch (30 cm) circle and place on top of the filling. Brush with 2 teaspoons olive oil. Repeat with last dough ball and brush again. Score the pie into serving pieces and bake for about 1 hour. Remove, let cool slightly, and serve, either warm or at room temperature.

If using chilled homemade or frozen commercial phyllo. For chilled, leave it out of the refrigerator for 2 hours to come to room temperature; for frozen, thaw overnight in the refrigerator, then leave out at room temperature for 2 hours before using.

Brush a 9 x 13-inch (23 x 33 cm) baking pan with olive oil and place 8 sheets of phyllo on the bottom, brushing each with olive oil as you layer them. Spread the filling over the top phyllo evenly and cover with an additional 6 sheets, brushing each of them with olive oil. Press down gently. If there is overhang, pinch the excess edges together and roll in to form a rim. Score into rectangular serving pieces and bake for about 50 minutes, or until the phyllo is golden.

Glykoksini Pita me Kolokytha, Stafides kai Tyri

SWEET-AND-SAVORY WINTER SQUASH PIE

serves 8 to 12

Here's a delicious savory winter squash pie with a sweet touch, inspired by the many traditional sweet-and-savory pumpkin and other winter squash pies found all over Greece. This is a wonderful breakfast pie, but also makes a nice snack, midday meal, or main course with a fresh green salad on the side. The store-bought phyllo must be thawed in the refrigerator overnight, so plan ahead.

1 pound (450 g) #7 chilled or frozen commercial phyllo

½ cup (120 ml) extra-virgin Greek olive oil, plus more as needed

4 pounds (1.8 kg) winter squash, such as butternut, pumpkin, or calabaza, peeled, halved, and seeded

1 large red onion, grated or finely chopped

¼ cup (9 g) dried mint, or 1 cup (50 g) chopped fresh mint

1 cup (145 g) Greek raisins or other seedless raisins

1½ cups (225 g) crumbled fresh myzithra, manouri, or ricotta salata cheese

½ cup (120 ml) *petimezi* (grape molasses)

½ to 1 cup (50 to 100 g) coarse plain dried bread crumbs

1 tablespoon ground cinnamon

½ teaspoon ground cloves

Salt

1 cup (80 g) ground walnuts

Thaw the frozen phyllo in the refrigerator overnight. When ready to use the thawed or chilled phyllo, remove it from the fridge and let it come to room temperature.

Preheat the oven to 350°F (175°C). Lightly oil a 9 x 13-inch (23 x 33 cm) baking pan.

Grate the squash using a food processor fitted with the grating disc or by hand on the large holes of a box grater. Set aside in a bowl.

In a large skillet, heat 2 tablespoons of the olive oil over medium heat. Add the onion and cook until wilted, about 8 minutes. Transfer to a bowl. In the same skillet, heat 2 tablespoons of the olive oil over medium heat. Add the squash and cook until all its moisture cooks off. Transfer the cooked squash to the bowl with the onion and let cool slightly.

Add the mint, raisins, cheese, *petimezi*, bread crumbs, cinnamon, and clove and season with salt.

Layer 7 phyllo sheets, one a time, inside the prepared baking pan, brushing each one with olive oil and sprinkling walnuts between each layer. Spread the filling over the surface of the seventh phyllo sheet, patting it down with a spatula to distribute it evenly. Cover with another 4 phyllo sheets, brushing each one with olive oil. Push the overhang down the sides of the pan and under the pie. Bake for 45 to 55 minutes, until the phyllo is golden and the filling set. Remove from the oven, let cool to room temperature, and serve.

Kotopita me Koukounaria, Stafides, Myrodika kai Tyria

CHICKEN PIE
with raisins, pine nuts, herbs, and two greek cheeses

serves 8

This is a great recipe for a Sunday brunch and a brown-bag lunch alike! The warm spices, raisins, and nuts transform ordinarily mild chicken into an exotic filling for one of the most sating Greek phyllo pies.

⅔ cup (160 ml) extra-virgin Greek olive oil

1 leek, trimmed, washed well, and chopped

2 cups (220 g) chopped red onions

2 garlic cloves, minced

½ cup (65 g) pine nuts

3 cups (400 g) shredded cooked chicken

1 cup (100 g) grated graviera cheese

½ cup (75 g) grated Greek feta

½ cup (75 g) Greek golden raisins

1 cup (50 g) chopped fresh mint, or 3 tablespoons dried

½ cup (25 g) chopped fresh parsley

1 teaspoon ground cinnamon

½ teaspoon ground cloves

1 teaspoon ground cumin

½ teaspoon freshly grated nutmeg

Salt and freshly ground black pepper

A few tablespoons rice, bulgur wheat, or quinoa, if needed

½ pound (225 g) #4 frozen or chilled commercial phyllo, thawed overnight if using frozen, and at room temperature

Preheat the oven to 350°F (175°C). Lightly oil a 12-inch (30 cm) round baking dish or tart pan.

In a large wide pot or deep skillet, heat 2 tablespoons of the olive oil over medium heat. Add the leek and onions and cook until soft and lightly browned. Stir in the garlic.

While the onion mixture is cooking, lightly toast the pine nuts in a separate small skillet and transfer to a plate to cool.

Transfer the onion-leek mixture to a bowl. Stir in the chicken, cheeses, raisins, mint, parsley, cinnamon, cloves, cumin, nutmeg, and the toasted pine nuts. Season to taste with salt and pepper. If the mixture is loose, add a handful of raw rice, bulgur, or quinoa.

Layer the first phyllo sheet on bottom of pan and brush with olive oil. Place the second one on top at a slight angle, so that it overlaps the first but widens the overhang, like a fan, in other words. Continue with 4 more sheets, oiling each. Spread the chicken mixture evenly over the surface, pressing down with a spatula. Cover with 5 sheets of phyllo, layering and oiling each the same as the one on the bottom.

Using kitchen shears or a sharp paring knife, cut away all but about 1½ inches (4 cm) of the overhanging phyllo. Pick up the bottom and top sheets, press them together and fold them inwards to form a decorative rim around the inside periphery. Brush the surface generously with olive oil. Place a small round plate or bowl, about 3 inches (7.5 cm) in diameter, in the center of the pan as a guide and score a circle around it. Score even-sized slices radiating from the inner circle to the edge. Remove the plate. Sprinkle the phyllo with cold water and bake for 45 minutes, or until the phyllo is crisp and golden. Remove from the oven, let cool, and serve.

Naousseiki Tyropita tis Soulas

SOULA'S NAOUSSA CHEESE PIE

serves 8 to 10

Naoussa, a once buzzing commercial town in Macedonia in northern Greece, is now known more for its delicious, tannic red wines, made with the xinomavro grape, than for the textile manufacturing that was once its lifeblood. On a search to find how wine has insinuated itself into the local cuisine, I visited various pastry shops, finding everything from xinomavro chocolate truffles to sourdough bread made with red wine starter. One such bakery was Soula's, who, in the true spirit of Greek hospitality, offered to take us to her home where she prepared a few local specialties. This pie, with its distinctly Macedonian phyllo pastry, bursting with butter and shaped into a coil, is her version of a traditional cheese pie from the area.

FOR THE PHYLLO

4 to 4½ cups (500 to 565 g) all-purpose flour, plus more for dusting

½ teaspoon salt

¼ cup (60 ml) extra-virgin Greek olive oil or vegetable oil, plus more for greasing

FOR THE FILLING

2 pounds (900 g) Greek feta, crumbled

4 large eggs

½ cup (1 stick / 115 g) butter, melted and clarified, plus more for brushing if desired

Olive oil, for brushing (optional)

Make the phyllo: In the bowl of a stand mixer fitted with the dough hook, combine the flour, salt, olive oil, and 1½ cups (360 ml) water. Mix on medium speed until the dough begins to come together in a mass. Knead for 8 to 10 minutes more, until the dough is smooth and doesn't stick to the sides of the bowl.

Lightly oil a large bowl. Turn the dough out of the mixer bowl, form it into a ball, and place it in the oiled bowl. Cover with plastic wrap and let rest at room temperature for at least 30 minutes or up to 3 hours.

Make the filling: Combine the feta and eggs in a medium bowl.

Divide the dough into two equal-size balls. Let rest, covered, for a few minutes. On a floured surface, roll out the first dough ball to a large circle, about 20 inches (50 cm) in diameter. Place a dessert plate in the center of the circle. Using a sharp paring knife and working at equal distances around the plate, cut strips, like radii, extending from the rim of the plate to the periphery of the dough circle.

Remove the plate and brush the entire surface of the pastry with some of the melted butter. Next, fold in the first strip like a flap over the center of the pastry circle. Brush the exposed surface with butter. Repeat with each of the strips, folding each over the center like a flap and brushing the exposed surface. Once all the strips have been folded and buttered, pat around the periphery of the pastry to form a smooth-edged circle. Repeat with the second ball.

Cover each circle with plastic wrap and let rest for 20 minutes at room temperature or transfer to the refrigerator and chill for up to 24 hours. If refrigerated, bring the dough to room temperature before using.

Preheat the oven to 350°F (175°C). Brush a 15-inch (37.5 cm) round baking pan with butter or olive oil.

Roll out the first dough ball on floured surface to a circle about 18 inches (45 cm) in diameter. Cut the circle into strips that are 3 inches (7.5 cm) wide. Brush each strip with melted butter. Spread about 2 tablespoons of the feta filling down the length of each strip and fold over to cover the filling, pressing all the edges to seal. Take the cheese-filled cylinder and place one end in the center of the prepared baking pan. Gently twist the cylinder to shape it into a coil inside the pan. Repeat with remaining phyllo pastry and filly, twisting and placing the next cylinder at the edge of the first one, and continuing so the entire pan is filled concentrically with the gently twisted pastry. Brush the surface with butter and bake for 45 minutes to 1 hour, until puffed and golden. Remove from the oven, let cool, and serve.

Evraiki Melitzanopita tis Salonikis

SIMPLE EGGPLANT PITA
from the jewish community of thessaloniki

serves 6 to 8

This is one of the classic Sephardic Jewish recipes of Thessaloniki.

2 pounds (900 g) eggplants

2 cups (300 g) crumbled Greek feta

Salt and freshly ground black pepper

1 large egg, lightly beaten

Olive oil, for brushing

12 sheets #4 commercial phyllo

1 egg yolk, whisked with 1 tablespoon water, for egg wash

½ cup (50 g) grated Kefalotyri, Kefalograviera, Pecorino Romano, or Parmesan cheese

Holding the eggplants with tongs, char them over a low open flame on a stovetop burner, turning them until soft and charred on all sides, about 15 minutes in total. (Alternatively, char them under the broiler or on a grill, turning them with tongs to char all sides.) Transfer to a large stainless steel bowl. Cover tightly with plastic wrap and let cool.

When cool enough to handle, peel the eggplants and place the flesh in a clean bowl. Mash the flesh with a fork. Mix in the feta, season to taste with salt and pepper, and stir in the egg.

Preheat the oven to 350°F (175°C). Lightly oil a 9 x 13-inch (23 x 33 cm) baking pan.

Spread the phyllo in front of you on a clean work surface and keep covered with a kitchen towel while working. Place the first sheet on the bottom of the oiled pan. Brush the sheet with olive oil. Repeat with next 7 sheets of phyllo.

Spread the eggplant mixture evenly over the surface of the phyllo and top with remaining 5 sheets, one at a time, brushing each with olive oil as you layer them.

Score the pie into squares or wedges, into serving pieces. Brush the surface with the egg wash and sprinkle with the cheese. Bake for 45 to 55 minutes, or until the phyllo is crisp and golden. If the top sheet begins to darken too much while baking, cover the pie loosely with a piece of parchment paper or aluminum foil. When the pie is done, remove from the oven and let cool for at least 30 minutes before serving.

GREEK MOUNTAIN CHEESE BREAD
with mastiha

makes three 6-inch (15 cm) round flatbreads

Inspired by one of the most popular and traditional cheese breads from northern Greece, I've taken a little liberty and added the Mediterranean's most seductive spice, mastiha, or mastic, a resin extracted from the sap of a unique tree that flourishes in the twenty-one mastiha *villages on the southern tip of Chios, in the eastern Aegean.* Mastiha *has many uses, both in the kitchen and in the medicine chest, and has been known since antiquity for its therapeutic value, especially as a salve for stomach and mouth ailments. In cooking, it's surprisingly versatile.*

½ teaspoon *mastiha* (mastic) crystals

Scant 1 teaspoon salt

1 tablespoon active dry yeast

1½ to 2 cups (360 to 480 ml) warm water

3½ to 4½ cups (440 to 565 g) all-purpose flour

1 tablespoon extra-virgin Greek olive oil

2 cups (300 g) crumbled Greek feta

1 cup (100 g) coarsely grated graviera or Kefalograviera cheese

½ teaspoon freshly ground black pepper

1 teaspoon dried mint or oregano

In a mortar with a pestle, pound together the *mastiha* and salt until the mixture is a fine powder.

In the bowl of a stand mixer, dissolve the yeast in the warm water and stir until it is diluted. Let stand for 5 minutes to proof. Fit the mixer with the dough hook. Add 3½ cups (440 g) of the flour and the salt-*mastiha* mixture. Knead on medium speed until a dough mass takes shape. Continue kneading, adding a little more flour if necessary, until the dough is silky smooth and doesn't stick to the sides of the bowl.

Oil a large bowl. Remove the dough from the mixer bowl, form it into a ball, and place it in the greased bowl. Cover with plastic wrap or a kitchen towel and set aside in a warm, draft-free place to rise until almost doubled in bulk, about 40 minutes.

Add the cheeses, pepper, and mint to the dough and knead briefly in the bowl to incorporate, then turn the dough out onto a lightly floured surface and knead until the ingredients are worked into the dough. Divide the dough into 3 equal-size balls, cover, and let rest for a few minutes.

Preheat the oven to 375°F (190°C). Lightly oil two baking sheets.

Place a dough ball on one of the prepared baking sheets and, using your hands, flatten it into an uneven circle 8 to 10 inches (20 to 25 cm) in diameter. Repeat with the remaining dough balls. Cover with a cloth and let rise for 30 minutes. Using the tips of your fingers, dimple the surface of the dough, pressing down and spreading it out a bit more. The surface should be similar to that of an Italian focaccia. Bake for about 30 minutes, or until the bread is golden. Remove from the oven and let cool before serving.

Ladenia

OLIVE OIL FLATBREAD

makes one 10- to 12-inch (25 to 30 cm) oval flatbread, or 6 to 8 servings

Milos and Kimolos, two islands in the Cyclades, are known for a few regional specialties, among them open-faced pies that are typically either sold at the local bread baker's or made at home. There are a few variations, including one topped with olives and another topped with watermelon mash. This recipe, with a topping of fresh tomatoes and oregano, makes a nice snack, a great addition to the table for a dinner party, or a good lunch, accompanied by a fresh greens salad.

FOR THE DOUGH

1 (¼-ounce / 7 g) package active dry yeast (2¼ teaspoons)

1½ cups (360 ml) warm water, plus more as needed

1¾ cups (235 g) bread flour

1½ cups (190 g) all-purpose flour

1 teaspoon salt

FOR THE TOPPING

⅓ cup (80 ml) extra-virgin Greek olive oil, plus more as needed

2 large onions, chopped

2 ripe but firm large tomatoes, chopped

2 tablespoons fresh oregano

Salt and freshly ground black pepper

In the bowl of a stand mixer, dissolve the yeast in the warm water and cover with a kitchen towel. Let stand for 5 minutes or until it starts to bubble.

In a separate bowl, mix together the two flours and the salt.

Fit the mixer with the dough hook attachment. With the mixer running on low speed, slowly add the flour mixture to the yeast mixture and knead with the dough hook until combined, then increase the speed to medium and knead until a dough mass forms. Add a little more warm water as needed if the mixture is too dense, or a little more flour if it is too loose. Knead on medium speed until the dough is smooth and nothing sticks to the sides of the bowl. Cover the bowl with plastic wrap and let stand in a draft-free place for 1 hour, or until the dough doubles in bulk.

Meanwhile, make the topping: In a large skillet, heat the olive oil over medium heat. Add the onions and cook for about 5 minutes, or until they start to soften. Add the chopped tomatoes, raise the heat to medium-high, and cook until most of the liquid has cooked off. Remove from the heat.

Preheat the oven to 325°F (160°C). Oil a large square or rectangular baking pan.

Gently punch down the dough and, using a rolling pin, roll it out on a lightly floured surface to the size of the prepared pan. Gently place the dough in the pan, cover, and let the dough rise again for 15 minutes.

Spread the tomato-onion mixture evenly over the dough. Season with the oregano and salt and pepper to taste. Bake for about 1 hour, or until the dough is crisp and the topping is lightly charred. Remove from the oven, let cool slightly, and serve.

CARNIVOROUS
PLEASURES

Η γριά κότα έχει το ζουμί

H gria kota ehei to zoumi

"Old hens have all the juice."

I've always had an ambivalent relationship to the whole subject of meat on the Greek and, by extension, Mediterranean table. Relegated to the smallest compartments of the Mediterranean diet pyramid, meat is often disparaged without really understanding its place in the culture and diet.

While consumption of animal protein was nowhere near as prevalent a generation or two ago as it is in Greece today, meat was—and still is—consumed for everyday meals and holiday feasts alike. In rural communities, the attitude toward meat consumption is one of both acceptance and reverence. Most country families keep a few animals, everything from chickens to a goat or two, maybe a pig, to perhaps some rabbits. At some point, after reaching the right age and weight, living well and being treated humanely until then, animals are regarded as food.

Like the vast array of seasonal plant-based specialties, meat, too, in the Greek kitchen, is seasonal. Traditionally, for example, pork was the winter meat, and its consumption has been a paean to nose-to-tail cooking long before the term ever became fashionable. To this day, the idea of wasting food is anathema to most Greeks, whether they live in cities or villages, mountains or islands.

Some meat is almost exclusively festive. Turkey, rooster, and spit-roasted or stuffed whole lambs and goats were and still are the centerpieces of celebratory tables, Christmas and New Year's for the former, Easter, of course, for sheep and goats.

In this chapter, most of the recipes are meant to be accessible as everyday meals. Greek meat cookery is both simple and deliciously aromatic. Warm spices like cinnamon and nutmeg, natural sweeteners such honey and *petimezi* (grape molasses), and a plethora of herbs and fresh and dried fruits all find a place in the heady, hearty meat dishes on the Greek table. The selection is both one of regional specialties and more contemporary interpretations on the classics. From easy chicken recipes to succulent lamb and a few rich stews, there is something here for carnivores of every ilk.

Psito Kotopoulo Yemisto me Elies kai Syka

ROASTED CHICKEN
stuffed with figs and olives

serves 4 to 6

The fig and the olive are a relatively new match for two of the oldest Mediterranean foods. Mastiha (mastic) infuses the stuffing as it bakes and adds one more undertone to this rich, flavorful, but simple chicken dish.

FOR THE FIG-OLIVE STUFFING

4 slices stale raisin-walnut bread, cut into cubes

½ cup (75 g) coarsely chopped green olives

1 large onion, coarsely chopped

1 shallot, coarsely chopped

½ cup (25 g) finely chopped fresh parsley

8 vacuum-packed, frozen peeled, or fresh chestnuts, boiled, peeled, and crumbled

6 dried figs, preferably Greek, chopped

⅓ cup (80 ml) mastiha liqueur or ouzo

½ to ¾ cup (120 to 180 ml) chicken broth

2 tablespoons butter, melted

Salt and freshly ground black pepper

FOR THE CHICKEN

2 tablespoons extra-virgin olive oil, plus more for the pan

1 large whole chicken, about 4 pounds (2 kg)

Salt and freshly ground black pepper

½ cup (120 ml) strained fresh orange juice

½ cup (120 ml) mastiha liqueur or ouzo

Make the stuffing: Mix all the ingredients for the stuffing together and set aside. Use ½ cup (120 ml) of the broth at first and if the stuffing seems dry, add as much of the remaining broth as needed to achieve a moist texture.

Make the chicken: Preheat the oven to 350°F (175°C). Lightly oil a baking pan large enough to hold the chicken.

Trim excess fat from the chicken and pat dry. Stuff the cavity of the chicken with the fig-olive stuffing. Place in the prepared pan and season generously with salt and pepper.

Whisk together the orange juice, mastiha liqueur, and olive oil in a small bowl and season with salt and pepper. Brush the mixture over the chicken. Bake for about 1¼ hours, brushing with the orange juice mixture every 15 minutes or so and basting the bird with the pan juices, until the chicken is very tender and browned, and an instant-read thermometer inserted into the thickest part of the thigh registers 165°F (75°C). Remove from the oven, let cool slightly, and serve.

Kykladitiko Yemisto Kotopoulo Tyria, Stafides kai Myrodika

CYCLADES-STYLE WHOLE STUFFED CHICKEN
with cheese, herbs, and raisins

serves 4 to 6

There are many recipes for stuffed meats, from chicken, rooster, and turkey to the paschal lamb or goat, throughout the Cyclades islands. This traditional recipe usually calls for a rooster, but I've reworked it with more pedestrian chicken.

1 cup (240 ml) extra-virgin Greek olive oil

1 chicken liver, rinsed and finely chopped (optional)

2 large red onions, finely chopped

4 garlic cloves, crushed

2 cups (480 ml) dry white wine

2 cups (60 g) plain croutons or coarsely chopped stale country bread

1 cup (50 g) finely chopped fresh parsley

½ cup (25 g) finely chopped fresh mint

½ cup (25 g) chopped fresh thyme

⅔ cup (95 g) dark or golden seedless raisins

1 cup (100 g) coarsely grated Kefalotyri, Kefalograviera, or other hard sheep's-milk cheese

Salt and freshly ground black pepper

1 large egg, lightly beaten

1 large roasting chicken, about 4½ pounds (2 kg), preferably organic

2 pounds (900 g) roasting potatoes, peeled and halved

Preheat the oven to 400°F (200°C).

In a large deep skillet, heat 2 tablespoons of the olive oil over medium heat. Add the chicken liver, if using, and cook, stirring, until lightly browned. Remove and set aside. Add the onions to the skillet and cook over medium-low heat until soft and lightly colored, about 12 minutes. Stir in the garlic. Return the liver to the pan, stir, and pour in 1 cup (240 ml) of the wine. Cook until the liquid has reduced by half. Transfer the mixture to a large bowl.

Add the croutons, parsley, mint, thyme, raisins, cheese, and salt and pepper to taste to the liver-onion mixture. Add the egg and combine well.

Pat dry the chicken. Spoon the stuffing into the cavity of the bird. Place the skin flap over the opening and secure closed with toothpicks or skewers. Rub the outside of the bird with 2 tablespoons of the olive oil and season generously with salt and pepper. Place in a large roasting pan.

In a large bowl, toss the potatoes, salt, pepper, and remaining ¾ cup (180 ml) olive oil. Place them around the chicken in the pan. Roast for 15 minutes. Pour in the remaining 1 cup (240 ml) wine and roast for about 1½ hours more, basting the chicken with the pan juices every 15 minutes, until an instant-read thermometer inserted into the thickest part of the chicken registers 165°F (75°C) and the potatoes are very tender. Remove from the oven, let cool slightly, and serve.

Sartsa apo ta Eptanisa

TOMATO CHICKEN OR GUINEA HEN
with kefalograviera cheese

serves 4 to 6

This old recipe from the Ionian islands originally called for guinea hen, aka frangokota, *or "French chicken," in Greek. In Corfu, it's called* faraona, *for Pharaoh, and, indeed, the ancient Greeks used to import the bird from Egypt. Guinea hens slipped into obscurity after the fall of the Roman Empire and resurfaced sometime in the sixteenth century, when Portuguese merchants began trading them from their West African colony to France, which might also account for why the bird is known as "French chicken" in many parts of Greece today.*

½ cup (120 ml) extra-virgin Greek olive oil

2 medium red onions, finely chopped

4 garlic cloves, chopped

2 cups (360 g) chopped plum tomatoes (canned are fine)

Salt

¼ cup (60 ml) red wine vinegar

2 small guinea hens (about 1½ pounds / 680 g each), or 1 medium chicken (about 3 pounds / 1.3 kg)

Freshly ground black pepper

½ cup (120 ml) white wine

2 tablespoons dried Greek oregano

1 cup (130 g) cubed graviera or Kefalograviera cheese

Preheat the oven to 350°F (175°C).

In a large heavy skillet, heat ¼ cup (60 ml) of the olive oil over medium heat. Add the onions and cook until soft and translucent, about 10 minutes. Stir in the garlic. Add the tomatoes. Season with salt, cover, reduce the heat to medium-low, and simmer for about 20 minutes, or until the sauce starts to thicken. Add the vinegar and simmer for 5 minutes more.

Generously season the guinea hens or chicken with salt and pepper. Place in a Dutch oven or deep, preferably ceramic or glass baking dish with a cover and pour the sauce over and around the bird(s). Pour in the wine and sprinkle in the oregano. Drizzle the remaining ¼ cup (60 ml) olive oil over and around the bird(s). Cover and bake until tender, about 1 hour. About 10 minutes before removing from the oven, add the cheese cubes to the pan. The cheese should be oozing but still hold its shape when you serve the hens or chicken.

Remove from the oven and serve.

Kotopoulo Psito me Haloumi, Manitaria kai Myrodika

ROASTED CHICKEN
with haloumi, mushrooms, and herbs

serves 6

I am always on the lookout for new, easy ways to roast a chicken. This recipe is hearty and gorgeous, especially good when the weather starts to get chilly. You can exchange the haloumi cheese, which is a specialty of Cyprus, for any firm cheese in the pasta filata family of cheeses, such as Greek formaella, provolone, scamorza, or caciocavallo.

1 whole chicken, about 4 pounds (1.8 kg), cut in half lengthwise and trimmed

3 tablespoons (45 ml) extra-virgin Greek olive oil

1 large onion, finely chopped

1 medium carrot, finely chopped

4 garlic cloves, minced

2 cups (290 g) teardrop or cherry tomatoes

3 cups (285 g) button mushrooms, trimmed and halved

Salt and freshly ground black pepper

2 cups (330 g) chopped canned tomatoes

½ cup (120 ml) dry white wine

2 tablespoons balsamic vinegar

1 tablespoon dried Greek oregano

2 bay leaves

1½ cups (195 g) ¾-inch (1.5 cm) cubes haloumi or other pasta filata cheese (see headnote)

3 tablespoons chopped fresh parsley, for garnish

Preheat the oven to 375°F (190°C).

Place the chicken on a clean cutting board and flatten each half by pounding them lightly with a meat mallet.

In a large wide pot, heat the olive oil over medium-high heat. Carefully place one chicken half inside, skin-side down. Sear until golden brown and turn carefully with kitchen tongs to brown lightly on the other side. Set aside in a baking dish large enough to hold both halves in a single layer. Repeat with the remaining chicken half. Cover the baking dish and set aside.

Drain all but 2 tablespoons of the fat from the pan. Heat the remaining fat over medium heat. Add the onion and carrot and cook until softened, about 8 minutes.

Add the garlic and stir for a minute. Add the whole tomatoes and shake them around in the pan for a few minutes. Add the mushrooms and gently stir to coat with the oil and soften slightly. Season lightly with salt and pepper.

Pour in the canned tomatoes, raise the heat to medium-high, and add the wine. As soon as the alcohol cooks off, reduce the heat to medium-low, add the vinegar, oregano, and bay leaves, and cook for about 10 minutes to allow the flavors to meld and to thicken the sauce slightly.

Season the chicken halves generously on both sides with salt and pepper. Spoon the sauce all around them and a little on top. Cover the baking dish with parchment paper, then aluminum foil, and roast for 25 minutes. Uncover and strew the haloumi cubes all around the chicken. Roast for 20 minutes more, until the chicken is tender and the haloumi is soft. Remove from the oven, sprinkle with the parsley, and serve hot.

CHICKEN LORE

If vase paintings are any indication, chicken has been a part of the Greek table since at least the sixth century BC. Pottery from Rhodes and Sparta dating to that period depicts images of world's most popular edible bird. One ancient name for the rooster was *alektryon*, meaning a creature that causes one to leave one's bed, *lektron*. In the Greek colonies of southern Italy, the Sybarites banned chickens . . . in favor of a little more shut-eye every morning.

To this day on the Greek table, the age, sex, and size of the bird determine how it will be cooked. Old hens, as they say, have the most juice, and so are reserved for soup. Larger chickens are stuffed and roasted.

Small guinea hens, which are called *frangokotes*, or "French hens," were mainly found in areas where there was a Catholic population, especially in the Ionian islands. Game hens can easily replace regular chicken in dishes such as the Roasted Chicken with Haloumi, Mushrooms, and Herbs on page 292.

Kotopoulo Psimmeno me Verikoka kai Yiaourti

ROASTED APRICOT CHICKEN MARINATED IN GREEK YOGURT

serves 6

An easy, delicious Sunday lunch or weeknight dinner. Greek yogurt helps tenderize the chicken. I sweeten up the apricots with some Greek raisins, too.

4 pounds (1.8 kg) chicken parts

Salt and freshly ground black pepper

6 tablespoons (90 ml) Greek yogurt

2 tablespoons apricot jam

2 teaspoons Dijon mustard

1 tablespoon balsamic vinegar

4 tablespoons (60 ml) extra-virgin Greek olive oil

Juice of 1 orange, strained

1 teaspoon ground cumin

1 teaspoon ground turmeric

½ teaspoon paprika

2 cinnamon sticks

1 large red onion, halved and sliced

8 dried apricots

2 tablespoons raisins

1 teaspoon sugar

½ cup (25 g) fresh mint leaves, cut into thin strips

Preheat the oven to 375°F (190°C).

Pat dry the chicken. Season with salt and pepper on all sides.

Whisk together the yogurt, jam, mustard, vinegar, 3 tablespoons of the olive oil, the orange juice, cumin, turmeric, and paprika. Toss the chicken in this mixture and marinate at room temperature for 15 minutes or cover and refrigerate for up to 6 hours.

Transfer the marinated chicken to a glass baking dish. Add the cinnamon sticks to the dish. Cover with parchment paper, then aluminum foil. Bake for about 45 minutes, or until the chicken is almost cooked through, or reaches 150°F (66°C).

In the meantime, in a heavy nonstick skillet, heat the remaining 1 tablespoon olive oil over medium heat. Add the onion, season with a little salt, and cook, stirring, until lightly browned and soft, 10 to 12 minutes. Add the apricots and raisins and sprinkle with the sugar. Cook until heated through, then gently stir in the mint.

Remove the parchment and foil and bake until the chicken begins to brown nicely. Spoon the pan juices over it. Add the onion-apricot mixture to the chicken and continue baking until the internal temperature of the chicken reaches 165°F/ 74°C .

Remove from the oven, let cool slightly, and serve.

Fterougies me Ouzo

OUZO-GLAZED CHICKEN WINGS

serves 5

You can use this glaze for chicken breasts or legs, beef or pork ribs, and roasted whole chicken or Cornish game hens, too. I like to use oregano-infused extra-virgin Greek olive oil for this dish.

3 tablespoons Dijon mustard

¼ cup (60 ml) Greek yogurt

¼ cup (60 ml) balsamic vinegar

½ cup (120 ml) extra-virgin Greek olive oil, preferably oregano-infused, plus more for the baking dish

2 tablespoons ouzo, or 1 teaspoon fennel seeds, pulverized in a spice grinder or with a pestle and mortar

3 tablespoons strained fresh orange juice

2 tablespoons Greek honey

3 garlic cloves, minced

2 teaspoons minced fresh ginger

½ teaspoon cayenne pepper, or more to taste

1 heaping teaspoon ground cumin

Salt

2 pounds (about 1 kg) chicken wings, preferably organic

Whisk together the mustard, yogurt, vinegar, olive oil, ouzo, orange juice, honey, garlic, ginger, cayenne, and cumin in large bowl and season with salt. Add the wings and toss to coat completely with the marinade. Cover and refrigerate for at least 30 minutes or up to 2 hours.

Preheat the oven to 375°F (190°C). Oil a large baking dish.

Place the chicken wings in the baking dish and roast until golden, turning several times so that they cook evenly, about 35 minutes total.

Aromatiko, Pikantiko Kotsi me Revithia

SPICY AROMATIC BRAISED LAMB SHANKS
with chickpeas

serves 6

In Greece, hearty stews that combined meat and vegetables or beans were a way to stretch a meal, providing a little animal protein to every member of the family, for example, while filling bellies on more economical raw ingredients such as chickpeas, an ancient legume in the eastern Mediterranean. This is a recipe originally from the islands of the eastern Aegean. Note that if you're using dried chickpeas, they need to soak overnight, so plan ahead, or used canned chickpeas.

1½ cups (275 g) dried chickpeas, picked over for debris and rinsed, or 4½ cups (747 g) canned chickpeas

6 fresh or dried bay leaves (optional)

2 large onions: 1 left whole, 1 finely chopped (optional)

¾ cup (180 ml) extra-virgin Greek olive oil

6 lamb shanks, about 1 pound (450 g) each

Salt and freshly ground black pepper

1 carrot, halved

2 celery stalks, very finely chopped

1½ cups (360 ml) white wine or brandy

6 allspice berries

1 cinnamon stick

1 (3-inch / 7.5 cm) whole dried chile (optional)

4 fresh thyme sprigs

2½ cups (415 g) chopped canned plum tomatoes

Water or chicken broth

½ cup (25 g) finely chopped fresh parsley

If using dried chickpeas, put them in a large bowl, add cold water to cover, and set aside at room temperature to soak overnight. Drain the chickpeas and place them in a large pot. Add water to cover by 3 inches (7.5 cm), 2 bay leaves, and the whole onion. Bring to a boil over medium-high heat, reduce the heat to low, and simmer for about 1½ hours, or until the chickpeas are about two-thirds cooked. Skip this step if using canned chickpeas.

While the chickpeas cook, preheat the oven to 375°F (190°C).

In a large skillet or wide shallow pot, heat 6 tablespoons (90 ml) of the olive oil. Working in batches, sear the lamb shanks, turning them with kitchen tongs to brown well on all sides. Season generously with salt and pepper. Remove with kitchen tongs and transfer to a large ovenproof clay or enamel casserole dish with a lid. Repeat to brown the remaining shanks.

In the same pan, heat a couple of tablespoons of the olive oil (if needed—there may be sufficient fat in the pan) over medium heat. Add the chopped onion, carrot, and celery. Carefully pour in the wine or brandy and stir to deglaze the pan. Reduce the heat to medium and cook, stirring, until the vegetables are softened, about 15 minutes.

When the chickpeas are done, drain them, discarding the bay leaves and onion. Whether using cooked or canned, place the chickpeas in the casserole, scattering them all around the shanks, and stir in the vegetables. Add the allspice, cinnamon stick, chile, thyme, tomatoes, and enough water or broth to barely cover the meat and chickpeas.

Cover and bake for about 2 hours, or until the meat is falling off the shanks and the chickpeas are tender. Check the liquid content during cooking; if there is not enough, add some more water or broth; if there is too much, remove the lid or covering about halfway through braising to allow it to evaporate. Season to taste with salt and pepper.

Remove from the oven, pour in the remaining olive oil, and stir it gently into the chickpeas. Let rest for 30 minutes. Serve sprinkled with the chopped parsley.

Mpouti Arnisio y Katsikisio Psito me xinomavro kai Myrodika

ROASTED LEG OF LAMB OR GOAT
with xinomavro wine and herbs

serves 6

Lamb is such a touchy subject, even among meat lovers. New Zealand? Australian? American? They all taste so different from the lambs (and goats) that graze on Greece's sea-sprayed rich natural grasses and flora. Greek lamb tends to be smaller and milder. Look for young lamb for this recipe.

FOR THE LAMB

15 garlic cloves

¼ cup (70 g) allspice berries

3 tablespoons whole black peppercorns, crushed

3 to 4 tablespoons coarse Greek sea salt, as needed

1½ cups (150 g) grated Kefalotyri or other sharp, hard, preferably Greek, sheep's-milk cheese, such as Kefalograviera, ladotyri, or hard myzithra (pecorino and Parmesan also work well)

1 (6½- to 7-pound / 3 kg) bone-in lamb or goat leg

2 to 3 tablespoons extra-virgin Greek olive oil

FOR THE ROASTING PAN

6 fresh rosemary sprigs

10 fresh thyme sprigs

10 fresh oregano sprigs

6 dried Greek sage leaves

3 onions, sliced

3 celery stalks, coarsely chopped

1 large fennel bulb, coarsely chopped

6 bay leaves

1 tablespoon whole black peppercorns

5 to 6 tablespoons (75 to 90 ml) extra-virgin Greek olive oil

Salt

2 cups (480 ml) xinomavro or other tannic red wine, plus more as needed

Preheat the oven to 400°F (200°C).

Prepare the lamb: In a mortar, working in batches if your mortar isn't large enough, combine the garlic, allspice, 1½ tablespoons of the peppercorns, and a little salt and pound with the pestle until the mixture is a damp, chunky paste. Transfer to a small bowl and stir in the grated cheese. Set aside until ready to use.

Rinse the lamb or goat leg and pat dry. Using a sharp paring knife, make about 25 incisions on all sides of the leg. Stuff a large pinch of the spice-cheese mixture into each of the incisions, pushing it in as deep as possible. Continue until you've used all the the mixture, making additional incisions as necessary.

Rub the olive oil over the surface of the leg and season generously with salt and the remaining 1½ tablespoons crushed peppercorns.

For the roasting pan, combine the rosemary, thyme, oregano, sage, onions, celery, fennel, bay leaves, peppercorns, and olive oil in a large bowl and season with salt. Spread the vegetable-herb mixture over the bottom of a large roasting pan. Place the meat over the vegetables. Pour ½ cup (120 ml) of the wine over the meat. Roast for 20 minutes, until the meat begins to brown. Reduce the oven temperature to 325°F (160°C).

Remove the pan from the oven and cover with parchment or waxed paper, then with aluminum foil. Return the pan to the oven and roast for 2 to 2½ hours more for medium-rare, uncovering the pan every 30 minutes and pouring the remaining wine over the leg in ½-cup (120 ml) increments, or until a meat thermometer inserted into the thickest part of the leg registers 145°F (65°C).

Remove from the oven and let the meat rest for 20 to 30 minutes before carving. If desired, strain the pan juices and drizzle over the slices of lamb as you serve.

Egaiopelagitiko Psito Arnaki

AEGEAN ISLAND STUFFED LAMB

serves 6

So many people associate Greek Easter with the outdoor feasts of spit-roasted lamb or goat that are traditional on the mainland that island recipes are sometimes overlooked. Easter on most Aegean islands is a feast in which stuffed roasted lamb takes center stage. The recipes are a wonderful mirror of what is on hand locally from island to island, and so tell a story of regionality that is still timely.

I've adapted the recipe to what an American cook is more likely to make: a stuffed boneless shoulder rather than a whole stuffed baby lamb or goat.

1 boneless lamb shoulder, about 3 pounds (1.4 kg)

Salt and freshly ground black pepper

8 garlic cloves, finely chopped

⅔ cup (160 ml) extra-virgin Greek olive oil, plus more as needed

1 red or yellow onion, finely chopped

6 scallions, finely chopped

1 cup (185 g) long-grain rice, such as Greek Carolina

3 cups dry white wine

Finely grated zest of 1 lemon

1 teaspoon fennel seeds

½ cup (25 g) snipped fresh dill

1 cup (50 g) chopped fresh mint leaves

1 cup (150 g) crumbled Greek feta

¼ cup (35 g) pine nuts, toasted

⅓ cup (50 g) raisins (optional)

1 large egg

3 pounds (1.4 kg) new potatoes, preferably organic, unpeeled

6 fresh rosemary sprigs

6 fresh oregano sprigs

Open the lamb up on a clean work surface and season generously on both sides with salt and pepper. Using a sharp paring knife, make small slits all over the surface of the lamb. Use one-quarter of the garlic (about 3 tablespoons, or 2 chopped cloves) to stuff the slits. Cover and refrigerate.

Preheat the oven to 375°F (190°C).

In a large deep skillet or wide pot, heat ⅓ cup (80 ml) of the olive oil over medium heat. Add the onion and scallions and cook, stirring occasionally, until wilted and translucent, about 8 minutes. Add the rice and toss to coat with the oil. Add one-third of the remaining garlic and stir. Pour in 1 cup (240 ml) water and 1 cup (240 ml) of the wine and cook until the liquids have been absorbed and the rice is al dente, about 12 minutes. The filling should be fairly dry. Season to taste with salt and pepper. Let the mixture cool.

Add the lemon zest, fennel seeds, dill, mint, feta, pine nuts, raisins (if using), and half the remaining garlic to the rice and stir well to combine. Taste and adjust the seasoning with additional salt and pepper. Stir in the egg and 3 tablespoons of the olive oil.

Remove the lamb from the fridge and return it to your work surface. Spread the filling over the surface of the meat, then roll up the lamb, securing the roll at a few points with butcher's twine or ovenproof elastic bands.

Place the lamb on a rack set inside a roasting pan. Place the potatoes around the lamb. Season generously with salt, pepper, and the remaining garlic. Add the rosemary and oregano sprigs to the roasting pan, and fill the pan with enough water to come about halfway up the potatoes. Roast, uncovered, for 20 minutes.

Pour the remaining 2 cups (480 ml) wine over the lamb and potatoes, cover with parchment paper, then aluminum foil, and slide back into the oven. Reduce the oven temperature to 375°F (190°C) and roast for 1 hour 10 minutes to 1 hour 20 minutes for medium, or until a meat thermometer inserted into the lamb registers 130°F (55°C).

Remove from the oven, let rest for 20 minutes, then slice and serve with the potatoes.

NOTE: If there is leftover rice filling, put it in an ovenproof casserole with enough water to cover by 1 inch (2.5 cm), cover with a lid, and bake it simultaneously with the lamb, for 35 to 40 minutes, until set and tender.

Teleia Arnisia Paidakia

THE BEST GREEK LAMB CHOPS

makes 4 chops, to serve 4

Classics hardly need an explanation. These simple, succulent lamb chops are always a big seller on restaurant menus, but there is no reason why we can't make them at home. I like the rack chops best, but if you want something a little meatier, try making this with loin chops instead.

4 rack-of-lamb chops, about 4 ounces (115 g) each

3 large garlic cloves, minced

2 tablespoons chopped fresh rosemary

1 tablespoon dried thyme

1 tablespoon dried Greek oregano or savory

1 cup (240 ml) dry red wine

½ cup (120 ml) extra-virgin olive oil

Salt and freshly ground black pepper

2 lemons, cut in half, for garnish

Trim, rinse, and pat dry the lamb chops.

Using a spice grinder or mortar and pestle, pulverize the garlic, rosemary, thyme, and oregano into a paste.

Rub the lamb chops all over with the herb-garlic mixture. Place in a single layer in a shallow bowl and pour in the wine and olive oil. Cover and marinate in the refrigerator for 2 to 24 hours. Let stand at room temperature for 30 minutes before grilling.

Heat a grill to medium-high.

Place the lamb chops over direct heat and grill, season with salt and pepper, and turn once about halfway through, seasoning the other side as well. Grill for 6 to 8 minutes for rare, 8 to 10 minutes for medium, or 12 to 15 minutes for well done. Season to taste with additional salt and pepper. Remove from the grill and serve hot, with the lemon halves on the side.

GRILLED BUTTERFLIED LEG OF LAMB

serves 8

Greeks in Greece tend to go out to restaurants for a grill-fest, rarely barbecuing at home, where outdoor space, especially in cities, is always limited. This recipe makes a great Greek-inspired barbecue dish. Try brushing it with sour cherry barbecue sauce (page 14) in addition to the spice rub.

1 (5-pound / 2.3 kg) boned leg of lamb, butterflied

3 large garlic cloves, minced

3 tablespoons chopped fresh rosemary

3 tablespoons dried thyme, marjoram, savory, or oregano

1 tablespoon whole black peppercorns

1 tablespoon extra-virgin olive oil

Salt and freshly ground black pepper

2 or 3 lemons, cut in half, for garnish

The butterflied leg of lamb should be about 2 inches (5 cm) thick. Once the butcher has butterflied it, have him pound it with a mallet to flatten out to the desired thickness. You can do this yourself, too: Place the lamb on a strong counter and bang it all over its surface, either with a heavy skillet or a mallet, until flattened to about 2 inches (5 cm).

Using a mortar and pestle or a spice grinder, pulverize the garlic, herbs, and peppercorns. Combine with the olive oil in a small bowl.

Season the butterflied leg generously with salt and pepper and rub the herb-garlic paste all over, pushing it into every nook and cranny within the meat. Let the lamb rest for 1 to 2 hours or up to 6 hours, covered and refrigerated.

Heat a grill to high.

Place the lamb directly over the heat and sear it for a total of about 10 minutes, turning once, to brown on all sides. Once seared, slide the lamb over to continue grilling over indirect heat. Rare lamb will take about 20 minutes more. About halfway through grilling, cut off a tiny piece to test for doneness. Remove from the heat when grilled to the desired doneness. Let the meat rest for 5 minutes before slicing. Slice into ½-inch (1.5 cm) pieces and serve, garnished with the lemon halves.

Exohiko me Hoirino

PORK MEDALLIONS BAKED IN PAPER

serves 4

I love to bake in paper. I love the whole idea of serving forth a surprise, like a gift everyone at the table gets to open. Exohiko means "of the countryside," and it's one of the most popular ways to cook meat throughout Greece.

2 pounds (about 1 kg) boneless shoulder of pork, cut into 2-inch (5 cm) medallions

2 tablespoons Greek or Dijon mustard

2 tablespoons strained fresh lemon juice

¼ cup (60 ml) white wine

¼ cup (60 ml) extra-virgin Greek olive oil

10 garlic cloves

10 dried sage leaves

Salt and freshly ground black pepper

Hot paprika (optional)

Grated zest of 1 lemon, preferably organic

8 fresh rosemary sprigs, each 3 to 4 inches (7.5 to 10 cm) long

1 leek, trimmed, washed well, and cut into thin rings

1 celery stalk, coarsely chopped or diced

12 (1-inch / 2.5 cm) cubes Kefalotyri or Kefalograviera cheese

Rinse the pork and pat dry.

In a medium metal bowl, whisk together the mustard, lemon juice, wine, and olive oil. Toss the pork in this mixture. Cover and refrigerate for 1 hour.

Preheat the oven to 350°F (175°C). Lightly oil a baking sheet. Cut four pieces of parchment paper large enough to hold the pork pieces.

In a mortar, grind together the garlic and sage leaves using the pestle.

Using a slotted spoon, transfer the pork to a bowl and pat dry. Season generously with salt and pepper, add the garlic-sage mixture, and toss. Place an equal portion of the pork on each piece of parchment. Sprinkle the contents of each packet judiciously with hot paprika, if desired. Sprinkle evenly with the lemon zest. Place 2 rosemary sprigs in each packet over the meat. Divide the leek and celery evenly over the pork in each packet. Add equal amounts of the cheese cubes to each. Drizzle in a little of the marinade.

Fold the long sides of the parchment over the pork and bring the two ends together, rolling them at the edges to close the parcel. Secure with kitchen string and place on the prepared baking sheet. Sprinkle a little water over the parcels. Bake the parcels for 1¾ hours, or until the pork is tender. During cooking, sprinkle more water in the baking sheet and over the parcels to keep the meat moist.

Remove from the oven and serve. Open the parcels carefully, because the steam that escapes is very hot.

Kontosouvli

"SHORT" SKEWERS FROM MAINLAND GREECE

serves 4 as a main course

Kontosouvli—*short skewers*—*are a specialty of the rolling hills and expansive plains of mainland Greece, perfect grazing ground, where meat is a staple. If anything differentiates this simple skewered barbecued lamb dish from all others in the Greek repertoire, it is probably that it is one of the few that is usually preferred without lemon squeezed over it once the meat is grilled. Note that the meat mixture needs to be refrigerated overnight before being grilled, so plan ahead.*

2 large red onions

1½ pounds (680 g) boneless pork, cut into 1½-inch (4 cm) cubes

⅓ cup (80 ml) extra-virgin olive oil

4 garlic cloves, minced

2 tablespoons dried Greek oregano

Salt and freshly ground white pepper

Grate the onions on the large holes of a box grater or using a food processor fitted with the grating disc. Do not discard the onions' juices.

Combine the meat, grated onions and their juices, olive oil, garlic, and oregano, in a bowl, season with salt and white pepper, and knead so that all the flavors meld. Cover well with plastic wrap and refrigerate overnight. Bring to room temperature before grilling.

When ready to cook the skewers, heat a grill to high.

Thread the meat onto four 10- or 12-inch-long (25 to 30 cm) metal skewers. Grill over direct heat for 15 to 20 minutes, turning to brown on all sides. Remove from the grill and serve immediately.

Kalogeros

SLICED VEAL
layered with eggplants and cheese

serves 4

Kalogeros, named for a mountain peak on Naxos, is one of the island's traditional recipes.

2 large eggplants, peeled and cut into ¼-inch (6 mm) rounds

Salt

2 pounds (900 g) boneless veal shoulder or beef chuck or shoulder, cut into ½-inch (1.5 cm) thick slices

All-purpose flour, for dredging

¾ cup (180 ml) extra-virgin Greek olive oil, plus more as needed

2 large onions, finely chopped

1 cup (240 ml) canned crushed tomatoes

1 cup (240 ml) dry white wine

2 bay leaves

½ teaspoon ground cinnamon

Freshly ground black pepper

6 ounces (170 g) Greek feta or local soft sour myzithra cheese, crumbled

2 ripe but firm large tomatoes, cut into very thin rounds

4 ounces (115 g) Graviera Naxos or Gruyère cheese

Layer the eggplant slices in a colander, sprinkling each layer with salt. Set the colander in the sink, place a plate over the eggplant slices and a weight (such as a large can of tomatoes) on top, and let sit for 30 minutes. Dredge the veal in the flour. In a large skillet, heat ½ cup (120 ml) of the olive oil over medium heat and add the veal and cook, turning, until browned on both sides. Remove with a slotted spoon and set aside.

Add the onions, reduce the heat to low, and cook, stirring, until the onions soften, about 8 minutes. Place the meat over the onions. Add the crushed tomatoes and bring to a boil. Add the wine. As soon as it steams up, add the bay leaves, cinnamon, and enough water to cover by 1 inch (2.5 cm). Season with salt and pepper. Cover, bring to a boil, and reduce the heat to low. Simmer for 1½ hours, until the veal is very tender.

While the veal cooks, rinse the eggplants very well, drain, and blot dry on paper towels. In a large skillet, heat the remaining ¼ cup (60 ml) olive oil over medium heat. Add the eggplant and cook, turning with tongs, until lightly browned and tender. Preheat the broiler with a rack positioned 8 inches (20 c) from the heat. Brush the eggplants with olive oil and place in an oiled baking pan. Broil, turning once, until soft. Remove and drain on paper towels.

Preheat the oven to 375°F (190°C). Lightly oil a glass baking dish large enough to hold the eggplant and veal slices. Place the eggplant pieces in one layer on the bottom of the prepared baking dish. Place the veal in one layer over the eggplant and sprinkle with the feta. Spread a layer of tomato rounds over the feta. Top with the Graviera. Pour the skillet juices and sauce over the top and bake for about 15 minutes, until the cheeses melt. Remove from the oven and serve.

To Agapimeno Kokinisto tou Yiou Mou

MY SON'S FAVORITE BEEF STEW

serves 8 to 10

One of the classics of Greek meat cookery is a one-pot stew called kokinisto, *which means "red," so named for the tomato that goes into it. This is a variation of that recipe, enriched with a complex nexus of herbs and spices that give the dish a rich, multifaceted flavor.*

4½ to 5 pounds (2 to 2.3 kg) boneless beef, cut into stew-size pieces

Extra-virgin Greek olive oil

1½ cups (270 g) fine semolina flour, for dredging

2 red onions, coarsely chopped

1 fennel bulb, chopped

2 large carrots, quartered lengthwise

6 garlic cloves, chopped

2 cups (480 ml) dry red wine, such as xinomavro or agiorgitiko

1 (14-ounce / 410 g) can plum or chopped tomatoes, with juices

12 pitted prunes: 8 whole, 4 very finely chopped

1 small orange, unpeeled, cut into 8 to 10 sections

4 bay leaves

1 large cinnamon stick

10 allspice berries

4 dried sage leaves

10 fresh thyme sprigs

Salt and freshly ground black pepper

3 tablespoons balsamic vinegar, plus more to taste

3 tablespoons *petimezi* (grape molasses), plus more to taste

2 to 3 tablespoons Greek honey, plus more to taste

2 tablespoons good-quality tomato paste

Rinse the meat and pat dry.

In a large wide pot or deep skillet, heat about ½ cup (120 ml) olive oil—enough to coat the surface of the pot—over medium-high heat. Place the semolina in a deep bowl. Working in batches, add some of the meat to the bowl and toss to coat in the semolina, shaking off the excess. Add the dredged meat to the hot oil and cook, turning as needed, until well browned on all sides. Transfer the browned meat to a bowl. Repeat with the remaining meat, adding more olive oil if needed between batches.

While the meat is browning, in a separate large wide pot or a Dutch oven, heat ½ cup (120 ml) olive oil over medium heat. Add the onions and fennel and cook until soft and translucent. Add the carrots and stir to coat with the oil. Stir in the garlic.

Add the browned meat to the onion mixture. As it starts to heat up, pour in the wine. As soon as the alcohol cooks off, add the tomatoes, the chopped prunes, orange, bay leaves, cinnamon

stick, allspice, sage leaves, thyme, and salt and pepper to taste. Add enough water to come just below the surface of the meat.

Cover, raise the heat to bring the liquid to a boil, then reduce the heat to low and simmer for about 2 hours, or until the meat just begins to get tender. Add the vinegar, *petimezi*, and honey. Simmer until the meat is tender, another half hour or so. About 15 minutes before removing from the heat, add the remaining whole prunes, stir in the tomato paste, taste, and adjust the seasoning with salt, pepper, and additional acidity (vinegar) or sweetness (*petimezi* or honey). Serve hot.

Spetzofai

SAUSAGES
braised with fresh, roasted, and pickled peppers

serves 6

Spetzofai, *after the word for "peppers" in the local dialect of Mount Pelion, where this dish orig-*
inated, is one of the heartiest of all winter meat recipes in Greece. It can be served alone or as a
sauce over pasta or rice. It's also great with fries, such as those on page 152.

1½ pounds (680 g) fresh pork or beef sausage, cut into 1-inch (2.5 cm) chunks

3 tablespoons extra-virgin Greek olive oil

1 large red onion, halved and sliced

3 garlic cloves

6 green bell peppers, seeded and cut into 1-inch (2.5 cm) strips

3 red Florina peppers in brine, drained, rinsed, and cut into strips

4 pickled pepperoncini peppers

½ cup (120 ml) white wine

2 cups (330 g) chopped canned tomatoes

2 tablespoons tomato paste

2 bay leaves

Salt and freshly ground black pepper

1 heaping teaspoon dried Greek oregano

In a large wide pot or deep skillet, sear the sausage pieces over medium-high heat until nicely browned. Remove with a slotted spoon and drain off the rendered fat from the pan.

In the same pan, heat the olive oil over medium heat. Add the onion and cook, stirring, until lightly browned. Stir in the garlic and cook for a few minutes to soften. Add the bell pepper strips and cook, stirring gently, until they begin to soften. Add the Florina peppers and pepperoncini. Cook, stirring, for a few minutes.

Return the sausage to the pan and stir to combine. Pour in the wine. As soon as the alcohol cooks off, add the tomatoes, tomato paste, bay leaves, and salt and black pepper to taste. Cover and simmer for about 25 minutes, or until the sausage is thoroughly cooked and the peppers are tender. Stir in the oregano a few minutes before removing from the heat. Taste and adjust the seasoning with salt and black pepper. Remove from the heat, remove the bay leaves, and serve.

FRESH
FROM THE
SEA

Sea Bass Carpaccio   320

Greek Sea Bass Baked with Santorini Assyrtiko Wine,
Capers Leaves, and Herbs   323

Mediterranean Sea Bass with Mushrooms
and Red Wine   324

Cod Fillets with Orange and Green Olive Salsa   325

Grilled Mackerel Stuffed with Carrots, Raisins,
Pine Nuts, and Herbs   327

Braised Octopus with Olives   330

Baked Sardines with Ouzo, Tomatoes,
Capers, and Lemon   332

Grilled Butterflied Sardines
with Red Onion and Herbs   333

Grilled Large Shrimp with Ouzo, Lemon, Pepper,
and Coriander   334

Shrimp and Mussels in Fresh Tomato-Basil Sauce   337

Mou epsise to psari sta heili

"She grilled the fish on my lips."
(Meaning: She tormented me or gave me a hard time.)

Fish cookery often seems more complicated than it really is, and yet it's probably the one thing most people associate very closely with the Greek table. Greek seafood restaurants the world over compete with one another for the most comprehensive and freshest display of fish, showcased on snowy ice in a corner of the dining room. But home cooks have less access to a broad variety of fish than restaurants do, and most people rely either on the frozen fish in supermarket freezers or on whatever fresh fish the market might carry.

Salmon, tilapia, cod, and pollock are probably among the most common. But none of these is native to the Aegean. In this chapter, the recipes call for Mediterranean varieties of fish and seafood that are available and accessible in the United States. Mediterranean sea bass is one of them, and what is available stateside (and what you find in most restaurants) is mainly the product of aquaculture, which I have come to appreciate more and more, knowing the care and quality with which fish are farmed in Greece, but also knowing how tenuous are the wild fish stocks in these days of overfishing and pollution. Greece, with its thousands of miles of coastline, is one of the world's premiere producers of farmed fish. A few innovative companies are even producing organic farmed fish. Sea bass, grouper, and some snapper are the main varieties, and they are flown fresh almost daily to reach American markets.

Oily fish such as sardines and mackerel are another favorite. Sardine is considered a poor man's fish in Greece, but nutritionally it's one of the richest, a great source of omega-3 fatty acids. Mackerel, tunny, and all related fish are equally popular.

The sea is everywhere evident in Greece, and for the most part fish cookery is simple. A fresh whole fish on the grill is still considered one of the best things in the world to savor, but it's something most people go out to a restaurant for.

Shellfish and cephalopods make up another vast category of fruits of the sea that define the flavors and ingredients of the Greek table. Many people have savored a piece of grilled octopus in Greek restaurants overseas or in Greece proper. I like to braise octopus, too, and have a deep appreciation for the many octopus stews that are part of the regional Greek table. One recipe here, cooked with olives, is a classic from the island of Lesvos, in the eastern Aegean.

In the recipes that follow, I've tried to incorporate flavors from all over Greece, reworking traditional recipes for modern home cooks, and to give a nod to the regional traditions that define fish cooking in this ancient maritime culture.

Lavraki Carpaccio

SEA BASS CARPACCIO

serves 2 to 4

There are a few very region-specific recipes for raw salted or marinated fish in the Greek kitchen, mostly in areas with a deeply rooted fishing tradition, such as Lesvos, where the local sardines are savored after just a few hours in salt. But the delicate crudo-type dishes that have become so popular—witness the poke *phenomenon—are newcomers to the Greek table and were initiated by the country's most creative chefs, who started a trend using Greek herbs and alcoholic beverages as marinades for raw fish. Mediterranean sea bass, one of the most important farmed fish in Greece, makes a beautiful carpaccio. Its delicate flesh pairs perfectly with the citrus flavors and dill that give this particular carpaccio a traditional Greek flair.*

FOR THE MARINADE

¼ cup (60 ml) ouzo

3 tablespoons strained fresh grapefruit juice

2 tablespoons strained fresh orange juice

2 tablespoons strained fresh lemon juice

¼ cup (60 ml) extra-virgin Greek olive oil

¼ teaspoon *boukovo* (Greek red pepper flakes) or red pepper flakes

1 teaspoon coarse salt

Freshly ground black pepper

2 (6-ounce) skinless sea bass fillets, thinly sliced crosswise on an angle

½ grapefruit, cut into 3 wedges, peeled, and sliced thin into triangular pieces

1 small orange, peeled, sectioned, and cut into thin triangular slices

1 small scallion, thinly sliced

1 tablespoon chopped fresh dill

Make the marinade: In a small saucepan, heat the ouzo over medium heat for about 5 minutes to cook off the alcohol. (Keep the kitchen fan off and stand away from the saucepan because the ouzo may ignite, which is natural when heating alcohol; the flame will die down in a few seconds.) Remove from the heat and let cool.

Whisk together all the marinade ingredients in a large bowl. Add the sea bass and marinate for 1 hour in the refrigerator.

Serve the fish on a large plate with the citrus slices, scallion, and dill and drizzle with a little of the marinade if desired.

Lavraki me Kaparofylla kai Assyrtiko Santorinis

GREEK SEA BASS BAKED
with santorini assyrtiko wine, caper leaves, and herbs

serves 6

This simple, robust sea bass recipe calls for a few of my absolute favorite Greek ingredients. Assyrtiko wine from Santorini, for example, lends a delicious minerality and acidity to the sauce. The caper leaves, another specialty from the island, imbue the dish with both texture and a subtle sealike brininess, since most caper bushes on the island grow wild along the coast. Both are great examples of the intensely flavored ingredients that mirror Santorini's unique volcanic terroir.

6 skin-on sea bass or sea bream fillets

1 cup (240 ml) Santorini assyrtiko wine

2 teaspoons Greek or Dijon mustard

2 garlic cloves, minced

1 fennel bulb, trimmed, halved, and sliced

1 red onion, halved and chopped

3 cups (435 g) cherry or teardrop tomatoes, whole

2 tablespoons capers, drained

2 tablespoons caper leaves, if available

½ cup (120 ml) extra-virgin Greek olive oil

Grated zest of 1 lemon

4 or 5 fresh thyme sprigs

Salt and freshly ground black pepper

3 tablespoons snipped fresh chives

½ cup (25 g) chopped fresh parsley

Preheat the oven to 375°F (190°C).

Score the skin side of sea bass or bream fillets with a sharp paring knife.

Whisk together ½ cup (120 ml) of the wine, the mustard, and half the garlic in a medium bowl. Gently toss the fillets in the marinade. Cover and refrigerate for 30 minutes.

Place the fennel, onion, remaining garlic, the cherry tomatoes, capers, caper leaves, olive oil, and remaining ½ cup (120 ml) wine in a glass or ceramic baking dish and toss to combine. Roast for 20 to 30 minutes, until thick and bubbling.

Place the fish fillets over the vegetables. Sprinkle with the lemon zest and thyme sprigs and season with salt and pepper. Cover and bake for 10 to 12 minutes, until the fillets are fork-tender. Remove from the oven, uncover, sprinkle with the chives and parsley, and serve.

Lavraki me Manitaria kai Kokino Krasi

MEDITERRANEAN SEA BASS
with mushrooms and red wine

serves 4

This recipe is one of the simplest to make in the entire book and one of my personal favorites, equally suitable for a quick midweek meal as it is for a more formal dinner party. The seemingly uncommon marriage of red wine and fish is balanced by the addition of mushrooms. Serve this on its own with a simple green salad and, yes, drink some Greek red wine, perhaps a tannic xinomavro from Macedonia or a more from supple agiorgitiko from Nemea in the Peloponnese.

1 pound (450 g) mixed fresh button, fresh portobello, and dried chanterelle mushrooms

4 tablespoons (60 ml) extra-virgin Greek olive oil

1 red onion, finely chopped

2 garlic cloves, finely chopped

⅔ cup (160 ml) dry Greek red wine, such as xinomavro

3 fresh thyme sprigs

Salt and freshly ground black pepper

2 teaspoons tomato paste

1 tablespoon Greek balsamic vinegar

4 skin-on Mediterranean sea bass fillets

3 tablespoons snipped fresh chives

Wipe all the mushrooms clean. Slice the button mushrooms and the portobellos. Place the dried chanterelles in a bowl with warm water just to cover and set aside to rehydrate for about 20 minutes.

In a large deep skillet, heat 2 tablespoons of the olive oil over medium heat. Add the onion and cook until soft and lightly colored, about 10 minutes. Stir in the garlic. Add the button and portobello mushrooms. Drain the chanterelles, reserving the soaking liquid. Add the rehydrated chanterelles to the skillet. Stir gently all together, reduce the heat to low, cover, and cook for 5 minutes to wilt the mushrooms.

Add the wine, raise the heat to medium, and bring to a simmer. Add the thyme. Season lightly with salt and pepper. Add the tomato paste and vinegar. Cook for 5 minutes, until the sauce thickens. Strain the reserved mushroom soaking liquid through a fine-mesh sieve into the skillet. Stir gently.

Lightly season the fish fillets with salt and pepper and place them skin-side up over the mushroom mixture. Cover and cook for about 7 minutes, until fork-tender. Sprinkle the chopped chives over the contents of the pan, drizzle with the remaining 2 tablespoons olive oil, and serve.

Freskos Bakaliaros me Portokali kai Prasines Elies

COD FILLETS
with orange and green olive salsa

serves 4

The salsa is what gives this easy cod dish its punch. You may serve the salsa with other fish, too, such as grilled or poached salmon, perch, fresh halibut, or snapper, and more.

FOR THE SALSA

1 small navel orange

4 plum tomatoes, peeled, seeded, and chopped

2 tablespoons strained fresh orange juice

2 tablespoons mastiha liqueur or ouzo

⅓ cup (35 g) finely chopped red onion

2 tablespoons strained fresh lemon juice

2 tablespoons extra-virgin Greek olive oil

½ cup (75 g) finely chopped pitted Greek cracked green olives

½ teaspoon crushed coriander seeds

½ teaspoon smoked paprika

2 tablespoons chopped fresh oregano

FOR THE FISH

Olive oil, for the baking dish

4 (6-ounce) cod or other white-fleshed fish fillets, such as halibut, snapper, or perch

Salt and freshly ground black pepper

2 teaspoons finely chopped lemon zest

Make the salsa: Grate the orange along the fine teeth of a Microplane and reserve 2 teaspoons of the zest for the fish. Peel the orange, removing the pith completely. Divide it into sections and cut each into thin triangular slices. Put the orange slices in a bowl and add all the remaining salsa ingredients, cover, and refrigerate for 1 hour. Remove from the refrigerator 15 to 20 minutes before serving.

Make the fish: Preheat the oven to 375°F (190°C). Lightly oil a glass baking dish large enough to fit the fish in one layer.

Season the fish on both sides with salt and pepper. Place in the pan and sprinkle with the lemon zest and reserved 2 teaspoons orange zest. Drizzle with olive oil. Bake for about 12 minutes, until the fish is fork-tender. Transfer to a platter, spoon over the salsa and any pan juices, and serve.

Mayiatiko Yemisto

GRILLED MACKEREL
stuffed with carrots, raisins, pine nuts, and herbs

serves 4

Mackerel, one of my favorite Mediterranean fish, with its smooth, unctuous flesh and deep flavor, is an excellent fish for the grill. The raisins, carrot, nuts, and croutons pressed into the mackerel's cavity make this a particularly filling entrée.

4 large whole mackerel, about 2 pounds (1 kg) each, deboned (see Note)

Salt and freshly ground black pepper

FOR THE STUFFING

⅓ cup (50 g) golden seedless raisins

⅓ cup (80 ml) brandy or dry white wine

⅓ cup (45 g) pine nuts

¼ cup (60 ml) extra-virgin Greek olive oil, plus more for brushing

1 large red onion, finely chopped

1 large carrot, finely diced

1 garlic clove, minced

2 cups (60 g) plain croutons or ¼-inch (6 mm) dried bread cubes made from stale, hard bread

½ cup (25 g) chopped fresh parsley

1 teaspoon dried thyme

Salt and freshly ground black pepper

Rinse and pat dry the deboned fish. Season inside and out with salt and pepper. Put them on a plate, cover, and refrigerate until ready to use.

Make the stuffing: Soak the raisins in the brandy for 30 minutes. Heat a small nonstick skillet over medium heat and toast the pine nuts, tossing continuously, until lightly golden on both sides. Transfer to a plate and set aside.

In a medium nonstick skillet, heat the olive oil over medium heat. Add the onion and carrot and cook, stirring, for about 7 minutes. Add the garlic and stir together for another minute or so. Remove from the heat and transfer to a large bowl.

Add the bread cubes, raisins and brandy, pine nuts, parsley, and thyme and season with salt and pepper. Toss well.

Heat a grill to medium. The grill rack should be about 5 inches (12.5 cm) from the heat source. Oil a flat, long-handled grill basket that has a top and bottom for holding whole fish in place securely. (You will need to use this to keep the stuffed fish together.) Tear off or cut four 14-inch (36 cm) squares of parchment paper and four equal-size pieces of aluminum foil. Set each parchment square over a square of foil.

Place one-quarter of the filling inside the cavity of each fish, pressing it in gently to be as compact as possible. Brush the surface of the fish, on both sides, with a little olive oil. Place each stuffed fish in the middle of a parchment-foil square. Bring the sides of both the parchment and foil up and around and fold closed securely and relatively tightly. There should be some room between the fish and the wrapping, but it should be fairly compact.

Place the wrapped fish in the prepared grill basket and place the basket over direct medium heat. Grill the fish for 25 to 35 minutes, flipping the basket once after about 15 minutes. Remove from the grill, unwrap carefully (any steam in the packets will be hot), and serve hot.

NOTE: Have your fishmonger debone the mackerel. Instead of grilling, you can also cook the fish over medium heat in a grill pan with a lid for 25 to 30 minutes. Alternatively, you can bake the fish: Put the wrapped fish in a baking pan and bake in a preheated 350°F (175°C) oven for 30 to 35 minutes.

VARIATION

You can make this with whole snapper or sea bass as well.

BRAISED OCTOPUS
with olives

serves 4 to 8

I asked my friend Nick Livanos, a New York restaurateur whose family roots are in the village of Molyvos on the island of Lesvos, what dish he most closely associates with the island. Without blinking an eye, he mentioned octopus cooked with olives. This is an adaptation of a local recipe, and one of the most delicious octopus stews I've ever enjoyed!

2 pounds (900 g) small white onions

4 pounds (1.8 kg) octopus

6 tablespoons (90 ml) extra-virgin Greek olive oil, plus more for serving

1 medium red onion, very finely chopped

1 medium fennel bulb, very finely chopped

4 garlic cloves, minced

1 star anise pod

3 bay leaves

½ teaspoon whole black peppercorns

5 fresh thyme sprigs

½ cup (120 ml) white wine

1 tablespoon good-quality tomato paste

Salt and freshly ground black pepper

2 cups (290 g) teardrop or cherry tomatoes

1 teaspoon chopped fresh thyme

¼ cup (60 ml) ouzo

2 tablespoons Greek balsamic vinegar

1 tablespoon Greek honey or *petimezi* (grape molasses)

1½ cups (230 g) pitted Greek black or green olives, rinsed

½ cup (25 g) chopped fresh parsley

Bring a pot of water to a rolling boil. Fill a large bowl with ice and water. Add the small white onions to the boiling water and blanch for 2 minutes. Remove with a slotted spoon and immediately place in the bowl of ice water. Drain. Using a paring knife, cut off their root ends. Pinch each onion to remove the skin, which will slip off very easily. Set aside in a bowl.

Clean the octopus: Cut off the head/sac just below the eyes and, using a sharp paring knife, dig out the beak and discard. (You can clean the inside of head by turning it inside out and removing the viscera while running it under cold water. I like to use it either by slicing it and cooking it together with the octopus, or in octopus *keftedes*—see page 90.) Cut the remaining octopus into 8 tentacles, put them in a bowl, and refrigerate until ready to use.

In a wide pot, heat 3 tablespoons of the olive oil over medium heat. Reduce the heat to low, add the red onion and fennel, and cook, stirring, until very soft and just on the verge of starting to brown, 10 to 12 minutes. Stir in half the garlic. Add the octopus tentacles, star anise, bay leaves, peppercorns, and thyme sprigs. Cover and cook over low heat for about 30 minutes, or until the octopus turns deep pink and has exuded its liquid. Add the wine. In about 5 minutes, when the alcohol has cooked off, stir in the tomato paste. Cook the octopus until tender but not stringy, 15 to 25 minutes more.

While to octopus is simmering, prepare the onions and tomatoes. In a large, deep, preferably nonstick skillet, heat the remaining 3 tablespoons olive oil over medium heat and add the peeled small onions. Sprinkle lightly with salt. Cook slowly, shaking the pan back and forth every few minutes, until the onions turn light amber in color. Add the whole tomatoes to the pan and raise the heat to medium-high. Taste and adjust the seasoning with salt and pepper. Add the remaining garlic and the chopped thyme. Shake back and forth in the pan until the tomato skins wrinkle. Add the ouzo, vinegar, and honey and cook for another minute or two, until the tomatoes start to brown. Toss in the olives and shake to combine.

About 7 minutes before removing the octopus from the heat, add the onion-tomato mixture. Add the parsley and stir very gently to combine. Remove the star anise, bay leaves, and thyme sprigs. Remove from the heat and serve.

Sardeles Psites me Ouzo, Ntomata, Kapari kai Lemoni

BAKED SARDINES
with ouzo, tomatoes, capers, and lemon

serves 6

This recipe is an homage to the island of Lesvos, home to most renowned sardines in Greece, culled from the rich Bay of Kalloni and from the other bays and coves that lace the island's coast. Lesvos is also home to some of the best ouzo makers in Greece. The refreshing anise flavor of Greece's national drink balances beautifully with the oily, rich flavor and texture of sardines.

½ cup (120 ml) extra-virgin Greek olive oil, plus more for the baking dish

2 pounds (900 g) fresh sardines

2 ripe but firm tomatoes, halved lengthwise, cored, and cut into slices about ⅛ inch (3 mm) thick

2 medium red onions, halved and cut into slices about ⅛ inch (3 mm) thick

2 lemons, halved lengthwise and cut into slices a little less than about ⅛ inch (3 mm) thick

3 tablespoons capers in brine, rinsed and drained

Juice of 1 lemon, strained

¼ cup (60 ml) ouzo

2 teaspoons Greek or Dijon mustard

2 tablespoons chopped fresh oregano leaves, or 2 teaspoons dried Greek oregano

Sea salt and freshly ground black pepper

Preheat the oven to 350°F (175°C). Lightly oil a rectangular glass or ceramic baking dish.

Clean the sardines: Using a sharp paring knife, cut off their heads from the spine toward the belly and pull down gently to remove the attached viscera. Run under cold water and scoop out any remaining viscera with a small spoon or your fingers. (You can wear gloves while doing this, as sardines have a strong, lingering fish smell thanks to all the healthy oils they contain.) Rinse the sardines well in a colander.

Place the sardines in the prepared baking dish one by one in neat rows, alternating the placement of each so that the first one sits plump end to tail, the second one snuggled next to it tail to plump end, etc., thus enabling the most efficient use of the space in the pan.

Take the tomato, onion, and lemon slices and snuggle them between the fish, alternating between each as much as possible. Sprinkle the capers over the fish evenly.

In a small bowl, whisk together the lemon juice, ouzo, mustard, oregano, and olive oil. Pour the mixture evenly over the contents of the baking dish. Season with salt and pepper. Cover with parchment or waxed paper, then aluminum foil, and bake for 20 minutes. Remove the paper and foil and bake for 7 to 10 minutes more, until lightly browned on top. Remove from the oven and serve immediately.

Sardelles Psites stin Schara me Oma Kremydia

GRILLED BUTTERFLIED SARDINES
with red onion and herbs

serves 4

Butterflied, grilled sardines topped with crunchy raw red onions are one of the great meze dishes of Thessaloniki, Greece's second largest city and a place renowned for its complex, rich, multi-faceted food history. The sardines available in Greek waters are small. Look for large Spanish sardines, which are readily available in the United States.

⅓ cup (80 ml) extra-virgin olive oil, plus more for the grill basket

⅓ cup (80 ml) strained fresh lemon juice

1 teaspoon dried Greek oregano

Salt and freshly ground white pepper

1 pound (450 g) large fresh sardines, gutted and butterflied

2 large red onions, sliced into paper-thin rings

1 teaspoon sweet paprika or a combination of sweet and hot paprika

3 tablespoons finely chopped fresh parsley

2 or 3 lemons, cut into 4 wedges each, for garnish

Whisk together the olive oil, lemon juice, oregano, and salt and pepper to taste in a large bowl. Toss the fish in the marinade, cover, and let stand at room temperature for about 20 minutes.

Heat a grill to medium. Set the grill rack about 4 inches (10 cm) from the heat source. Lightly oil a flat, long-handled grill basket that has a top and bottom for holding whole fish in place securely.

Place one-third of the butterflied fish, one next to the other, in a neat row inside the prepared grill basket. Close the top to secure them in the basket and set the basket on the grill over medium-high heat. Grill for 6 to 8 minutes, flipping the basket once, until the sardines are tender. Brush with the marinade while the fish grills. Transfer from the grill basket to a tray, oil the basket again, and repeat to grill the second and third batches of fish.

To serve the fish, spread half the onions over a serving platter and sprinkle half the paprika over them. Place the sardines on top and cover with the remaining onions. Sprinkle with the remaining paprika and the parsley. Serve with the lemon wedges on the side.

Garides Stin Schara me Marinata apo Ouzo, Lemoni kai Koliandro

GRILLED LARGE SHRIMP
with ouzo, lemon, pepper, and coriander

serves 4

Greece in the summer is about being outside, under the hot sun, near the water, sea salt spraying on the breeze and seafood sizzling nearby. The quaff of choice is often a glass of milky-white ouzo on ice, the perfect foil to smoky seafood. This simple grilled shrimp dish is flavored with Greece's national spirit.

2 pounds (900 g) large shrimp, unpeeled

1 teaspoon whole black peppercorns

½ teaspoon coriander seeds

Grated zest of 1 lemon

1 garlic clove, minced

Salt

1 cup (240 ml) strained fresh lemon juice

½ cup (120 ml) ouzo

Devein the shrimp, but leave the shells and tails intact.

In a mortar, crush the peppercorns, coriander seeds, lemon zest, garlic, and salt using the pestle until the mixture is a thick paste. Transfer the spice mixture to a large stainless steel bowl, add the lemon juice and ouzo, and whisk to combine. Add the shrimp, toss well, cover, and refrigerate for at least 30 minutes or up to 3 hours.

Heat a grill to high.

Thread 4 shrimp each onto four 8-inch (20 cm) metal skewers, skewering them through at their thickest point, near the upper part of their body. Grill for about 4 minutes on each side, or until the shells turn bright red. Remove from the grill and serve, either on the skewers or off.

Garides kai Mydia se Saltsa apo Freskia Tomata kai Vasiliko

SHRIMP AND MUSSELS
in fresh tomato-basil sauce

serves 6

This aromatic, easy shrimp-mussel dish can be served on its own or as a sauce over pasta.

6 ripe tomatoes

4 tablespoons (60 ml) extra-virgin Greek olive oil

1 large red onion, minced

3 garlic cloves, smashed

1 cup (240 ml) dry white wine

Sea salt and freshly ground black pepper

1½ pounds (680 g) medium shrimp, peeled and deveined

24 mussels, scrubbed and debearded

1 cup (50 g) chopped mixed varieties of fresh basil (Italian, cinnamon, purple, tiny-leaved)

½ cup (25 g) chopped fresh oregano

Chop 3 tomatoes and puree the remaining 3 in the bowl of a food processor.

In a large wide shallow pot, heat 2 tablespoons of the olive oil over medium heat. Add the onion and garlic and cook, stirring, for about 7 minutes, until soft. Add the chopped tomatoes and the pureed tomatoes. Bring to a simmer and pour in ½ cup (120 ml) of the wine. Season to taste with salt and pepper. Reduce the heat to low, cover the pot with the lid ajar, and simmer for 40 to 45 minutes, until the sauce thickens.

While the sauce is simmering, in a large nonstick skillet, heat the remaining 2 tablespoons olive oil over high heat. Add the shrimp and cook, stirring, for 3 to 4 minutes, until they turn bright pink.

Place the remaining ½ cup (120 ml) wine, the mussels, and ¼ cup (60 ml) water in a large nonreactive pot. Cover the pot, bring to a boil over high heat, and steam for 6 to 7 minutes, until the mussels open; discard any that don't.

Strain the mussel cooking liquid through a coffee filter or fine-mesh sieve and add it to the tomato sauce. Bring to a simmer. Stir in the mixed basils, oregano, sautéed shrimp, and steamed mussels. Cook gently for a few minutes for the flavors to meld, then serve.

SWEET
ENDS

Kalio lahano me glyka, para ahari me pikra

"Better to have cabbage with sweetness, rather than sugar with bitterness."
(Meaning: It's better to be poor and happy than rich and miserable.)

Perhaps more than in any other chapter in this book, the sweet end is also the most creative few pages. In a conscious decision to avoid the clichés, such as baklava, *kataifi*, *galaktoboureko*, and all the other sweets one can find in countless Greek cookbooks, including my own older ones, I wanted to honor the present.

Greek pastry has seen a revolution in the past few years, as more and more chefs in Greek restaurants the world over experiment with traditional ingredients and transform them into contemporary dreamscapes.

Mastiha, for example, the resinous spice from the island of Chios, has gone from being an ingredient from my mother's generation used once or twice a year in holiday breads to one that graces everything from chocolate to Hellenized versions of panna cotta. Liqueurs, traditional spoon sweets (seasonal fruits, immature nuts, and young vegetables put up in sugar syrup), honey, tahini, and other Old World ingredients or preparations are now showcased in wonderful contemporary Greek desserts.

In these next few pages, I create a new Greek sweet end for home cooks to enjoy.

Flogeres me Tahini kai Meli

TAHINI-HONEY PHYLLO FLUTES

makes 30 pieces

You can make this phyllo dessert without butter! Note that frozen phyllo needs to defrost in the refrigerator overnight, so plan ahead.

1 pound (450 g) #7 chilled or frozen commercial phyllo, thawed in the refrigerator overnight if frozen

½ cup (120 ml) extra-virgin olive oil, plus more for the baking sheets

2 cups (480 ml) tahini

1½ cups (400 g) granulated sugar

½ cup Greek honey

3 cups (240 g) finely ground walnuts

2 teaspoons ground cinnamon

3 to 4 cups (375 to 500 g) confectioners' sugar, as needed, for dusting

Quince, *neratzi* (bitter orange), or orange spoon sweets, for serving (see Note)

Remove the phyllo from the refrigerator and let it come to room temperature. Preheat the oven to 350°F (175°C). Lightly oil two baking sheets.

In the bowl of a stand mixer fitted with the whisk attachment, whip together the tahini, granulated sugar, and honey on high speed until smooth and creamy, drizzling in water in ¼-cup (60 ml) increments (up to 1½ cups / 360 ml) until the tahini mixture is creamy and spreadable, about the consistency of peanut butter. Stir in the walnuts and cinnamon by hand. Set aside.

Place the phyllo sheets horizontally in front of you on a clean work surface. Cut them crosswise into three 6-inch-long (15 cm) strips. Stack the phyllo strips and keep them covered with a kitchen towel. Take one strip, place it vertically in front of you, and brush it sparingly with some of the olive oil. Place a second strip on top. Place a tablespoon of the filling in the bottom center of the strip, fold in the sides, and roll up to form a tight cylinder. Place the cylinder seam-side down in the prepared baking pan. Continue with the remaining phyllo and filling until you have used all of one or the other. Bake until lightly golden, 8 to 12 minutes. Remove from the oven and let cool slightly. While the pastry is still warm, sift confectioners' sugar over it generously.

Serve topped with quince, *neratzi*, or orange spoon sweets. Store any leftovers in tins in a cool, dry place for about 5 days.

NOTE: These spoon sweets are available online or in Greek grocery stores.

Psimeni Krema me Mastiha

GREEK YOGURT–MASTIHA PANNA COTTA
with spoon sweets

serves 6

Panna cotta has been co-opted by Greek professional and home cooks alike, and it's morphed into an Italo-Greco hybrid, made nowadays with the likes of Greek yogurt and flavored with spoon sweets, Greek liqueurs, even herbal teas. This recipe is simple and elegant.

2 cups (480 ml) milk

1 cup (240 ml) Greek yogurt

1 cup (240 ml) heavy cream

2 tablespoons mastiha liqueur, or ½ teaspoon *mastiha* (mastic) crystals pounded with 1 teaspoon sugar in a mortar with a pestle

3 long strips lemon zest (peeled with a vegetable peeler)

4 teaspoons unflavored gelatin powder

½ cup (100 g) sugar

Orange preserves or Greek orange or *neratzi* (bitter orange) spoon sweets (see Note, page 342), for garnish

¼ cup (60 ml) Greek honey, for garnish

In a medium saucepan, combine 1½ cups (360 ml) of the milk, the yogurt, cream, mastiha liqueur (or pulverized crystals), and lemon zest and whisk to combine. Cover and bring to a simmer over low heat. Remove from the heat and let the mixture stand for 1 hour.

Sprinkle the powdered gelatin over the remaining ½ cup (120 ml) milk in a small bowl to soften.

Return the milk-yogurt mixture to a simmer over medium heat, then remove from the heat. Pour in the gelatin mixture and the sugar and whisk until smooth. Strain through a fine-mesh sieve into a pitcher. Pour the panna cotta mixture into six ⅔-cup (150 ml) ramekins and chill until set, at least 2 hours.

To serve: Run a knife around each of the ramekins to loosen the panna cotta and invert onto individual serving plates. Top each with 2 teaspoons of the preserves or spoon sweet and drizzle with honey. Serve immediately.

Manouri stin Schara me Syka Posé

GRILLED MANOURI CHEESE
with ouzo-poached figs

serves 4

Here's a dessert that can almost double as a starter!

16 dried figs, preferably Greek

½ teaspoon *mastiha* (mastic) crystals

½ cup (100 g) plus 2 teaspoons sugar

½ cup (120 ml) honey

½ cup (120 ml) mastiha liqueur

8 whole black peppercorns

Olive oil for greasing

4 (½-inch / 1.5 cm) round slices manouri cheese or ricotta salata

Fresh mint, for garnish

Soak the dried figs in water to cover for 1 hour. Drain, reserving the soaking water.

In a mortar, pound the *mastiha* crystals and 2 teaspoons of the sugar to a fine powder using the pestle.

In a medium saucepan, combine 1½ cups (360 ml) of the fig soaking water, the remaining ½ cup (100 g) sugar, the *mastiha*-sugar mixture, and the honey and bring to a boil over medium-high heat, stirring until the sugar has dissolved. Add the mastiha liqueur and peppercorns.

Simmer for about 7 minutes, stirring gently, until the syrup thickens slightly, enough to loosely coat the back of a spoon. Add the figs and poach for 7 minutes. Remove from the heat.

Heat a grill to medium or heat a nonstick grill pan over medium-high heat. Oil the grill grates or brush the pan very lightly with oil.

Grill the cheese rounds over a medium-hot part of the grill or in the grill pan, turning, until they just begin to acquire grill marks, about 2 minutes per side.

Place a round of cheese on each of four serving plates and place 4 poached figs over each. Drizzle with the poaching syrup, garnish with mint, and serve.

Mpananes Stin Schara me Sokolata kai Pasteli

GREEK BANANA SPLIT
with chocolate-nut paste, *pasteli,* cinnamon, and honey

serves 4

My daughter, now a young adult, used to hide jars of Merenda, the Greek equivalent of the chocolate-hazelnut spread Nutella, hoarding it for a rainy day. My son also grew up licking the last gooey bits of the chocolate-hazelnut cream from the spoon. It's become part of Greek popular food culture, and I work it into a very American banana split, topped with a bit of ancient crunch in the form of pasteli, *the sesame-honey confection that's been around for millennia.*

3 ounces (85 g) Greek *pasteli* (sesame-honey brittle) or other sesame or nut brittle

FOR THE SAUCE

½ cup (120 ml) Merenda, Nutella, or other chocolate-hazelnut spread

¼ cup (60 ml) heavy cream

1 teaspoon pure almond extract

FOR THE BANANAS

1 tablespoon unsalted butter

4 large, firm bananas, peel on, stem tips removed, halved lengthwise

3 tablespoons brandy or orange liqueur

2 tablespoons honey, preferably Greek thyme or pine honey

Scant 1 teaspoon ground cinnamon

8 scoops vanilla or chocolate ice cream, for serving

Place the *pasteli* on a sturdy work surface over a piece of parchment paper. Cover with another piece of parchment and, using a kitchen mallet, hammer until crumbled. Set aside. (You can crush the *pasteli* up to a week ahead of time and store it in an airtight container in a cool, dry place.)

Prepare the sauce: In the top of a double boiler, melt the chocolate-hazelnut spread over medium heat. Add the cream and almond extract and stir until blended. Cover with plastic wrap and keep warm in the double boiler.

Prepare the bananas: Heat a grill pan over medium heat and brush the pan with the butter. Place the bananas cut-side down in the pan and cook for 2 to 3 minutes, until the bananas are lined with grill marks.

In the meantime, whisk together the brandy, honey, and cinnamon in a small bowl. Turn the bananas over so that the flesh side is up, brush generously with the brandy mixture, cover the pan, and cook for 2 to 3 minutes more, until the bananas are cooked through. Remove carefully and set aside until cool enough to handle. Peel the banana halves.

Place two grilled banana halves in each serving dish. Top with two scoops of ice cream, drizzle with the sauce, and garnish with the crushed *pasteli*. Serve immediately.

Tzizkeik me Mastiha

GREEK YOGURT CHEESECAKE
with mastiha

serves 8

This Greek-American hybrid is an easy cheesecake to make. The faintly bitter, earthy flavor of the mastiha (mastic) adds an exotic dimension. You can try using crumbled Greek melomakarona cookies, available in Greek stores or online, as a base, too.

1¾ cups (210 g) crumbled graham cracker or cinnamon cookies

3 tablespoons Greek honey

2 (8-ounce / 225 g) package cream cheese

1 cup (200 g) sugar

6 egg whites

2 teaspoons pure vanilla extract

½ teaspoon *mastiha* (mastic) crystals, pounded with 1 teaspoon sugar in a mortar with a pestle

Pinch of salt

3 cups (720 ml) Greek yogurt

Greek spoon sweet of your choice (see Note, page 342), such as bergamot, orange rind, or pistachio, for topping

Preheat the oven to 375°F (190°C).

Combine the crumbled cookies and honey in the bowl of a food processor and pulse to combine. Press into the bottom and up the sides of a 9-inch (22 cm) springform pan. Place in the refrigerator until ready to use.

In the bowl of a stand mixer fitted with the paddle attachment, whip the cream cheese until smooth. Add the sugar and beat to combine. Add the egg whites one at a time, mixing well after each addition before adding the next. Scrape down the sides of the bowl. Add the vanilla, *mastiha* powder, and salt and beat to combine. Add the yogurt and beat to combine.

Pour the mixture over the prepared crust and bake for 40 to 45 minutes, until set. The filling will still look soft. Leave the cheesecake in the oven with the door ajar for 1 hour. Remove from the oven and let stand at room temperature for 1 hour before topping.

Spread some Greek spoon sweets over the top and chill for a few hours until completely set before serving.

Mous Pikris Sokolatas me Ouzo

DARK CHOCOLATE OUZO ORANGE MOUSSE

serves 8

Ouzo and chocolate are a match made in heaven.

2 cups (480 ml) chilled heavy cream

4 large egg yolks

3 tablespoons granulated sugar

Pinch of salt

3 tablespoons ouzo

3 tablespoons orange liqueur

7 ounces (200 g) good-quality bittersweet chocolate, chopped

FOR GARNISH

1 cup (240 ml) heavy cream

2 teaspoons confectioners' sugar

2 teaspoons ouzo

Mint sprigs or orange slices (optional)

In a small heavy saucepan, heat ¾ cup (180 ml) of the cream over low heat just until hot. Do not allow to boil.

In a medium metal bowl, whisk together the egg yolks, granulated sugar, and salt until combined. While whisking, add the hot cream in a slow stream and whisk continuously until combined.

Transfer the custard to saucepan and cook over low heat, stirring continuously, until it registers 160°F (70°C) on a candy thermometer. Strain the mixture through a fine-mesh sieve into a bowl and stir in the ouzo and orange liqueur.

In the top of a double boiler, melt chocolate, stirring frequently. Whisk the custard into the melted chocolate until smooth. Remove the top of the double boiler and set aside to cool.

In the bowl of a stand mixer fitted with the whisk attachment, beat the remaining 1¼ cups (300 ml) cream until it holds stiff peaks. Whisk a quarter of the whipped cream into the cooled chocolate custard to lighten it, then fold in the remaining whipped cream. Spoon the mousse into eight wineglasses or 6-ounce ramekins, cover, and refrigerate for at least 6 hours.

Remove the custards from the refrigerator 20 minutes before serving.

For the garnish, in the bowl of a stand mixer fitted with the whisk attachment, whisk the cream, confectioners' sugar, and ouzo until the cream holds stiff peaks. Spoon a little of the whipped cream over the mousse and serve, garnished with mint sprigs or orange slices, if desired.

Revani me Gefsi Karyda kai Anana

PIÑA COLADA REVANI

serves 8 to 12

Revani or ravani *is one of the most traditional Greek nut-based, syrup-soaked cakes. There are many such cakes in the Greek kitchen, made with a base of almonds, as revani is, or walnuts. Over the years chefs have experimented with them, adding a modern twist here and there. This recipe was inspired by a dessert I originally came across in a wonderful book by the British chef Silvena Rowe, who transforms traditional eastern Mediterranean dishes into contemporary delights.*

FOR THE SYRUP

3 cups (600 g) sugar

1 cinnamon stick

1 (1-inch-wide / 2.5 cm) strip lemon zest (peeled with a vegetable peeler)

1 tablespoon Greek brandy

2 cups (330 g) small-diced fresh or drained canned pineapple

FOR THE REVANI

1 cup (2 sticks / 225 g) unsalted butter, plus more for the pan

2 cups (360 g) coarse semolina

1 tablespoon baking powder

1 cup (200 g) plus 2 teaspoons sugar

6 large eggs, separated

2 tablespoons brandy

1 tablespoon strained fresh orange juice

1 tablespoon finely ground blanched almonds

½ cup (45 g) unsweetened shredded coconut

FOR THE GARNISH

½ cup (100 g) sugar

Fresh pineapple rings or chunks

Greek yogurt or vanilla or coconut ice cream (optional)

Prepare the syrup: In a medium saucepan, combine the sugar and 1½ cups (320 ml) water and bring to a boil. Add the cinnamon stick, lemon zest, brandy, and pineapple and simmer over medium heat for 5 to 7 minutes. Remove the pan from the heat and strain through a fine-mesh sieve into a bowl. Let the syrup cool to room temperature.

Make the *revani*: Preheat the oven to 375°F (190°C). Line a 9- or 10-inch (22 or 25 cm) springform pan with parchment paper and butter the sides and bottom.

Sift together the semolina and baking powder into a small bowl.

In the bowl of a stand mixer fitted with the whisk attachment, whip the butter on high speed until creamy, about 4 minutes. Gradually add 1 cup (200 g) of the sugar and continue beating. Add the egg yolks one by one, whisking well after each addition before adding the next.

(CONTINUED)

Remove the whisk attachment and replace it with the paddle attachment. Add the brandy, orange juice, and semolina–baking powder mixture and beat on medium speed until smooth. Add the ground almonds and coconut and beat until the mixture is well combined.

In a large bowl using a whisk or handheld mixer, beat the egg whites until frothy. Slowly add the remaining 2 teaspoons sugar and continue beating until the egg whites hold stiff peaks. Gently fold the egg whites into the semolina mixture.

Pour the batter into the prepared pan and bake for 30 to 35 minutes, until the cake turns golden brown with a thin, soft, sponge-like surface and a toothpick or metal or wooden skewer inserted into the center of the cake comes out clean.

Remove the *revani* from the oven, place it on a rack, and pour the syrup over it gradually, while it is still in the pan. Let sit for at least 2 hours, turning it over if necessary for the syrup to go everywhere (if you flip it upside down, make sure you place it on a plate before doing so!).

To garnish: Spread the sugar over a flat plate and dip pineapple rings or chunks into the sugar, turning to coat both sides. Either have the broiler lit or use a crème brûlée torch to lightly brown the pineapple pieces until the sugar burns slightly and starts to caramelize.

Serve each wedge of *revani* with a piece of "burnt" pineapple and a dollop of either Greek yogurt or ice cream.

Poutinga me Gefsi Elliniko Kafe

GREEK COFFEE BREAD PUDDING

serves 6 to 8

Like the Greek coffee baklava on page 352, this, too, was born of the quest for modernizing traditional recipes. The flavors are very soothing, almost caramel-like.

Butter, for greasing

4 large eggs

1½ cups (330 g) brown sugar

2 cups (480 ml) heavy cream, plus more for serving if desired

1 cup (240 ml) milk

1 cup (240 ml) strained Greek coffee or regular brewed coffee, chilled (see page 353)

2 teaspoons pure vanilla extract

Pinch of ground cinnamon

Grated zest of ½ lemon

6 cups cubes stale brioche, *tsoureki*, or egg bread

½ cup (75 g) raisins

Preheat the oven to 350°F (175°C). Butter a 9 x 13-inch (23 x 33 cm) baking pan.

Whisk together the eggs and brown sugar in a medium bowl. Add the cream, milk, coffee, vanilla, cinnamon, and lemon zest. Stir well.

Put the bread cubes and raisins in a large bowl. Pour the egg mixture over the bread cubes and allow to sit for 20 minutes.

Transfer the mixture to the buttered pan. Place the pan inside a larger pan and fill the larger pan halfway with water. Place in the oven and bake for 40 to 50 minutes, until puffed and golden. Remove from the oven, let cool slightly, cut into squares or circles, and serve, if desired, with a drizzle of cream.

Baklavas me Siropi apo Elliniko Kafe

GREEK COFFEE BAKLAVA

makes 48 (2-inch / 5 cm) cylinders

I am always looking for cool ways to repurpose tradition. Baklava with Greek coffee syrup is one of the many modern desserts born of that desire! Note that the phyllo will need to defrost overnight in the fridge, so plan ahead.

1 pound (450 g) #7 commercial phyllo, thawed overnight in the refrigerator

½ cup ground Greek coffee

4 cups (400 g) walnuts, ground in a food processor (about 5 cups whole)

½ cup (100 g) sugar, plus more as needed for the syrup

2 teaspoons ground cinnamon

½ to 1 teaspoon ground cloves

½ to 1 teaspoon ground cardamom

½ teaspoon freshly grated nutmeg

Grated zest of 1 orange

½ cup (1 stick / 115 g) unsalted butter, melted and preferably clarified (see Note)

Vanilla ice cream, for serving (optional)

Remove the thawed phyllo from the refrigerator and let it come to room temperature.

In a saucepan, stir together the ground coffee and 5 cups (1.2 L) water and heat over medium heat until the mixture foams up and simmers. Remove from the heat and let cool slightly. Carefully pour the liquid part only into a bowl, leaving the thick sludge to settle on the bottom of the pot. Discard that.

In a large bowl using a fork, combine the walnuts, sugar, spices, orange zest, and 3 tablespoons of the prepared Greek coffee.

Preheat the oven to 350°F (175°C). Lightly oil or butter a 9 x 13-inch (23 x 33 cm) baking pan.

Open the phyllo, lay it flat, and cover it with a kitchen towel. Take one sheet of phyllo at a time and spread it open on a clean work surface so that it is horizontally in front of you. Brush the surface with some of the melted butter and fold the phyllo sheet in half horizontally. Spread about 5 level tablespoons of the filling across the bottom of the phyllo, about ½ inch (1.5 cm) in from the edge. Roll up the phyllo to form a cylinder about 1 inch (2.5 cm) in diameter. Place it seam-side down inside the buttered pan. Repeat with remaining sheets and filling, placing each long cylinder of baklava snugly next to the other, until the baking pan is filled and either the phyllo or the filling has been used up. The cylinders will most likely be longer than the inside of the pan, so cut off the excess and discard. Use a small, sharp serrated knife to cut into pieces about 2 inches (5 cm) long. Brush generously with some of remaining melted butter. Bake, uncovered, until the phyllo is lightly browned, about 30 minutes.

While the baklava is baking, measure out the remaining coffee and pour it into a saucepan. Add an equal volume of sugar. Bring to a simmer and cook until the syrup starts to thicken but is still quite loose, about 8 minutes. Remove and let cool.

Remove the hot baklava from the oven and, using a ladle, spoon over enough of the cooled coffee syrup for the baklava to absorb it without getting too soggy or overly wet. Let the baklava sit for a few hours at room temperature, or even overnight, to absorb the syrup.

If desired, cook down the remaining syrup until it is dense and thick, almost as thick as honey. Set aside.

Cut a few pieces of baklava and serve them snugly next to one another on a plate, with a scoop of vanilla ice cream. Drizzle with the reduced coffee syrup, if desired, and serve.

NOTE: To clarify butter, melt it in a small pot over medium heat or in the microwave for a few minutes until the butter is liquid and the milk solids have separated and accumulated on the surface. Using a spoon, skim off and discard the solids. What remains is clarified butter.

HOW TO MAKE GREEK COFFEE

To make Greek coffee, in a small pot or *briki*, the long-handled, tapered Greek coffee pot, place the desired amount of ground coffee and water. For a basic demitasse cup, for example, you will need 1 heaping teaspoon ground Greek coffee and ¾ demitasse cup water. For a medium-sweet coffee, the coffee-to-sugar ratio is 1:1—in other words, 1 teaspoon ground coffee per 1 teaspoon sugar.

Bring to a simmer, stirring. As soon as the coffee starts to foam up, remove from the heat and let it set. Pour the liquid into the cup. Serve.

For the two recipes in this chapter that require prepared Greek coffee (pages 352 and 353), make the coffee in a saucepan without sugar, let the muddy sediment settle on the bottom of the pan, and pour the coffee off as needed.

XINOMAVRO CHOCOLATE CAKE

serves 6 to 8

In the northern Greek environs of Naoussa, one of Greece's premier red wine–producing regions, the xinomavro grape reigns supreme. A visit up there while we were filming the show taught me that locals don't just drink their beloved tannic red wine, they also use it to cook with. Grape molasses cookies with red wine jelly, xinomavro-filled chocolates, sourdough bread starter with the wine, and xinomavro biscuits were just a few of the novelties I came across. The tannic red wine pairs beautifully with chocolate, so I created a dark chocolate cake to honor the match.

6 tablespoons (¾ stick / 85 grams) unsalted butter, at room temperature, plus more for the pan

1 cup (125 g) plus 1 tablespoon all-purpose flour, plus more for the pan

¾ cup (165 g) firmly packed dark brown sugar

¼ cup (50 g) granulated sugar

1 large whole egg, at room temperature

1 large egg yolk, at room temperature

1 teaspoon pure vanilla extract

¾ cup (180 ml) xinomavro or other dry, tannic red wine

½ cup (50 grams) Dutch-process cocoa powder

⅛ teaspoon baking soda

½ teaspoon baking powder

¼ teaspoon ground cinnamon

¼ teaspoon table salt

FOR THE SYRUP

1 cup (240 ml) xinomavro or other dry, tannic red wine

¾ cup (150 g) granulated sugar

1 cinnamon stick

6 whole black peppercorns

3 whole cloves

FOR GARNISH

8 to 10 small clusters of red seedless grapes

Whipped cream (optional)

Cocoa powder or a grinding of black pepper

Preheat the oven to 325°F (160°C). Line the bottom of an 8-inch (20 cm) round cake pan with parchment paper and either butter and lightly flour the parchment and exposed sides of the pan or spray the interior with a nonstick spray.

In the bowl of a stand mixer fitted with the paddle attachment, cream the butter on medium speed until smooth. Add the brown sugar and granulated sugar and beat until fluffy, about 3 minutes.

Add the egg and egg yolk and beat well, then add the vanilla and wine and beat to combine.

(CONTINUED)

Stop the mixer and sift the flour, cocoa, baking soda, baking powder, cinnamon, and salt together directly into the wet ingredients. Mix until almost combined, then remove the bowl from the mixer and fold together with a rubber spatula until fully combined.

Spread the batter in the prepared pan. Bake for 30 to 35 minutes, or until a cake tester inserted into the center comes out clean. The top of the cake should be shiny and smooth. Remove the cake and let it cool on a wire rack.

While the cake is cooling, prepare the syrup and the garnish: For the syrup, combine the wine, granulated sugar, cinnamon stick, peppercorns, and cloves in a small saucepan and cook over medium heat until the mixture has reduced by about half and reaches the consistency of a thick syrup. Strain it and discard the cinnamon, peppercorns, and cloves.

For the garnish, when the cake is done, raise the oven temperature to 375°F (190°C). Place the grape clusters on a shallow baking pan lined with parchment paper and roast for about 20 minutes, turning, until wrinkled and pleasantly "leathery." Remove and set aside.

To serve: Cut the cake into serving pieces and top each piece with a few individual roasted grapes or a small cluster of roasted grapes. Drizzle with the syrup and spoon a little whipped cream, if desired, onto the plate or cake. Sift a little cocoa onto the plate or grind a little black pepper over and around the plate and serve.

En Plo Glyko

FLOATING GREEK ISLAND
in a wine-dark sea

serves 4

I love meringues, and I've always wanted to put this simple dessert, named for the wine-dark sea of Homer and the Greek islands that mystify the horizon, on a menu. It's nothing more than a simple fruit soup with meringues. Truth be told, it's a lot easier to buy meringues for this than to make them. My intention was to provide a recipe for something easy but impressive. Happy sailing . . .

3 cups thawed frozen (660 g) or trimmed fresh (435 g) strawberries, quartered or coarsely chopped

3 tablespoons sugar, or more to taste

½ cup (120 ml) red wine

2 tablespoons Greek honey

2 tablespoons strained fresh lemon juice

2½ ounces (70 g) dark chocolate

4 small meringues (see sidebar, page 358)

2 fresh strawberries, for garnish

Mint sprigs, for garnish

Combine the strawberries, sugar, and wine in a medium saucepan and bring to a simmer. Cook until the sugar has dissolved and the alcohol has cooked off. Add the honey and lemon juice. Using a blender or immersion blender, puree the soup. Chill thoroughly.

When ready to serve, melt the chocolate in the top of a small double boiler. Ladle the soup into serving bowls. Place 2 meringues inside each soup bowl. Drizzle with the melted chocolate and garnish with a strawberry and a few mint sprigs. Serve.

HOW TO MAKE MERINGUES

It's obviously a lot easier to buy ready-made meringues. If you opt to make
them yourself, here's how: You'll need 2 large egg whites, a pinch of salt,
and 4 ounces (115 g) sugar. Preheat the oven to 280°F (140°C). Line two
baking sheets with parchment paper. Place the egg whites and salt in the bowl
of a stand mixer fitted with the whisk attachment and whisk on low speed for
1 minute. Increase the speed to medium and continue whisking for 2 to 3
minutes more, until the whites hold stiff peaks. Continue whisking, adding
1 tablespoon of the sugar at a time, until the whites are very stiff and glossy,
5 to 8 minutes. Take a heaping spoonful at a time of the whipped whites and
drop them at intervals of 2 inches (5 cm) onto the prepared baking sheets.
Bake for 30 to 40 minutes, or until the meringues are dry. Turn off the oven,
open the oven door slightly and leave it ajar. Leave the meringues in the oven
until cool (1–2 hours). Store in a cool, dry place.

Semifreddo me Mastiha kai Rodakina

PEACH MASTIHA GREEK YOGURT SEMIFREDDO

makes one 8½ x 4½-inch (21 x 11 cm) loaf, to serve 6

Another hybrid that takes a classic Italian technique and pairs it with traditional Greek ingredients. This easy dessert is great on a summer day.

2 ripe peaches, unpeeled, pitted and sliced, or 4 canned peach halves (preferably Greek canned peaches, which are excellent), very well drained

1¼ cups (250 g) sugar

½ cup (120 ml) mastiha liqueur

3 large egg whites, at room temperature

⅛ teaspoon salt

1 cup (240 ml) Greek yogurt

3 tablespoons strained fresh lemon juice

½ cup (25 g) finely chopped fresh mint

Line an 8½ x 4½-inch (21 x 11 cm) loaf pan with two pieces of plastic wrap, leaving a generous overhang on all sides.

In a large skillet, cook the peaches and ¼ cup (50 g) of the sugar over medium heat, stirring occasionally, until peaches are softened and the sugar has dissolved, about 5 minutes. Carefully add the mastiha liqueur and cook until the alcohol has cooked off.

Transfer to a blender and puree until smooth. Let cool.

In the top of a double boiler, whisk together the egg whites, salt, and remaining 1 cup (200 g) sugar. Cook, whisking continously, until sugar has dissolved and the mixture is warm to the touch, 2 to 4 minutes. Remove the top of the double boiler. Using a handheld mixer, beat the egg mixture on high speed until tripled in volume, glossy, and completely cool, up to about 10 minutes.

Whisk together yogurt and lemon juice in a large bowl, then stir in the mint. Gently fold in the egg white mixture until combined.

Transfer half the yogurt mixture to the prepared pan; smooth the surface. Spoon on half the peach mixture and swirl it into yogurt layer, then repeat with the remaining yogurt and peach mixtures. Fold the plastic wrap overhang over the top to seal and freeze for at least 8 hours, until firm.

Unwrap the semifreddo and, using the plastic overhang, gently lift it from the pan. Invert the semifreddo onto a cutting board, remove the plastic wrap, and let sit for at least 10 minutes to soften. Slice into 6 even slices, about 1½ inches (4 cm) thick; transfer to plates and serve.

The semifreddo can be frozen for up to 3 days.

Glyko Elliniko Haos

MY BIG FAT GREEK MESS

serves 6

In these days of Brexits and Grexits, I wanted to pay homage to a mess! Taking a cue from the classic English dessert Eton Mess, and always on the lookout for quick crowd-pleasers that look impressive, I created—without much trouble, I should add—my own Greek mess, a mélange of broken meringues, Greek spoon sweets, toasted almonds, and tangy Greek yogurt whipped cream. Don't worry about who will clean this mess up . . . you'll lick the bowls clean for sure!

2 cups (480 ml) chilled heavy cream

1 tablespoon confectioners' sugar

½ teaspoon pure almond or vanilla extract

1 cup (240 ml) Greek yogurt

1½ cups (375 ml) Greek *vyssino* (sour cherry) spoon sweet (see Note, see page 342)

6 meringue rounds (see page 358), about 4 inches (10 cm) in diameter, broken up by hand into small chunks

⅔ cup (95 g) blanched almonds, toasted

In the bowl of a stand mixer fitted with the whisk attachment, whisk the heavy cream on medium-high speed until it begins to stiffen. Add the sugar and almond or vanilla extract and whip until the cream holds stiff peaks. Using a spatula, fold the yogurt into the cream.

Assemble the mess: Place a dollop of the cream-yogurt mixture in each of six glass goblets or dessert bowls. Drizzle 1 teaspoon of the sour cherry spoon sweet and its syrup on top. Add a few pieces of broken meringue, then a few toasted almonds, and a little more of the sour cherries and their syrup. Continue layering the meringues, cream mixture, sour cherries, and almonds, finishing with a drizzling of the sour cherry syrup and a sprinkling of the toasted almonds. Serve immediately.

GREEK
WINES
AND
SPIRITS

GREEK WINES: A LONG HISTORY

I CAN IMAGINE THE EXCITEMENT OF AN ARCHEOLOGIST IN EASTERN MACEDONIA, absorbed in the puzzle of his or her work, of piecing together an image of life in prehistoric Greece, meticulously brushing away dirt and debris to unearth some vessel or ancient ditch to find charred pits and the gossamer residuals of pressed grapes. A eureka moment, perhaps, revealing a wine making history that stretches as far back as eight thousand years. So old is the vine and its pleasure-giving juice in this country where almost everything edible and imbibed has been savored in one uninterrupted continuum to this very day.

Wild then domesticated *Vitis vinifera* grapes were part of life in Greece from the deepest recesses of history. Wine has been a prized commodity almost as long as the grape has existed in Greece. Homer mentions the wine trade between islands in the northern Aegean and Asia Minor, and writes of renowned wines such as the Pramnios Oinos of Ikaria—by some accounts the same wine with which Odysseus plied the cyclops to get him drunk enough so that he and his men could escape! By the time the Minoan civilization on Crete and the Mycenaean in the Peloponnese flourished, wine was being shipped and traded all over the known world.

The ancient Greeks were the first to develop a system of identifying provenance and quality, the precursor to today's designations of origin, a way to help identify specific areas whose unique microclimate helps produce wines of distinct character and extraordinary quality.

Of course, as the Greeks colonized the Mediterranean, they took their farming techniques and crops with them, spreading not only the love of wine, but also the very grapes needed for making it.

Wine's importance spurred innovations in the ceramic arts, for the old skins and pouches used to transport wine were inefficient and thus the amphorae were born. And how to seal those porous clay vessels, all the better to keep wine from spoiling in the hulls of ships as they bounced on choppy waters? With a brushing of pine resin, of course, the first incarnation of retsina came to be, arguably Greece's most famous wine and one that's seen a glorious reinvention today.

Ancient vintners studied and perfected their art, leaving a legacy of techniques and varietals that are still part of Greece's wine lore. Sweet wines made with sun-dried grapes were first envisioned by those ancient imbibers. Today, some of the most esteemed wines produced in Greece, such as the honey-gold muscats of Samos and Limnos and the chocolaty Vinsanto of Santorini, are produced from grapes left to dehydrate under the hot Greek sun. The ancient Greeks flavored their wines with honey and herbs; today, in a place I am most familiar with, Ikaria, my native island, winemakers still abide by the ancient tradition of aging wine in amphorae buried in the ground (to keep it cool), and stopping the slab-like cover with sprigs of laudanum, a wild plant that is said to repel insects and keep microbes away. That continuum . . . rearing its beautiful head in common countryside practices.

There is a vase at the Benaki Museum in Athens that always stirs my heart and imagination. It depicts one of the most detailed scenes of ancient Greeks partaking in one of the most civilized of all human activity: enjoying a meal with wine and company during the course of an ancient symposium. Wine fueled these cultural salons. Indeed, the word symposium means to drink together. Ancient Greek winemaking reached its zenith during the Classical Period and the Golden Age of Athens. The writers and philosophers of the day waxed poetic about the great wines of antiquity, which, I can only guess, helped them, in turn, free thought and tongue so that food, wine, and philosophy were all intimately connected. It was during this time that the idea of wine as an accompaniment to food was first embraced.

Modern Greek grape cultivation and winemaking owe a tremendous debt to the foundations that were established during the Classical Period. It was then, for example, that a system of protected designations of origin was first organized, based on the unique qualities and characteristics of specific places and vineyards. Provenance, *terroir*, the appreciation of aromas, and the language to describe the experience were born in that unique, seminal period of human—and Greek—history. Wine flowed from that glorious Classical world into Hellenistic, Roman, Byzantine, Ottoman, and, finally, modern times, filling cups and coffers and finding a seminal place in the rituals of Eastern Orthodoxy.

The Classical Period ended with the death of Alexander the Great, whose conquests had played a seminal role in the dispersal and dissemination of wine and the vine. For one, his armies had to be supplied with wine, not only for recreational use but also for antiseptic reasons, as a "safe" quaff, which meant that through Hellenistic times, Macedonian ships sailed the Aegean and Mediterranean to deliver wine to the likes of Rhodes and Kos, Cyprus, the Asia Minor coast, Lesvos, and Egypt, all outposts of Alexander's vast army. Many of these places developed wine-making industries of their own; Alexandria's was especially renowned.

The pleasure-loving Romans adapted many of customs and traditions of the Greeks, including, of course, the love of wine. Greek wines were much in demand throughout the Roman Empire. Horace nicknamed Homer and his epics *Homerus vinosus*; Virgil waxed poetic about Greek grape varietals; and Pliny catalogued Greek wines with detailed descriptions. Taking a cue from Hippocrates, the Golden-Age Greek father of medicine, two Greek doctors who lived during the Roman period, Dioskourides and Galenos, wrote of the therapeutic value of wine, a precursor, at least to my mind, of how the Greek-Mediterranean way of eating and living impart both physical and emotional well-being. Moderation—παν μέτρον άριστον to the ancient Greeks—has always been the way Greeks sip and savor their beautiful wines.

As the ancient world faded and Christianity took root, Greek wine continued to flourish. The vine is ever present in Byzantine iconography; monasteries throughout the Christian world, and especially the Orthodox Christian world, were beacons of viticulture and winemaking. To this day, some of the finest wines in Greece are produced on Mount Athos, the thousand-year-old monastic community in the Halkidiki peninsula of northern Greece. The sacrament of Holy Communion in Eastern Orthodoxy is expressed with a sip of dark, sweet Greek red wine, symbolic of the blood of Christ. There was a time, just a few centuries ago, when the famed sweet wine of Santorini, vinsanto, was exported almost exclusively to Russia to supply churches with the wine for Holy Communion.

With the fall of the Byzantine Empire and the rise of the Ottoman, which dominated most of Greece for four hundred years, wine was surprisingly undisturbed for the simple reason that taxes trumped religion. Despite the Muslim ban on wine consumption, the Ottomans saw wine as a source of income and levied both vineyards and wines with taxes.

During the almost eight thousand years of wine production on Greek soil, its continuity was genuinely threatened only three times. The first was during the Greek War of Independence, in 1821, and in the six or so years that followed, as able-bodied Greeks abandoned their fields to take up arms, but also as the Ottoman Turks employed a scorched-earth policy to much of Greek agriculture, destroying vineyards, olive groves, and more as their stronghold waned. When the young nation was firmly rooted, its agriculture rebounded, propitiously for the grape, since at the time, toward the end of the nineteenth century, France was experiencing the devasting effects of the phylloxera blight, which wiped out most of its vineyards, making room for the need to import wine. Greece was a ready supplier. One of the most prized of all Greek wines in demand in France was the sweet muscat of Samos.

It would take but a few decades for most of the Greek vineyards to fall prey to the same blight. Santorini, with some of the oldest continuously producing vineyards in the world, was one of the few places not hit, something that the island's vintners like to boast when they say that their vines are three thousand years old.

During the twentieth century, the war years and massive immigration wrought havoc on Greece's historic wine production. It wasn't until the 1980s that a glimmer of light started to shine again on the vines and wines of Greece. A new generation of oenologists emerged, having studied both inside and outside of Greece, mainly in France and Germany. Today, many young oenologists study at U.C. Davis. A few visionary winemakers took this generation under their wings and let them fly, so to speak, creating a kind of critical mass of talent, ambition, education, and opportunity. Today, there are over six hundred vineyards throughout Greece and the Greek vineyard is renowned for both its indigenous varieties—those very same grapes that were so prized in antiquity—but also for the international grapes that flourish and find new expression on Greek soil.

GREEK WINE TODAY: THE GREEK VINEYARD

GREEK VINEYARDS ARE AMONG THE WORLD'S OLDEST, THANKS LARGELY TO THE COUN-try's temperate climate, which is so conducive to grape cultivation.

The Greek landscape is 80 percent mountains, and most Greek wines are, indeed, produced in mountainous and semi-mountainous regions, something reflected in the country's number of Protected Designation of Origin (PDO) products, which come from these regions. The second most important areas for Greek wine production are the coastal areas, such as Halkidiki in Nothern Greece, as well as the coastal areas of Thrace, Kavala, continental Greece, the Peloponnese, and, of course, the islands, with the exception of Santorini, which is in a category all its own. Santorini's volcanic soil provides the most distinct of all microclimates in Greece and, arguably, in the world.

Like all agriculture in Greece, grape cultivation, and, so by extension, winemaking, is done on a human scale. Wine-producing areas are small and vineyards are family-owned. The mountainous terrain is often so difficult to cultivate that many vineyards are planted on terrace-like steps carved out of mountain slopes. Mechanical cultivation is almost impossible because machinery simply doesn't fit on these plots. The same, by the way, holds true for olive cultivation, with groves family-owned and small and cultivation largely manual, even to this day.

WINE CATEGORIES AND APPELLATIONS

IN EUROPE, THERE IS AN APPELLATION SYSTEM THAT SETS APART THE WINE AND FOOD products from specific areas that are distinct either because of tradition or unique geographic characteristics. You may have seen abbreviations such as AOC and AOQS on French wines, for example; in Greece, these are called PDO (Protected Designation of Origin). There are twenty-nine such regional wines, and the nomenclature is displayed on the wines' labels. PDO wines can display vintage years.

The PDO Wines of Greece are: PDO Anchialos; PDO Amynteo; PDO Archanes; PDO Goumenissa; PDO Dafnes; PDO Zitsa; PDO Lemnos; PDO Mantinia; PDO Mavrodaphne of Cephalonia; PDO Mavrodaphne of Patras; PDO Messenikola; PDO Monemvassia-Malvasia; PDO Muscat of Cephalonia; PDO Muscat of Lemnos; PDO Muscat of Patras; PDO Muscat of Rio Patras; PDO Muscat of Rhodes; PDO Naoussa; PDO Nemea; PDO Paros; PDO Patras; PDO Peza; PDO Slopes of Meliton; PDO Rapsani; PDO Rhodes; PDO Robola of Cephalonia; PDO Samos; PDO Santorini; and PDO Sitia.

There is another category called Protected Geographic Indication (PGI), also displayed on wine labels, a category which basically covers all regional wines and any of the wines of "traditional designation." To confuse things even further (God bless the EU!), there are three PGI levels: PGI Regional Wines, PGI District Wines, and PGI Area Wines. Essentially, the PGI tag lets the consumer know that the wine has some traditional and authentic standing in the local agricultural history of a place. It's a broader distinction than PDO, but PGI wines can also display vintage years.

Other categories in the wine appellation system include a new one, Varietal Wines, which can display vintage years, and Table Wines, which are neither PDO nor PGI and are not in the Varietals category, either. Vintage years are not allowed to be displayed on table wines. In the Table Wine category for Greek wines is a subcategory called "Wines of Traditional Designation," which basically refers to retsina.

UNIQUE GRAPE VARIETALS

IF THERE IS ANYTHING TO REMEMBER ABOUT GREEK WINES, IT IS THAT MOST ARE PRO-duced by distinctly Greek grapes. There are dozens, if not hundreds, of indigenous, regional grape varietals in Greece, and these are what give Greek wines their unique, fascinating character, a far cry from the monotony of chardonnay and pinot noir!

That said, there are also two broad categories of Greek wines: those produced from exclusively Greek grapes and those produced with a blend of Greek and international varieties. The range is available to American consumers.

Four Greek grape varietals are considered the noblest and most commercially important: xinomavro and agiorgitiko among the reds, and assyrtiko and moschofilero among the whites.

XINOMAVRO is one of the world's most singular grapes, producing a vast range of dry red wines that are noted for their deep red color, acidity, strong tannings, and ability to age well. They can be compared to the great Nebbiolo-based reds of Barolo and Barbaresco, or the pinot noirs of Burgundy. Xinomavro is synonymous with the regions of Naoussa and Amynteo in northern Greece, the two most important xinomavro appellations. There are two other appellations as well for xinomavro, in Goumenissa, north of Thessaloniki, and in Rapsani, on the eastern slopes of Mount Olympus.

AGIORGITIKO is the other great red varietal of Greece, native to the Nemea region in the Peloponnese, a two-hour drive from Athens and well worth a visit. Nemea was once called St. George, Agios Giorgios, which is where the grape gets its name. The wine is also sometimes referred to as the "blood of Hercules," because it is here in this region that Hercules slayed the famed lion, one of his twelve labors.

The agiorgitiko variety is one of the oldest indigenous Greek grapes and it thrives in its native land, a lovely terrain of rolling hills. Agiorgitiko is a dark, ruby red with concentrated red-berry flavor and lively aromas. They are softer than xinomavro and often compared to merlot.

Agiorgitiko wines are produced in a range of styles, from light and subtle to complex and ageworthy. They are among the most drinkable, food-friendly wines produced in Greece.

MOSCHOFILERO is one of the two most important white grape varietals, a native of the Mantinia region of the Peloponnese. Its name means "aromatic leaf," and the wines produced from this grape are, indeed, characterized by a floral intensity, but also by a surprising freshness, tangy crispness, and aromatic nose. Moschofilero also produces some of the finest sparkling wines as well as delicious rosés in Greece. It's a great wine to pair with seafood, even the likes of sushi, and goes beautifully with the heady flavors of robust Greek cuisine as well as with the spice and aromas of Middle Eastern and Far Eastern foods.

The ASSYRTIKO grape from Santorini is perhaps the most unique of all Greek grapes, cultivated in some of the world's most ancient vineyards, on the chalky volcanic soil of Santorini, for more than three thousand years. Assyrtiko produces dry white wines that can be enjoyed both fresh and aged. The assyrtiko from Santorini is renowned for its intense minerality and crisp citrusy aromas, but also for its body and density, especially when barrel-aged. It has the unusual ability to retain high acidity as it ripens, but also to accumulate sugar, like a fine Riesling. The vineyards on Santorini are the most unique anywhere, as the island is a volcano, characterized by punishing aridity, intense summer heat, whipping winds, and cool, moist, evenings. To protect the grapes, vintners on the island long ago developed a traditional pruning method called *kouloures*, in which the vine is trained into a basket shape with the grapes growing on the inside.

OTHER INDIGENOUS GREEK VARIETIES

I would be doing an injustice to Greek winemaking if I did not mention at least some of the other important grapes that help make the Greek vineyard so distinct and so worthy of exploration.

ATHIRI (a-THEE-ree). This is another white grape, common to the islands of the southern Aegean (Rhodes) and Halkidiki, in eastern Macedonia. Athiri produces food-friendly wines with lovely floral aromas.

DEBINA (de-BEE-na). A white variety from Epirus that produces wines noted for their refreshing acidity, aromas of green apple and pear, and finesse. Debina is also one of the white varietals in Greece that are used to produce sparkling wines.

KOTSIFALI (ko-tsee-FA-lee). Kotsifali, from Crete, produces "juicy" wines that have a slightly plummy taste. Kotsifali is usually blended with another Greek island variety, mantilaria.

LIATIKO (lee-A-tee-ko). One of the oldest Greek red grape varieties, this grape is native to Crete and produces wines that have high alcohol potential.

LIMNIO (lee-mnee-O): Limnio is an ancient a red grape varietal native to the island of Limnos. Today it is cultivated throughout northern Greece, especially in Halkidiki, and produces beautiful, silky wines with exotic notes of wild cherries and violets.

MALAGOUZIA (ma-la-ghoo-zee-A). One of the most interesting Greek white grape varietals to be sure, with a long, illustrious history to boot. Malagouzia is related to the Medieval wine Malvasia and had almost completely disappeared until a few visionary Greek producers revived it. Malagouzia produces aromatic, floral, and structured wines that can be quite complex. It's a great match for fish and seafood prepared any way—fried, grilled, marinated, or baked.

MANTILARIA (man-dee-la-ree-A). This "rough," earthy red Aegean variety flourishes on the islands of Paros, Rhodes, and Crete and is usually blended with other varieties that balance out its unruly character.

MAVRODAPHNE (ma-vro-THA-fnee). One of the best-known varieties for the production of sweet dessert wines, mavrodaphne is cultivated mainly in the Patras area of the Peloponnese and on the Ionian island, Cephalonia. Although mavrodaphne is one of the best-known dessert wines in Greece, a few innovative winemakers have been producing some delicious dry mavrodaphne wines that are well worth seeking out.

MAVROTRAGANO (ma-vroe-TRA-ga-noe) is one of the most intriguing, if least-known, Greek grapes. It is indigenous to Santorini and can produce great, full-bodied but balanced red wines.

MOSCHATO (moss-HA-toe), or muscat, is cultivated in several places but is most closely associated with the great sweet wines of Samos, which are dense and full-bodied, with amazing aromas of pear and apple. Older Samos muscats have delicious hints of caramel and chocolate.

ROBOLLA (ro-BO-la). A famed white grape from the island of Cephalonia, robolla produces elegant wines with bright but subtle hints of lemon.

RODITIS (ro-THEE-tees). Roditis is a kind of all-purpose red grape varietal that is best known for producing white wines. It is cultivated all over Greece but most closely associated with the western Peloponnese, Thessaly, and parts of Macedonia. Wines made with the roditis grape are light and friendly, easy to drink, with fresh notes of citrus, apple, and pear. Roditis pairs beautifully with all types of fish, as well as with chicken, pork, and light pasta dishes. Roditis is also one of the two main grape varietals used to produce retsina.

SAVATIANO (sa-va-tee-a-NO). One of the most ubiquitous Greek white grape varietals, Savatiano is synonymous with Attica, the area around Athens, but is also grown all over central Greece. Along with roditis, it is the main grape in the production of retsina.

VILANA (vee-LA-na). A traditional variety from Crete, vilana produces pleasant wines with flowery and fruity aromas.

A WORD ABOUT RETSINA

RETSINA, ONE OF THE MOST FAMOUS WINES OF GREECE, IS ONE OF TWO OFFICIALLY designated Traditional Wines. It is produced from the savatiano and roditis varietals in Attica, Viotia, and Evia. There is also a rosé retsina called *kokineli*.

Classic retsina is made just like any white wine, with one exception: a small amount of resin from the Aleppo pine, which dominates the landscape in Attica, Evia, and Corinth and flourishes all over the Mediterranean, is added during the fermentation process.

Resinated wines have existed in Greece since antiquity, when thick pine resin was used to seal the amphorae in which wine was transported, making it less permeable. The resin is also a natural antiseptic. Over time, retsina became stigmatized because too many mediocre vintners used resin to camouflage subpar wines. That's totally changed now, and retsina is seeing its own little renaissance as a few very visionary Greek winemakers are producing some light, crisp exceptional retsinas worth looking for.

Retsina goes with everything, which makes it the perfect wine to pair with a Greek *meze* platter or meal. It's also great with succulent grilled octopus and other seafood and stands up well to all the heady, robust cheeses and other foods of Greece.

GREEK DESSERT WINES

SOME OF THE MOST SEDUCTIVE—AND FAMOUS—GREEK WINES ARE SWEET.

The moschato, or muscat, grape dominates the sweet wine shelf, with exceptional and very different expressions of the grape produced in Samos, an island in the northeastern Aegean, and in nearby Limnos, as well as Rhodes, in the southern Aegean, Cephalonia in the Ionian, and Patras in the Peloponnese. The most widely available in the United States is the range of sweet Samos muscats, which are also among the most highly prized value-for-money wines anywhere in the world.

One of the most unique Greek dessert wines is the luscious vinsanto of Santorini, produced from the island's sun-dried white assyrtiko grape, which otherwise makes bone-dry, crisp wines.

Mavrodaphne, a dark, sweet red wine produced in Patras and Cephalonia, is also fairly easy to find in the United States, and is a wine for anyone who loves the flavors of dried fruit and a velvety mouthfeel.

ONLINE SOURCES FOR GREEK FOODS

BY NO MEANS COMPLETE, HERE IS A LIST OF THE LARGEST AND MOST INTERESTING online sources for Greek food products.

TITAN FOODS (www.titanfoods.net)—By far one of the largest, if not *the* largest, online retailers of Greek food products. Titan began as a brick-and-mortar Greek supermarket in Astoria, New York, and is still a bustling emporium where you can find just about everything Greek and edible. They also produce a range of Greek sweets and phyllo specialties in-house. The online shop has a vast range of Greek foods that cover both gourmet and more everyday products.

MANI IMPORTS (www.maniimports.com/shop)—This online retailer is based on the West Coast, in Sacramento, and has a good selection of Greek cheeses, wines, olives, olive oils, and other Greek products, as well as products from around the Mediterranean.

YOLENIS (www.yolenis.com/en-us/?country=US)—A new source for Greek foods online, Yolenis has a good range of Greek gourmet and other products. Availability of products can sometimes be an issue, but the range is interesting.

KLIO TEA (kliotea.com) is a great source for a wide range of Greek herbal teas and regional, artisan Greek honeys, including the famed "longevity" honey of Ikaria, a Blue Zone.

DEMETER'S PANTRY (demeterspantry.com)—A good source of organic Greek food products and some genuinely rare and fascinating regional and artisanal fare.

GREEK INTERNET MARKET (www.greekinternetmarket.com)—Like Titan and Parthenon Foods, this site is an online Greek supermarket. The selection is a little smaller than what the other two Greek online behemoths carry but the descriptions are very thorough.

GREEKSHOPS.COM (www.greekshops.com)—A nice selection of everyday Greek ingredients, herbs and spices, coffees and teas, and cooking accessories. No cheeses, but they do offer some prepared appetizers and a range of mixes that many Greeks use to make sweets and desserts for those who don't want to cook from scratch.

iGOURMET GREEK SHOP (www.igourmet.com/greekfood.asp)—iGourmet offers several pages of Greek products including cheese, olives, premium olive oils, coffee, gift baskets, honey, and other fairly high-end products at reasonable prices.

PARTHENON FOODS (www.parthenonfoods.com)—Like Titan, Parthenon Foods is a site with a huge variety of Greek food products, from traditional pastas to Greek sea salt and more.

MASTIHASHOPNY (mastihashopny.com)—Mastiha Shop is an online site for all things related to *mastiha* (mastic), the natural resin that is both one of Greece's most seductive spices as well as a salve for all sorts of ailments. This online shop sells everything from the crystal form of the spice to cookies and chocolates flavored with *mastiha*, as well as a great line of health and beauty products, such as shampoo and moisturizer, perfumed with the substance.

INDEX